INTERNATIONAL MONEY AND FINANCE

INTERNATIONAL MONEY AND FINANCE

Ninth Edition

MICHAEL MELVIN

STEFAN NORRBIN

ACADEMIC PRESS
An imprint of Elsevier

ELSEVIER

Notices

Knowledge and best practice in this field are constantly changing. As new research and
experience broaden our understanding, changes in research methods, professional practices,
or medical treatment may become necessary.

Practitioners and researchers must always rely on their own experience and knowledge
in evaluating and using any information, methods, compounds, or experiments described
herein. In using such information or methods they should be mindful of their own safety
and the safety of others, including parties for whom they have a professional responsibility.

To the fullest extent of the law, neither the Publisher nor the authors, contributors, or
editors, assume any liability for any injury and/or damage to persons or property as a
matter of products liability, negligence or otherwise, or from any use or operation of any
methods, products, instructions, or ideas contained in the material herein.

British Library Cataloguing-in-Publication Data
A catalogue record for this book is available from the British Library

Library of Congress Cataloging-in-Publication Data
A catalog record for this book is available from the Library of Congress

ISBN: 978-0-12-804106-2

For Information on all Academic Press publications
visit our website at https://www.elsevier.com/books-and-journals

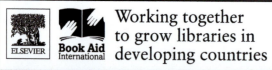

Working together
to grow libraries in
developing countries

www.elsevier.com • www.bookaid.org

Publisher: Nikki Levy
Acquisition Editor: Scott Bentley
Editorial Project Manager: Susan Ikeda
Production Project Manager: Jason Mitchell
Designer: Matthew Limbert

Typeset by MPS Limited, Chennai, India

CONTENTS

Part II   International Parity Conditions

Part III   Risk and International Capital Flows

Part IV   Modeling the Exchange Rate and Balance of Payments

PREFACE

International finance is one of the growth areas of the finance and economics curricula. Today's financial marketplace is truly global. No student of economics or finance can fully understand current developments without some background in international finance. If, after studying this text, a student can pick up *The Wall Street Journal* and understand the international financial news, along with its implications, then we feel that we have succeeded as teachers. To this end, *International Money and Finance* offers a concise yet comprehensive overview of the subject. The basics of the foreign exchange market and the balance of payments are presented, along with accessible discussions of the most recent research findings related to exchange rate determination. Topics covered range from the nitty-gritty of financing international trade to intuitive discussions of overshooting exchange rates and currency substitution.

The first edition of *International Money and Finance* grew from the lecture notes used to teach undergraduate students at Arizona State University. The notes, as well as the book, summarized the current literature in international finance, with only elementary math as a prerequisite. It was extremely gratifying to find that instructors at other institutions found the earlier editions to be useful texts for undergraduate and MBA students. In fact, the adoption list ranged from the leading MBA schools in the country to small rural 4-year colleges. The fact that the text has proved successful with students of varying abilities and backgrounds is a feature that we have strived to retain in preparing this eighth edition.

Users of the past editions will find the ninth edition updated and substantially revised to keep pace with the rapidly changing world of international finance. There are several major changes in this edition. Chapter 1, The Foreign Exchange Market, has been updated to reflect the current foreign exchange market, while Chapter 2, International Monetary Arrangements, has been updated to include more detail on central bank intervention, SDRs, and the foreign reserve buildup in China. Chapter 3, The Balance of Payments, has had a major revision to reflect the changes to the Balance of Payments classification system. In addition, a section has been added to discuss "twin deficit" and saving/investment imbalances as possible sources of current account deficits/surpluses. Chapter 4, Forward-Looking Market Instruments, has updated discussion of forwards, futures, and options prices. Chapter 5, The Eurocurrency Market, has an added section discussing the old versus new LIBOR and the cheating that lead to the changing methodology for collecting the LIBOR. Chapter 6, Exchange Rates, Interest Rates, and Interest Parity and Chapter 7, Prices and Exchange Rates, have updated discussion of parity conditions. Chapter 10, International Investment, has been updated to include several different types of foreign investment, whereas Chapter 11, Direct Foreign Investment and International Lending, now focuses on international lending and crises. In particular the chapter has been updated with a detailed discussion of the Greek debt crisis.

The ninth edition has been written in the same spirit as the first eight—to provide a concise survey of international finance suitable for undergraduate and MBA classes.

ACKNOWLEDGMENTS

We are grateful to all who have offered comments leading to the revision of *International Money and Finance*. They include countless former students and instructors at other institutions, who provided informal comments on style and content. Earlier editions were reviewed by Mamadou K. Diallo of East Stroudsburg University, B.D. Elzas of Erasmus University, Judy L. Klein of Mary Baldwin College, Vibhas Madan of Drexel University, Kiminori Matsuyama of Northwestern University, Thomas Russell of Santa Clara University, Larry J. Sechrest of Sul Ross State University, Robert Sedgwich of Sheffield Hallam University, Darrel Young of St. Edward's University, Carl Beidleman of Lehigh University, Glenn W. Boyle of Louisiana State University, David Ding of Memphis State University, Chen Jia-sheng of the University of Denver, Francis A. Lees of St. Johns University, Chu-Ping Vijverberg of the University of Texas at Dallas, Robert Flood of Northwestern University, Samuel Katz of Georgetown University, Donald P. Stegall of California State University at Fresno, Clas Wihlborg of the University of Southern California, Bernard Gauci of Hollins University, Bang Nam Jeon of Drexel University, Chris Neely of the Federal Reserve Bank of St. Louis, Helen Popper of Santa Clara University, and Felix Rioja of Georgia State University, Lance Girton of the University of Utah, Bijou Yang Lester of Drexel University, Peter Pedroni of Williams College, Miguel Ramirez of Trinity College, Julie Ryan of Immaculata College, Niloufer Sohrabji of Simmons College, and Mark Wohar of the University of Nebraska. While we could not incorporate all of their thoughtful suggestions, we appreciate their comments and have no doubt that the text has been much improved by their reviews.

Finally, we welcome comments and criticism from users of the eight editions of *International Money and Finance*. Our hope is that the book will evolve over time to best suit your needs.

TO THE STUDENT

WHY STUDY INTERNATIONAL FINANCE?

Why study the subject of international money and finance? One reason is that career goals are paramount to many people, and in this regard the topic of the text is related to a growth area in the labor market. This book provides a background in international finance for those who expect to obtain jobs created by international investment, international banking, and multinational business activity. Other readers may have a more scholarly concern with "rounding out" their economic education by studying the international relationships between financial markets and institutions. Although a course in principles of economics is the only prerequisite assumed for this text, many students may have already taken intermediate macroeconomics, money and banking, or essentials of finance courses. But for those interested in international economic relationships, such courses often lack a global orientation. The economic models and discussions of the typical money and banking course focus on the *closed economy*, closed in the sense that the interrelationships with the rest of the world are ignored. Here we study the institutions and analysis of an integrated world financial community, thus giving a better understanding of the world in which we live. We will learn that there are constraints as well as opportunities facing the business firm, government, and the individual investor that become apparent only in a worldwide setting.

FINANCE AND THE MULTINATIONAL FIRM

A *multinational firm* is a firm with operations that extend beyond its domestic national borders. Such firms have become increasingly sophisticated in international financial dealings because international business poses risk and return opportunities that are not present in purely domestic business operations. A US multinational firm may have accounts payable and receivable that are denominated in US dollars, Japanese yen, British pounds, Mexican pesos, Canadian dollars, and euros. The financial managers of this firm face a different set of problems than the managers of a firm doing business strictly in dollars. It may be true that "a dollar is a dollar," but the dollar value of yen, euros, or pesos can and does change over time. As the dollar value of the yen changes, the value of yen-denominated contracts will change when evaluated in terms of dollars.

Multinational finance responds to this new set of challenges with a tool kit of techniques and market instruments that are used to maximize the return on the firm's investment, subject to an acceptable level of risk. Once we extend beyond the domestic economy, a rich variety of business opportunities exist that must be utilized with the appropriate financial arrangements. This book intends to cover many aspects of these international financial transactions that the financial manager may encounter. The financial side of international business differs from the study of international trade commonly encountered in international economics courses. Courses in international trade study the determinants of the pattern and volume of world trade—formally referred to as the theory of *comparative advantage*. If country A produces and exports shoes in exchange for country B's food, we say that A has a comparative advantage in shoes and B has a comparative advantage in food. Besides comparative advantage, such courses also examine the movement of factors of production, labor, and capital goods between nations. Obviously, these subjects are important and deserve careful study, but our purpose is to study the monetary consequences of such trade. Although we will not explicitly consider any theories of comparative advantage—such theories are usually developed without referring to the use of money—we will often consider the impact of monetary events on trade in real goods and services. Our discussions range from the effects of the currency used in pricing international trade (Chapter 12) to financing trade in the offshore banking industry (Chapter 5). We will find that monetary events can have real consequences for the volume and pattern of international trade.

THE ACTORS

This course is not simply a study of abstract theories concerning the international consequences of changes in money supply or demand, prices, interest rates, or exchange rates. We also discuss the role and importance of the institutional and individual participants. Most people tend to think immediately of large commercial banks as holding the starring role in the international monetary scene. Because the foreign exchange market is a market where huge sums of national currencies are bought and sold through commercial banks, any text on international finance will include many examples and instances in which such banks play a major part. In fact, Chapter 1 begins with a discussion of the role of banks in the foreign exchange market.

Besides commercial banks, other business firms play a key part in our discussion, since the goods and services they buy and sell internationally effect a need for financing such trade. The corporate treasurer of any multinational firm is well versed in foreign exchange trading and hedging and international investment opportunities. What is hedging? How are international investment opportunities related to domestic opportunities? These are subjects we address in Chapters 4 and 6. Finally, we examine the role of government. Central banks, such as the Federal Reserve in the United States, are often important actors in our story. Besides their roles of buying, selling, lending, and borrowing internationally, they also act to restrict the freedom of the other actors. The policies of central governments and central banks are crucial to understanding the actual operation of the international monetary system, and each chapter will address the impact of government on the topic being described.

PLAN OF ATTACK

This book can be thought of in terms of four main sections. To aid our understanding of the relationships among prices, exchange rates, and interest rates, we will consider existing theories, as well as the current state of research that illuminates their validity. For those students who choose to proceed professionally in the field of international finance, the study of this text should provide both a good reference and a springboard to more advanced work—and ultimately employment. Chapters 1, The Foreign Exchange Market, Chapter 2, International Monetary Arrangements, Chapter 3, The Balance of Payments identify the key institutions and the historical types international monetary system as well as discussing the current system. In Chapters 4, Forward-Looking Market Instruments, Chapter 5, The Eurocurrency Market, Chapter 6, Exchange Rates, Interest Rates, and Interest Parity; Chapter 7, Prices and Exchange Rates, the international monetary system is expanded by allowing payments to be due in a future time period. This results in a need for hedging instruments and expands the interaction between financial variables in different countries.

Chapter 8, Foreign Exchange Risk and Forecasting; Chapter 9, Financial Management of the Multinational Firm; Chapter 10, International Portfolio Investment; Chapter 11, International Portfolio Investment, are devoted to applied topics of interest to the international financial manager. Issues range from the "nuts and bolts" of financing imports and exports to the evaluation of risk in international lending to sovereign governments. The topics covered in these chapters are of practical interest to corporate treasurers and international bankers.

Chapter 12, Determinants of the Balance of Trade, Chapter 13; The IS-LM-BP Approach; Chapter 14, The Monetary Approach; Chapter 15, Extensions to the Monetary Approach of Exchange Rate Determination, cover the determinants of balance of payments and exchange rates. Government and industry devote many resources to trying to forecast the balance of payments and exchange rates. The discussion in these chapters includes the most important recent developments. Although there is some disagreement among economists regarding the relative significance of competing theories, as far as possible in an intermediate-level presentation, the theories are evaluated in light of research evidence. Altogether, these chapters present a detailed summary of the current state of knowledge regarding the determinants of the balance of payments and exchange rates.

At the beginning of this introduction we asked: Why study international money and finance? We hope that the brief preview provided here will have motivated you to answer this question. International finance is not a dull "ivory tower" subject to be tolerated, or avoided if possible. Instead, it is a subject that involves dynamic real-world events. Since the material covered in this book is emphasized daily in the newspapers and other media, you will soon find that the pages in *International Money and Finance* seem to come to life. To this end, a daily reading of *The Wall Street Journal* or the London *Financial Times* makes an excellent supplement for the text material. As you progress through the book, international financial news will become more and more meaningful and useful. For the many users of this text who do not go on to a career in international finance, the major lasting benefit of the lessons contained here will be the ability to understand the international financial news intelligently and effectively.

PART I

The International Monetary Environment

CHAPTER 1

The Foreign Exchange Market

Contents

Foreign exchange trading refers to trading one country's money for that of another country. The need for such trade arises because of tourism, the buying and selling of goods internationally, or investment occurring across international boundaries. The kind of money specifically traded takes the form of bank deposits or bank transfers of deposits denominated in foreign currency. The *foreign exchange market*, as we usually think of it, refers to large commercial banks in financial centers, such as New York or London, that trade foreign-currency-denominated deposits with each other. Actual *bank notes* like dollar bills are relatively unimportant insofar as they rarely physically cross international borders. In general, only tourism or illegal activities would lead to the international movement of bank notes.

FOREIGN EXCHANGE TRADING VOLUME

The foreign exchange market is the largest financial market in the world. Every 3 years the Bank for International Settlements conducts a survey of trading volume around the world and in the 2016 survey the average amount of currency traded *each business day* was $5,088 billion. Thus the foreign exchange market is an enormous market. Fig. 1.1 shows that the

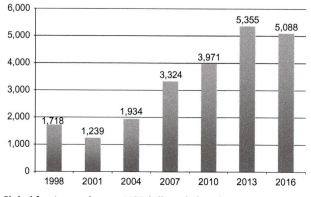

Figure 1.1 Global foreign exchange, USD billion daily volume.

Table 1.1 Top ten currency pairs by share of foreign exchange trading volume

Currency pair	Percent of total
US dollar/euro	23.0
US dollar/Japanese yen	17.7
US dollar/UK pound	9.2
US dollar/Australian dollar	5.2
US dollar/Canadian dollar	4.3
US dollar/China yuan renminbi	3.8
US dollar/Swiss franc	3.5
US dollar/Mexico peso	2.1
Euro/UK pound	2.0
US dollar/Singapore dollar	1.9

Source: Bank for International Settlements, Triennial Central Bank Survey, September 2016.

foreign exchange market has been growing rapidly in the last decade. In 2001 the trading volume of foreign exchange was $1,239 billion. In 2007 the foreign exchange market had almost tripled in volume, and by 2013 the foreign exchange market had grown another $2 trillion.

The US dollar is by far the most important currency, and has remained so even with the introduction of the euro. The dollar is involved in 87% of all trades. Since foreign exchange trading involves pairs of currencies, it is useful to know which currency pairs dominate the market. Table 1.1 reports the share of market activity taken by different currencies. The largest volume occurs in dollar/euro trading, accounting for 23% of the total. The next closest currency pair, the dollar/yen, accounts for slightly less than 18%. After these two currency pairs, the volume drops off dramatically. For example, the dollar/UK pound is roughly half as much foreign currency trading as the dollar/yen. The US dollar is represented in nine of the top ten currency pairs. Thus, the currency markets are dominated by dollar trading.

GEOGRAPHIC FOREIGN EXCHANGE RATE ACTIVITY

The foreign exchange market is a 24-hour market. Currencies are quoted continuously across the world. Fig. 1.2 illustrates the 24-hour dimension of the foreign exchange market. We can determine the local hours of major trading activity in each location by the country bars at the top of the figure. Time is measured as Greenwich Mean Time (GMT) at the bottom of the figure. For instance, in New York 7 a.m. is 1200 GMT and 3 p.m. is 2000 GMT. Fig. 1.2 shows that there is a small overlap between European trading and Asian trading, and there is no overlap between New York trading and Asian trading.

Dealers in foreign exchange publicize their willingness to deal at certain prices by posting quotes on electronic networks such as Reuters or EBS. When a dealer at a bank posts a quote, that quote then appears on computer monitors sitting on the desks of other foreign exchange market

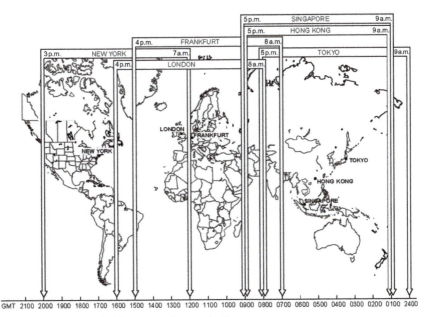

Figure 1.2 The world of foreign exchange dealing.

participants worldwide. This posted quote is like an advertisement, telling the rest of the market the prices at which the quoting dealer is ready to deal. In addition to the electronic trading venues, there is still bilateral direct-dealing in the market where one person speaks with a bank dealer to arrange a trade. These bilateral transactions and the quantities and prices that are transacted are proprietary information and are known only by the two participants in a transaction. The quotes on the electronic trading networks are the best *publicly* available information on the current prices in the market.

In terms of the geographic pattern of foreign exchange trading, a small number of locations account for the majority of trading. Table 1.2 reports the average daily volume of foreign exchange trading in different countries. The United Kingdom and the United States account for more than half of the total world trading. The United Kingdom has long been the leader in foreign exchange trading. In 2016, it accounted for just over 37% of total world trading volume. While it is true that foreign exchange trading is a round-the-clock business, with trading taking place somewhere in the world at any point in time, the peak activity occurs during business hours in London, New York, and Tokyo.

Fig. 1.3 provides another view of the 24-hour nature of the foreign exchange market. This figure shows the average number of quotes on the Japanese yen/US dollar posted to the Reuters foreign exchange network. Fig. 1.3 reports the hourly average number of quotes over the business week. Weekends are excluded since there is little trading outside of normal business hours. The vertical axis measures the average number of

Table 1.2 Top ten foreign exchange markets by trading volume

Country	Total volume (billions of dollars)	Percent share
United Kingdom	2426	37.1%
United States	1272	19.4%
Singapore	517	7.9%
Hong Kong	437	6.7%
Japan	399	6.1%
France	181	2.8%
Switzerland	156	2.4%
Australia	135	2.1%
Germany	116	1.8%
Bulgaria	86	1.3%

Source: Bank for International Settlements, Triennial Central Bank Survey, September 2016.

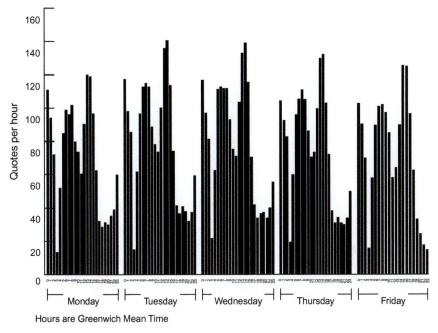

Figure 1.3 Average hourly weekday quotes, Japanese yen per US dollar.

quotes per hour, and the horizontal axis shows the hours of each weekday measured in GMT. A clear pattern emerges in the figure—every business day tends to look the same. Trading in the yen starts each business day in Asian markets with a little more than 20 quotes per hour being entered. Quoting activity rises and falls through the Asian morning until reaching a daily low at lunchtime in Tokyo (0230–0330 GMT).

The lull in trading during the Tokyo lunch hour was initially the result of a Japanese regulation prohibiting trading during this time. Since December 22, 1994, trading has been permitted in Tokyo during lunchtime, but there still is a pronounced drop in activity because many traders take a lunch break. Following the Tokyo lunch break, market activity picks up in the Asian afternoon and rises substantially as European trading begins around 0700 GMT. There is another decrease in trading activity associated with lunchtime in Europe, 1200–1300 GMT. Trading rises again when North American trading begins, around 1300 GMT, and hits a daily peak when London and New York trading overlap. Trading drops substantially with the close of European trading, and then rises again with the opening of Asian trading the next day.

Note that every weekday has this same pattern, as the pace of the activity in the foreign exchange market follows the opening and closing of business hours around the world. While it is true that the foreign exchange market is a 24-hour market with continuous trading possible, the amount of trading follows predictable patterns. This is not to say that there are not days that differ substantially from this average daily number of quotes. If some surprising event occurs that stimulates trading, some days may have a much different pattern. Later in the text we consider the determinants of exchange rates and study what sorts of news would be especially relevant to the foreign exchange market.

SPOT EXCHANGE RATES

A spot exchange rate is the price of one money in terms of another that is delivered today. Table 1.3 shows selected spot foreign exchange rate quotations for a particular day. All rates are in foreign currency per dollar terms. For example, in the table we see that on July 15, 2016, the US dollar traded for 0.9812 Swiss francs. Note that this exchange rate is quoted at a specific time, since rates will change throughout the day as supply and demand for the currencies change, and involves amounts traded that are greater than $1 million. If the amount was smaller than $1 million the cost of foreign exchange would be higher. The smaller the quantity of foreign exchange purchased, the higher the price. Therefore if you travel to a foreign country the exchange rate will be much less favorable for you as a tourist.

While the exchange rate just discussed is the Swiss franc price of the US dollar, we can always convert this into a US dollar price of the Swiss

Table 1.3 Selected spot currency exchange rates

Country (currency)	July 15, 2016		February 15, 2016
	Mid-price	Bid–offer	Mid-price
Canada (dollar)	1.2913	1.2911–914	1.3827
Australian (dollar)	1.3118	1.3116–119	1.4001
Japan (yen)	105.693	105.683–702	114.001
Euro area (euro)	0.9004	0.9003–005	0.8931
Sweden (krona)	8.5156	8.5128–184	8.4565
Switzerland (franc)	0.9812	0.9811–813	0.9826
UK (pound)	0.7450	0.7499–501	0.6903

Source: Oanda.com.

franc by taking the reciprocal of the exchange rate, or 1/exchange rate, For instance, the exchange rate of 0.9812 Swiss francs per dollar is converted into dollars per Swiss franc by calculating the reciprocal: $1/0.9812 = 1.019$. It will always be true that when we know the Swiss franc price per dollar (SF/\$), we can find the dollar price per Swiss franc by taking the reciprocal $1/(SF/\$) = (\$/SF)$.

Note that the exchange rate quotes in the first column in Table 1.3 are mid-price rates. For convenience we often talk about the spot rate as if it is one rate. Often this rate is the mid-price rate. However, the spot rate always involves two rates. Banks *bid* (buy) foreign exchange at lower rates than they *offer* (sell), and the difference between the selling and buying rates is called the *spread*. The *mid-price* is the average of the buying and selling rates. Table 1.3 lists the spreads for the currencies in the second column. The bid/offer prices is quoted so that one can see the *bid* (buy) price, and one can find the *offer* (sell) price by dropping the last three digits of the buy quote and replacing them with the second number. For example, the Swiss franc *bid–offer* price is 0.9811–813. Thus, the bank is willing to buy dollars for Swiss francs at 0.9811, and sell dollars at 0.9813 Swiss francs. The spread (the bank's profit) between the buy and sell rates is very small. The spread for the Swiss franc can be measured in percentage terms as the (ask-bid)/mid-price. Using the information in Table 1.3, we can compute the spread in percentage terms as $[(0.9813-0.9811)/0.9812 = 0.0002]$, or 2/100 of 1%. This spread is indicative of how small the normal spread is in the market for major traded currencies. The existing spread in any currency will vary according to the individual currency trader, the currency being traded, and the trading bank's overall view of conditions in the foreign exchange market. The spread quoted will tend to increase for more thinly traded currencies (i.e., currencies that do not generate a large volume of trading) or when the bank perceives that the risks associated with trading in a currency at a particular time are rising.

Let us look at an example of using the buy and sell rates. If you were a US importer buying watches from Switzerland at the dollar price of \$10 million, a bank would sell \$10 million worth of Swiss francs to you for 0.9811 Swiss francs per dollar. Note that Table 1.3 shows what banks are willing to bid and offer when buying or selling dollars for Swiss franc. We want to sell our dollars for Swiss franc so we need to use the bid rate for the bank in Table 1.3. You would receive SF9,811,000 to settle the account with the Swiss exporter.

$\$10,000,000 * 0.9811\ SF/\$ = SF9,811,000$

Table 1.4 International currency symbols

Country	Currency	Symbol	ISOcode
Australia	Dollar	A$	AUD
Austria	Euro	€	EUR
Belgium	Euro	€	EUR
Canada	Dollar	C$	CAD
Denmark	Krone	DKr	DKK
Finland	Euro	€	EUR
France	Euro	€	EUR
Germany	Euro	€	EUR
Greece	Euro	€	EUR
India	Rupee	₹	INR
Iran	Rial	RI	IRR
Italy	Euro	€	EUR
Japan	Yen	¥	JPY
Kuwait	Dinar	KD	KWD
Mexico	Peso	Ps	MXN
Netherlands	Euro	€	EUR
Norway	Krone	NKr	NOK
Saudi Arabia	Riyal	SR	SAR
Singapore	Dollar	S$	SGD
South Africa	Rand	R	ZAR
Spain	Euro	€	EUR
Sweden	Krona	SKr	SEK
Switzerland	Franc	SF	CHF
United Kingdom	Pound	£	GBP
United States	Dollar	$	USD

Thus far, we have discussed trading Swiss francs and Canadian dollars using the symbols SF and C$, respectively. Table 1.4 lists the commonly used symbols for several currencies along with their international standard (ISO) code. Exchange rate quotations are generally available for all countries where currencies may be freely traded. In the cases where free markets are not permitted, the state typically conducts all foreign exchange trading at an official exchange rate, regardless of current market conditions.

This chapter discusses the buying and selling of foreign exchange to be delivered on the spot (actually, deposits traded in the foreign exchange market generally take two working days to clear); this is called the *spot market*. In Table 1.3 the first column shows the spot market on July 15, 2016, whereas the last column shows what the spot market looked like 6 months prior on February 15, 2016. Comparing the quotes in the two spot markets we can see what has happened to the exchange rate in this 6-month period. If the exchange rate increases in value we say that the currency *appreciated*. If the currency falls in value then the currency *depreciated*. For example, the yen/dollar rate fell from 114.001 to 105.693. The dollar depreciated against the yen, because the value of a dollar decreased in terms of yen. Because of the reciprocal nature of exchange rates, a depreciating dollar means that the yen appreciated against the dollar. In contrast, we can see that the UK pound depreciated against the US dollar. In fact, the UK pound depreciated by almost 8%, a substantial fall for such a short period.

In Chapter 4, Forward-Looking Market Instruments, we will consider the important issues that arise when the trade contract involves payment at a future date. First, however, we should consider in more detail the nature of the foreign exchange market.

CURRENCY ARBITRAGE

The foreign exchange market is a market where price information is readily available by telephone or computer network. Since currencies are homogeneous goods (a dollar is a dollar regardless of where it is traded), it is very easy to compare prices in different markets. Exchange rates tend to be equal worldwide. If this were not so, there would be profit opportunities for simultaneously buying a currency in one market while selling it in another. This activity, known as *arbitrage*, would raise the exchange rate in the market where it is too low, because this is the market in which you would buy, and the increased demand for the currency would result in a higher price. The market where the exchange rate is too high is one in which you sell, and this increased selling activity would result in a lower price. Arbitrage would continue until the exchange rates in different locales are so close that it is not worth the costs incurred to do any further buying and selling. When this situation occurs, we say that the rates are "transaction costs close." Any remaining deviation between exchange rates will not cover the costs of additional arbitrage transactions, so the arbitrage activity ends.

For instance, suppose the following quotes were available for the Swiss franc/US dollar rate:

- Citibank is quoting 0.8745–755
- Deutsche Bank is quoting 0.8725–735

This means that Citibank will buy dollars for 0.8745 francs and will sell dollars for 0.8755 francs. Deutsche Bank will buy dollars for 0.8725 francs and will sell dollars for 0.8735 francs. This presents an arbitrage opportunity. We call this a *two-point arbitrage* as it involves two currencies. We could buy $10 million at Deutsche Bank's offer price of 0.8735 and simultaneously sell $10 million to Citibank at their bid price of 0.8745 francs. This would earn a profit of SF0.0010 per dollar traded, or SF10,000 would be the total arbitrage profit.

If such a profit opportunity existed the arbitrage would result in changes in the banks changing the rates as arbitrageurs enter the market. An increase in the demand to buy dollars from Deutsche Bank would cause them to raise their offer price above 0.8735, while the increased willingness to sell dollars to Citibank at their bid price of 0.8745 francs would cause them to lower their bid. In this way, arbitrage activity pushes the prices of different traders to levels where no arbitrage profits can be earned. Suppose the prices moved to where Citibank is quoting the Swiss franc/dollar exchange rate at 0.8740–50 and Deutsche Bank is quoting 0.8730–40. Now there is no arbitrage profit possible. The offer price at Deutsche Bank of 0.8740 is equal to the bid price at Citibank. The difference between the bid and offer prices of each bank is equal to the spreads of SF0.001. In the wholesale banking foreign exchange market, the bid–offer spread is the only transaction cost. When the quotes of two different banks differ by no more than the spread being quoted in the market by these banks, there is no arbitrage opportunity.

Arbitrage could involve more than two currencies. Since banks quote foreign exchange rates with respect to the dollar, one can use the dollar value of two currencies to calculate the *cross rate* between the two currencies. The *cross rate* is the implied exchange rate from the two actual quotes. For instance, if we know the dollar price of pounds ($/£) and the dollar price of Swiss francs ($/SF), we can infer what the corresponding pound price of francs (£/SF) would be. From now on we will explicitly write the units of our exchange rates to avoid the confusion that can easily arise. For example, $/£ = $1.76 is the exchange rate in terms of dollars per pound.

Suppose that in London $/£ = $1.76, while in New York $/SF = $1.10. The corresponding *cross rate* is the £/SF rate. Simple algebra shows that if $/£ = $1.76 and $/SF = 1.1, then £/SF = ($/SF)/($/£), or 1.10/1.76 = 0.625. If we observe a market where one of the three exchange rates—$/£, $/SF, £/SF—is out of line with the other two, there is an arbitrage opportunity, in this case a *triangular arbitrage*. Triangular arbitrage, or *three-point arbitrage*, involves three currencies.

Table 1.5 Triangular arbitrage

Location	$/SF	$/£	£/SF
New York	1.100	1.600	–
London	–	1.600	0.625
Geneva	1.100	–	0.625

To simplify the analysis of arbitrage involving three currencies, let us ignore the bid–offer spread and assume that we can either buy or sell at one price. Suppose that in Geneva, Switzerland the exchange rate is £/SF = 0.625, while in New York $/SF = 1.100, and in London $/£ = $1.600, as shown in Table 1.5. Examining Table 1.5 it appears to have no possible arbitrage opportunity, but astute traders in the foreign exchange market would observe a discrepancy when they check the cross rates. Computing the implicit cross rate for New York, the arbitrageur finds the implicit cross rate to be £/SF = ($/SF)/($/£), or 1.100/1.600 = 0.6875. Thus the cost of SF is high in New York, and the cost of £ is low.

Assume that a trader starts in New York with 1 million dollars. The trader should buy £ in New York. Selling $1 million in New York (or London) the trader receives £625,000 ($1 million divided by $/£ = $1.60). The pounds then are used to buy Swiss francs at £/SF = 0.625 (in either London or Geneva), so that £625,000 = SF1 million. The SF1 million would be used in New York to buy dollars at $/SF = $1.10, so that SF1 million = $1,100,000. Thus the initial $1 million could be turned into $1,100,000, with the *triangular arbitrage* action earning the trader $100,000 (costs associated with the transaction should be deducted to arrive at the true arbitrage profit).

As in the case of the two-currency arbitrage covered earlier, a valuable product of this arbitrage activity is the return of the exchange rates to internationally consistent levels. If the initial discrepancy was that the dollar price of pounds was too low in London, the selling of dollars for pounds in London by the arbitrageurs will make pounds more expensive, raising the price from $/£ = $1.60. Note that if the pound cost increases to $/£ = $1.76 then there is no arbitrage possible. However, the pound exchange rate is unlikely to increase that much because the activity in the other markets would tend to raise the pound price of francs and lower the dollar price of francs, so that a dollar price of pounds somewhere between $1.60 and $1.76 would be the new equilibrium among the three currencies.

Since there is active trading between the dollar and other currencies, we can look to any two exchange rates involving dollars to infer the cross rates. So even if there is limited direct trading between, for instance, Mexican pesos and yen, by using pesos/\$ and \$/¥, we can find the implied pesos/¥ rate. Since transaction costs are higher for lightly traded currencies, the depth of foreign exchange trading that involves dollars often makes it cheaper to go through dollars to get from some currency X to another currency Y when X and Y are not widely traded. Thus, if a business firm in small country X wants to buy currency Y to pay for merchandise imports from small country Y, it may well be cheaper to sell X for dollars and then use dollars to buy Y rather than try to trade currency X for currency Y directly.

SHORT-TERM FOREIGN EXCHANGE RATE MOVEMENTS

Understanding the "market microstructure" allows us to explain the evolution of the foreign exchange market in an intradaily sense, in which foreign exchange traders adjust their bid and offer quotes throughout the business day.

A foreign exchange trader may be motivated to alter his or her exchange rate quotes in response to changes in his or her position with respect to orders to buy and sell a currency. For instance, suppose Helmut Smith is a foreign exchange trader at Deutsche Bank, who specializes in the dollar/euro market. The bank management controls risks associated with foreign currency trading by limiting the extent to which traders can take a position that would expose the bank to potential loss from unexpected changes in exchange rates. If Smith has agreed to buy more euros than he has agreed to sell, he has a *long position* in the euro and will profit from euro appreciation and lose from euro depreciation. If Smith has agreed to sell more euros than he has agreed to buy, he has a *short position* in the euro and will profit from euro depreciation and lose from euro appreciation. His position at any point in time may be called his *inventory*. One reason traders adjust their quotes is in response to inventory changes. At the end of the day most traders balance their position and are said to *go home "flat."* This means that their orders to buy a currency are just equal to their orders to sell. Thus, the profit the bank receives is from trading activity, not from speculative activity.

FAQ: What Is a Rogue Trader?

Many bank traders are required to balance their positions daily. This is done to eliminate the risk that the overnight position changes in value dramatically. Note that in the arbitrage case the buying and selling is almost instantaneous. Therefore, there is practically no risk. The longer one has to wait for an offsetting position, the more risk there is. Thus, there is a speculative risk when a bank adopts a one-sided bet. An overnight position would be too much risk for most banks to accept, as this is a high-risk speculation.

However, banks have been subject to fraud at times where they seem to be unable to control what traders do. If traders take on their own bets in exception to the bank's risk controls then they have become "rogue traders." In September 2011, UBS bank discovered that one of their traders, Kweku Adoboli, had entered into upward of $10 billion in trades with fictitious offset trades. Effectively this created risky positions that lost UBS as much as $2.3 billion.

The most famous "rogue trader" is Nick Leeson, who lost $1.3 billion while working for Barings Investment bank in the early 1990s. He bought futures contracts without any offsetting transactions, claiming that they were purchase orders on behalf of a client. The loss to Barings Investment bank was so high that the well-respected bank that had existed over 200 years had to declare bankruptcy. Nick received a prison sentence in a Singapore jail for 6.5 years. For more on the life of Nick Leeson, see Leeson (2011) or watch Ewan McGregor starring as Nick Leeson in the movie *Rogue Trader*.

Let us look at an example. Suppose Helmut Smith has been buying and selling euros for dollars throughout the day. By early afternoon his position is as follows:

dollar purchases: $100,000,000

dollar sales: $80,000,000

In order to balance his position, Smith will adjust his quotes to encourage fewer dollar purchases and more dollar sales. For instance, if the euro is currently trading at $1.4650–60, then Helmut could raise the bid and offer quotes to encourage others to sell him euros in exchange for his dollars, while deterring others from buying more euros from him. For instance, if he changes the quote to 1.4655–65, then someone could sell him euros (or buy his dollars) for $1.4655 per euro. Since he has raised the dollar price of a euro, he will receive more interest from people wanting to sell him euros in exchange for his dollars. When Helmut buys euros from other traders, he is selling them dollars, and this helps to balance his inventory and reduce his long position in the dollar. At the same time Helmut has raised the sell rate of euros to $1.4665. This discourages other traders from buying more euros from Helmut (giving him dollars as payments).

This *inventory control* effect on exchange rates can explain why traders may alter their quotes in the absence of any news about exchange rate fundamentals.

In addition to the inventory control effect, there is also an *asymmetric information* effect, which causes exchange rates to change due to traders' fears that they are quoting prices to someone who knows more about current market conditions than they do. Even without news regarding the fundamentals, information is being transmitted from one trader to another through the act of trading. If Helmut posts a quote of 1.0250–260 and is called by Ingrid Schultz at Citibank asking to buy $5 million of euros at Helmut's offer price of 1.0260, Helmut then must wonder whether Ingrid knows something he doesn't. Should Ingrid's order to trade at Helmut's price be considered a signal that Helmut's price is too low? What superior information could Ingrid have? Every bank receives orders from nonbank customers to buy and sell currency. Perhaps Ingrid knows that her bank has just received a large order from Daimler Benz to sell dollars, and she is selling dollars (and buying euros) in advance of the price increase that will be caused by this nonbank order being filled by purchasing euros from other traders.

Helmut does not know why Ingrid is buying euros at his offer price, but he protects himself from further euro sales to someone who may be better informed than he is by raising his offer price. The bid price may be left unchanged because the order was to buy his euros; in such a case the spread increases, with the higher offer price due to the possibility of trading with a better-informed counterparty who wants him to sell euros.

The inventory control and asymmetric information effects can help explain why exchange rates change throughout the day, even in the absence of news regarding the fundamental determinants of exchange rates. The act of trading generates price changes among risk-averse traders who seek to manage their inventory positions to limit their exposure to surprising exchange rate changes and limit the potential loss from trading with better-informed individuals.

LONG-TERM FOREIGN EXCHANGE MOVEMENTS

Thus far we have examined short-run movements in exchange rates. For the most part we are interested in long-term movements in this book. Since the exchange rate is the price of one money in terms of another, changes in exchange rates affect the prices of goods and services traded internationally. Therefore most of this book is concerned with why exchange rates move and how we can avoid these effects. In this section we will introduce a simple but powerful tool, called the *trade flow model*. The trade flow model argues that the exchange rate responds to the demand for traded goods by countries.

We can use a familiar diagram from principles of economics courses—the supply and demand diagram. Fig. 1.4 illustrates the market for the yen/dollar exchange rate. Think of the demand for dollars as coming from the Japanese demand for US goods (they must buy dollars in order to purchase US goods). The downward-sloping demand curve illustrates that the higher the yen price of the dollar, the more expensive US goods are to Japanese buyers, so the smaller the quantity of dollars demanded. The supply curve is the supply of dollars to the yen/dollar market and comes from US buyers of Japanese goods (in order to obtain Japanese products, US importers have to supply dollars to obtain yen). The upward-sloping supply curve indicates that as US residents receive more yen per dollar, they will buy more from Japan and will supply a larger quantity of dollars to the market.

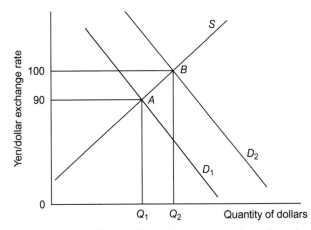

Figure 1.4 Traders' increased demand for dollars increases the dollar value.

The initial equilibrium exchange rate is at point *A*, where the exchange rate is 90 yen per dollar. Now suppose there is an increase in Japanese demand for US products. This increases the demand for dollars so that the demand curve shifts from D_1 to D_2. The equilibrium exchange rate will now change to 100 yen per dollar at point *B* as the dollar appreciates in value against the yen. This dollar appreciation makes Japanese goods cheaper to US buyers.

In the above example the demand for US dollars changed. The supply may also change. Such an example is illustrated in Fig. 1.5. Assume that the US starts at point B with a 100 yen/$ exchange rate. If US consumers start liking Japanese products more than before, this will result in a supply curve shift. US importers will be more eager to give up their dollars in exchange for yen. This shifts the supply curve out to the right, from S_1 to S_2, and lowers the value of the dollar. The new equilibrium is at point C, where the yen/dollar rate is at 85.

The examples above illustrate that the trade flow model can be a useful model to show the exchange rate changes in response to changes in demand for products in two countries. In the next chapter we will expand the trade flow model by adding central bank intervention. Later in the text we will examine other models that can explain exchange rate movements.

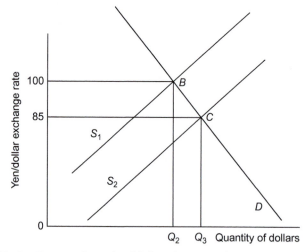

Figure 1.5 Traders' increased supply of dollars decreases the dollar value.

SUMMARY

1. The foreign exchange market is a global market where foreign currency deposits are traded. Trading in actual currency notes is generally limited to tourism or illegal activities.
2. The dollar/euro currency pair dominates foreign exchange trading volume, and the United Kingdom is the largest trading location.
3. A spot exchange rate is the price of a currency in terms of another currency for current delivery. Banks buy (bid) foreign exchange at a lower rate than they sell (offer), and the difference between the selling and buying rates is called the spread.
4. Arbitrage realizes riskless profit from market disequilibrium by buying a currency in one market and selling it in another. Arbitrage ensures that exchange rates are transaction costs close in all markets.
5. The factors that explain why exchange rates vary so much in the short run are inventory control and asymmetric information.
6. In the long run, economic factors (e.g., demand/supply of foreign and domestic goods) affect the exchange rate movements. The trade flow model is useful for discussing fundamental changes in the foreign exchange rate.

EXERCISES

1. Suppose Nomura Bank quotes the ¥/$ exchange rate as 110.30–.40. Assume you need ¥100,000. How much dollars do you need to pay Nomura Bank to buy ¥100,000. Explain.
2. Compute the cross rate for the following quotes.
   a. Compute the C$/€ using the following C$/$ = 1.5613, $/€ = 1.0008
   b. Compute the £/¥ using the following ¥/$ = 124.84, $/£ = 1.5720
   c. Compute the SF/C$ using the following SF/$ = 1.4706, C$/$ = 1.5613
3. Suppose Citibank quotes the ¥/$ exchange rate as 110.30–.40 and Nomura Bank quotes 110.40–.50. Is there an arbitrage opportunity? If so, explain how you would profit from these quotes. If not, explain why not.

4. Suppose that the spot rates of the US dollar, British pound, and Swedish kronor are quoted in three locations as the following:

	$/£	$/SKr	SKr/£
New York	2.00	0.25	–
London	2.00	–	10.00
Stockholm	–	0.25	10.00

Is there an arbitrage opportunity? If so, explain how you, as a trader who has $1,000,000, would profit from these quotes. If not, explain why not.

5. Consider the market for Japanese yen using the trade flow model. What would happen to the value of the Japanese yen (dollar per yen) if Japanese people like American automobiles more than before? Explain graphically.

FURTHER READING

Bank for International Settlements, 2016. Triennial Central Bank Survey of Foreign Exchange and OTC Derivatives Markets in 2016, Basel, September.

Berger, D.W., Chaboud, A.P., Chernenko, S.V., Howorka, E., Wright, J., 2008. Order flow and exchange rate dynamics in electronic brokerage system data. J. Int. Econ. 75 (1), 93–109.

Evans, M., Lyons, R., 2002. Order flow and exchange rate dynamics. J. Polit. Econ. 110 (1), 170–180.

N. Leeson, 2011. <www.nickleeson.com>.

Lyons, R.K., 1995. Tests of microstructural hypotheses in the foreign exchange market. J. Financ. Econ. 39, 321–351.

Norrbin, S., Pipatchaipoom, O., 2007. Is the real dollar rate highly volatile? Econ. Bull. 6 (2), 1–15.

APPENDIX A TRADE-WEIGHTED EXCHANGE RATE INDEXES

Suppose we want to consider the value of a currency. One measure is the bilateral exchange rate—say, the yen value of the dollar. However, if we are interested in knowing how a currency is performing globally, we need a broader measure of the currency's value against many other currencies. This is analogous to looking at a consumer price index to measure how prices in an economy are changing. We could look at the price of shoes or the price of a loaf of bread, but such single-good prices will not necessarily reflect the general inflationary situation—some prices may be rising while others are falling.

In the foreign exchange market it is common to see a currency rising in value against one foreign currency while it depreciates relative to another. As a result, exchange rate indexes are constructed to measure the average value of a currency relative to several other currencies. An *exchange rate index* is a weighted average of a currency's value relative to other currencies, with the weights typically based on the importance of each currency to international trade. If we want to construct an exchange rate index for the United States, we would include the currencies of the countries that are the major trading partners of the United States.

If half of US trade was with Canada and the other half was with Mexico, then the percentage change in the trade-weighted dollar exchange rate index would be found by multiplying the percentage change in both the Canadian dollar/US dollar exchange rate and the Mexican peso/ US dollar exchange rate by one-half and summing the result. Table A.1 lists two popular exchange rate indexes and their weighting schemes.

Table A.1 Percentage weights used in 2016 for the major and broad exchange rate indexes

	Exchange rate index	
Country	**Major**	**Broad**
Euro area	38.9	16.6
Canada	29.7	12.7
Japan	15.2	6.5
United Kingdom	7.7	3.3
Switzerland	4.0	1.7
Australia	2.8	1.2
Sweden	1.6	0.7
Mexico		12.1
China		21.6
Taiwan		2.4
Korea		3.9
Singapore		1.7
Hong Kong		1.3
Malaysia		1.5
Brazil		2.1
Thailand		1.4
Philippines		0.6
Indonesia		1.0
India		2.0
Israel		1.0
Saudi Arabia		1.0
Russia		1.4
Argentina		0.6
Venezuela		0.3
Chile		0.8
Colombia		0.7
Total	100.0	100.0

Source: Board of Governors of the Federal Reserve System, Table H.10; Authors' calculation.

Figure A.1 The dollar value for two different exchange rate indices (1975–2015). *Source: Federal Reserve Bank of St. Louis, FRED data, Authors' calculation.*

The indexes listed are the Federal Reserve Board's *Major Currency Index*, (TWEXMMTH) and the *Broad Currency Index* (TWEXBMTH).

Since the different indexes are constructed using different currencies, should we expect them to tell a different story? It is entirely possible for a currency to be appreciating against some currencies while it depreciates against others. Therefore, the exchange rate indexes will not all move identically. Fig. A.1 plots the movement of the various indexes over time.

Fig. A.1 indicates that the value of the dollar generally rose in the early 1980s—a conclusion we draw regardless of the exchange rate index used. Differences arise in the 1990s where the dollar stayed fairly constant against the major currencies, but appreciated according to the broad currency index. In the 2000s both indexes again tell the same story, with both indexes showing a depreciating dollar, until 2015 when the dollar appreciates according both indexes.

Since different indexes assign a different importance to each foreign currency, the different movement of the dollar for the two indexes is not surprising. For instance, if we look at the weights in Table A.1, then a period in which the dollar appreciated rapidly against the Mexican peso relative to other currencies would result in the Major Currency Index to record a smaller dollar appreciation relative to the Broad Currency Index. This is because the peso accounts for 12.1 percent of the Broad Currency Index, but zero for the Major Currency Index.

Exchange rate indexes are commonly used analytical tools in international economics. When changes in the average value of a currency are important, bilateral exchange rates (between only two currencies) are unsatisfactory. Neither economic theory nor practice gives a clear indication of which exchange rate index is best. In fact, for some questions there is little to differentiate one index from another. In many cases, however, the best index to use will depend on the question addressed.

APPENDIX B THE TOP FOREIGN EXCHANGE DEALERS

Foreign exchange trading is dominated by large commercial banks with worldwide operations. The market is very competitive, since each bank tries to maintain its share of the corporate business. *Euromoney* magazine provides some interesting insights into this market by publishing periodic surveys of information supplied by the treasurers of the major multinational firms.

When asked to rank the factors that determined who got their foreign exchange business, the treasurers responded that the following factors were the most important: The speed with which a bank makes foreign exchange quotes was ranked third. A second-place ranking was given to competitiveness of quotes. The most important factor was the firm's relationship with the bank. A bank that handles the other banking needs of a firm is also likely to receive its foreign exchange business.

The significance of competitive quotes is indicated by the fact that treasurers often contact more than one bank to get several quotes before placing a deal. Another implication is that the foreign exchange market will be dominated by big banks, because only the giants have the global activity to allow competitive quotes on a large number of currencies. *Euromoney* conducts an annual survey of major financial market participants to create a view of who does the most business. Table B.1 gives the rankings of the *Euromoney* survey. According to the rankings, Citi receives more business than any other bank. Note also that the big two—Citi and Deutsche Bank—dominate the foreign exchange market. The top ten banks are responsible for over ¾ of all foreign exchange trade in the world.

What makes Citi the world's best foreign exchange dealer? Many factors have kept them on top of the heap. An important factor is simply sheer size. Citi holds the bank accounts for many corporations, giving it a natural advantage in foreign exchange trading. Foreign exchange trading

Table B.1 The top ten foreign exchange dealers by market share

Rank	Bank	Market share
1	Citi	16.1%
2	Deutsche Bank	14.5%
3	Barclays	8.1%
4	JPMorgan	7.7%
5	UBS	7.3%
6	Bank of America Merrill Lynch	6.2%
7	HSBC	5.4%
8	BNP Paribas	3.7%
9	Goldman Sachs	3.4%
10	RBS	3.4%

Source: Euromoney FX Survey–Global FX Market Share, May 2015.

has emerged as an important center for bank profitability. Since each trade generates revenue for the bank, the volatile foreign exchange markets of recent years have often led to frenetic activity in the market with a commensurate revenue increase for the banks.

CHAPTER 2

International Monetary Arrangements

Contents

Like most areas of public policy, international monetary relations are subject to frequent proposals for change. Fixed exchange rates, floating exchange rates, and commodity-backed currency all have their advocates. Before considering the merits of alternative international monetary systems, we should understand the background of the international monetary system. Although an international monetary system has existed since monies have been traded, it is common for most modern discussions of international monetary history to start in the late 19th century. It was during this period that the gold standard began.

THE GOLD STANDARD: 1880–1914

Although an exact date for the beginning of the gold standard cannot be pinpointed, we know that it started during the period from 1880 to 1890.

Under a *gold standard*, currencies are valued in terms of their gold equiva-lent (an ounce of gold was worth $20.67 in terms of the US dollar over the gold standard period). The gold standard is an important beginning for a discussion of international monetary systems because when each cur-rency is defined in terms of its gold value, all currencies are linked in a system of fixed exchange rates. For instance, if currency A is worth 0.10 ounce of gold, whereas currency B is worth 0.20 ounce of gold, then 1 unit of currency B is worth twice as much as 1 unit of A, and thus the exchange rate of 1 currency $B = 2$ currency A is established.

Maintaining a gold standard requires a commitment from participating countries to be willing to buy and sell gold to anyone at the fixed price. To maintain a price of $20.67 per ounce, the United States had to buy and sell gold at that price. Gold was used as the monetary standard because it is a homogeneous commodity (could you have a fish standard?) world-wide that is easily storable, portable, and divisible into standardized units like ounces. Since gold is costly to produce, it possesses another important attribute—governments cannot easily increase its supply. A gold standard is a *commodity money standard*. Money has a value that is fixed in terms of the commodity gold.

One aspect of a money standard that is based on a commodity with relatively fixed supply is long-run price stability. Since governments must maintain a fixed value of their money relative to gold, the supply of money is restricted by the supply of gold. Prices may still rise and fall with swings in gold output and economic growth, but the tendency is to return to a long-run stable level. Fig. 2.1 illustrates graphically the relative stabil-ity of US and UK prices over the gold standard period as compared to later years. However, note also that prices fluctuated up and down in the short run during the gold standard. Thus, frequent small bursts of inflation and deflation occurred in the short run, but in the long run the price level remained unaffected. Since currencies were convertible into gold, national money supplies were constrained by the growth of the stock of gold. As long as the gold stock grew at a steady rate, prices would also follow a steady path. New discoveries of gold would generate discontinuous jumps in the price level, but the period of the gold standard was marked by a fairly stable stock of gold.

People today often look back on the gold standard as a "golden era" of economic progress. It is common to hear arguments supporting a return to the gold standard. Such arguments usually cite the stable prices, eco-nomic growth, and development of world trade during this period as

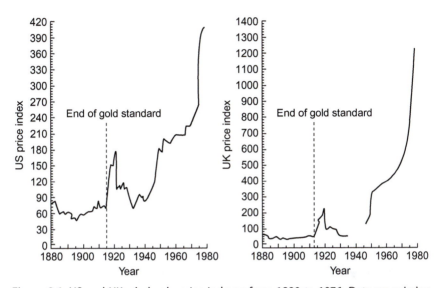

Figure 2.1 US and UK wholesale price indexes from 1880 to 1976. Data are missing for World War II years in the United Kingdom. *Source: Roy W., Jastram, 1977. The Golden Constant, Wiley, New York.*

evidence of the benefits provided by such an orderly international monetary system. Others have suggested that the economic development and stability of the world economy in those years did not necessarily reflect the existence of the gold standard but, instead, the absence of any significant real shocks such as war. Although we may disagree on the merits of returning to a gold standard, it seems fair to say that the development of world trade was encouraged by the systematic linking of national currencies and the price stability of the system. Since gold is like a world money during a gold standard, we can easily understand how a balance of payments disequilibrium may be remedied. A country running a balance of payments (official settlements) deficit would find itself with net outflows of gold, which would reduce its money supply and, in turn, its prices. A surplus country would find gold flowing in and expanding its money supply, so that prices rose. The fall in price in the deficit country would lead to greater net exports (exports minus imports), and the rise in price in the surplus country would reduce its net exports, so that balance of payments equilibrium would be restored.

In practice, actual flows of gold were not the only, or even necessarily the most important, means of settling international debts during this period. Since London was the financial center of the world, and England the world's leading trader and source of financial capital, the pound also served as a world money. International trade was commonly priced in pounds, and trade that never passed through England was often paid for with pounds.

THE INTERWAR PERIOD: 1918–1939

World War I ended the gold standard. International financial relations are greatly strained by war, because merchants and bankers must be concerned about the probability of countries suspending international capital flows. At the beginning of the war both the patriotic response of each nation's citizens and legal restrictions stopped private gold flows. Since wartime financing required the hostile nations to manage international reserves very carefully, private gold exports were considered unpatriotic. Central governments encouraged (and sometimes mandated) that private holders of gold and foreign exchange sell these holdings to the government.

Because much of Europe experienced rapid inflation during the war and in the period immediately following it, it was not possible to restore the gold standard at the old exchange values. However, the United States had experienced little inflation and thus returned to a gold standard by June 1919. The war ended Britain's financial preeminence, since the United States had risen to the status of the world's dominant banker country. In the immediate postwar years the pound fluctuated freely against the dollar in line with changes in the price level of each country.

In 1925, England returned to a gold standard at the old prewar pound per gold exchange rate, even though prices had risen since the pre-war period. As John Maynard Keynes had correctly warned, the overvalued pound hurt UK exports and led to a deflation of British wages and prices. By 1931, the pound was declared inconvertible because of a run on British gold reserves (a large demand to convert pounds into gold), and so ended the brief UK return to a gold standard. Once the pound was no longer convertible into gold, attention centered on the US dollar. A run on US gold at the end of 1931 led to a 15% drop in US gold holdings. Although this did not lead to an immediate change in US policy, by 1933 the United States abandoned the gold standard.

The depression years were characterized by international monetary warfare. In trying to stimulate domestic economies by increasing exports, country after country devalued, so that the early to mid-1930s may be characterized as a period of *competitive devaluations*. Governments also resorted to foreign exchange controls in an attempt to manipulate net exports in a manner that would increase gross domestic product (GDP). Of course, with the onslaught of World War II, the hostile countries utilized foreign exchange controls to aid the war-financing effort.

THE BRETTON WOODS AGREEMENT: 1944–1973

Memories of the economic warfare of the interwar years led to an international conference at Bretton Woods, New Hampshire, in 1944. At the close of World War II there was a desire to reform the international monetary system to one based on mutual cooperation and freely convertible currencies.

There was a need for a system that fixed currencies relative to each other, but did not fix each currency in terms of gold. The Bretton Woods agreement solved this problem by requiring that each country fix the value of its currency in terms of an anchor currency, namely the dollar (this established the "par" value of each currency and was to ensure parity across currencies). The US dollar was the key currency in the system, and *$1 was defined as being equal in value to 1/35 ounce of gold.* Since every currency had an implicitly defined gold value, through the link to the dollar, all currencies were linked in a system of fixed exchange rates.

Nations were committed to maintaining the parity value of their currencies within 1% of parity. The various central banks were to achieve this goal by buying and selling their currencies (usually against the dollar) on the foreign exchange market. When a country was experiencing difficulty maintaining its parity value because of balance of payments disequilibrium, it could turn to a new institution created at the Bretton Woods Conference: *the International Monetary Fund (IMF)*. The IMF was created to monitor the operation of the system and provide short-term loans to countries experiencing temporary balance of payments difficulties. Such loans are subject to IMF conditions regarding changes in domestic economic policy aimed at restoring balance of payments equilibrium.

In the case of a fundamental disequilibrium, when the balance of payments problems are not of a temporary nature, a country could apply for permission from the IMF to devalue or revalue its currency. Such a permanent change in the parity rate of exchange was rare. Table 2.1

Table 2.1 Exchange rates of the major industrial countries over the period of the Bretton woods agreement

Country	Exchange rates[a]
Canada	Floated until May 2, 1962, then pegged at C$1.081 = $1. Floated again on June 1, 1970.
France	No official IMF parity value after 1948 (although the actual rate hovered around FF350 = $1) until December 29, 1958, when rate fixed at FF493.7 = $1 (old francs). One year later, rate was FF4.937 = $1 when new franc (one new franc was equal to 100 old francs) was created. Devaluation to FF5.554 = $1 on August 10, 1969.
Germany	Revalued on March 6, 1961, from DM4.20 = $1 to DM4.0 = $1. Revalued to DM3.66 = $1 on October 26, 1969.
Italy	Pegged at Lit625 = $1 from March 30, 1960, until August 1971.
Japan	Pegged at ¥360 = $1 until 1971.
Netherlands	Pegged at F13.80 = $1 until March 7, 1961, when revalued at F13.62 = $1.
United Kingdom	Devalued from $2.80 = £1 to $2.40 = £1 on November 11, 1967.

[a]Relative to the US dollar.

summarizes the history of exchange rate adjustments over the Bretton Woods period for the major industrial countries. The Bretton Woods system, although essentially a fixed, or pegged, exchange rate system, allowed for changes in exchange rates when economic circumstances warranted such changes. In actuality, the system is best described as an *adjustable peg*. The system may also be described as a gold exchange standard because the key currency, the dollar, was convertible into gold for official holders of dollars (such as central banks and treasuries).

CENTRAL BANK INTERVENTION DURING BRETTON WOODS

By signing the Bretton Woods agreement, countries agreed to protect their exchange rate from moving up or down from the agreed-upon rate. This agreement implied that central banks had to take on a more active role in making sure that market pressure did not change the exchange rate. The various central banks achieved this goal by buying and selling their domestic currencies on the foreign exchange market. The central bank

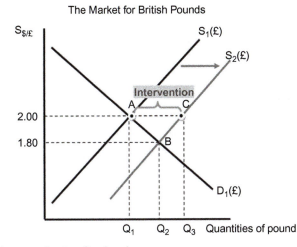

Figure 2.2 Intervention in a fixed exchange rate system.

intervention can be illustrated using the trade flow model developed in Chapter 1, The Foreign Exchange Market. Assume that the United States and the United Kingdom are trading with each other, and that the UK residents start demanding more Fords (a US good). In the first chapter you learned that this would imply a shift in the supply curve for pounds. UK traders would be more willing to supply their pounds to banks in exchange for dollars, because the traders want to buy US goods. Banks see more customers supplying pounds and demanding dollars, causing banks to want to depreciate the pound. Fig. 2.2 illustrates the shift in the supply curve causing the banks to want to depreciate the pound from a starting dollar/pound exchange rate of 2.00 to a new equilibrium exchange rate of 1.80.

To prevent the pound from depreciating the Bank of England (the central bank in the United Kingdom) has to intervene in the foreign exchange market. The Bank of England must intervene by buying up pounds and selling dollars that they have already stored in their bank vaults. Fig. 2.2 shows that the Bank of England has to buy a quantity of pounds equivalent to the distance from Q_1 to Q_3, and sell a quantity of dollars equal to the quantity of pounds multiplied by the 2.00 exchange rate. This action would supply enough dollars to prevent private banks and traders from changing the exchange rate.

FAQ: What Are Special Drawing Rights?

There is one odd currency that is priced in any currency table, but does not physically exist, namely the Special Drawing Right (SDR). This "currency" was issued by the IMF, but never existed in physical form. Instead it has been used as a unit of account for a long time. For example, all of IMF's own accounts are quoted in SDRs.

The SDR first appeared in 1969. The SDR was used to support the Bretton Woods fixed exchange rate system. Participating countries in the Bretton Woods agreement needed more official reserves to support the domestic exchange rate. However, at that time, the supply of gold and US dollars was insufficient for the rapid growth of world trade. The SDR provided more liquidity to the world markets and allowed countries to continue to expand trade. The SDR does not exist as notes and coins, but has value because all member countries of the IMF have agreed to accept it.

Allocations of SDRs are rare, and have only happened four times in history. The first allocation was in 1970–72 (SDR 9.3 billion) in the very end of the Bretton Woods system. The next one was in 1979–81 (SDR 12.1 billion). After that no more SDRs were allocated until the Great Recession. In August 28, 2009 SDR 161.2 billion were allocated and 21.5 billion SDRs were allocated shortly thereafter in September 9, 2009. Further information about the SDRs can be obtained from http://www.imf.org/external/np/exr/facts/sdr.HTM.

The table below shows the value of an SDR. On January 13, 2017 one SDR was worth $1.3513. The value is computed by the weighted value of the yuan, euro, the Japanese yen, the pound sterling and the US dollar. The weights are revisited every five years and these weights were established On October 1, 2016.

SDR Valuation

Friday, January 29, 2016

Currency	Currency amount under Rule O-1	Exchange rate	US Dollar equivalent
Chinese Yuan	1.0174	6.8490	0.14854
Euro	0.3867	1.06465	0.411711
Japanese yen	11.90	114.665	0.103781
Pound sterling	0.0859	1.21810	0.104691
US dollar	0.5825	1	0.5825
			1.3513
		US$1.00 = SDR	0.7400
		SDR1 = US$	1.3513

Source: IMF.org.

Note that the model used to illustrate the intervention is a flow model. This means that in each period the situation will occur. For example, if the period is a year, then the excess supply of pounds will exist every year, as long as the new demand for Fords exists. Thus, the Bank of England has to intervene each year and buy pounds and sell dollars. If the excess supply persists too long, the Bank of England may run out of dollars in their vaults, and would be forced to apply for permission from the IMF to devalue their currency to be in line with the new market exchange rate (in this example 1.80).

THE BREAKDOWN OF THE BRETTON WOODS SYSTEM

The Bretton Woods system worked well through the 1950s and part of the 1960s. In 1960, there was a dollar crisis because the United States had run large balance of payments deficits in the late 1950s. Concern over large foreign holdings of dollars led to an increased demand for gold. Central bank cooperation in an international gold pool managed to stabilize gold prices at the official rate, but still the pressures mounted. Although the problem of chronic US deficits and Japanese and European surpluses could have been remedied by revaluing the undervalued yen, mark, and franc, the surplus countries argued that it was the responsibility of the United States to restore balance of payments equilibrium.

The failure to realign currency values in the face of fundamental economic change spelled the beginning of the end for the gold exchange standard of the Bretton Woods agreement. By the late 1960s the foreign dollar liabilities of the United States were much larger than the US gold stock. The pressures of this "dollar glut" finally culminated in August 1971, when President Nixon declared the dollar to be inconvertible and provided a close to the Bretton Woods era of fixed exchange rates and convertible currencies.

THE TRANSITION YEARS: 1971–1973

In December 1971, an international monetary conference was held to realign the foreign exchange values of the major currencies. The *Smithsonian agreement* provided for a change in the dollar per gold exchange value from $35 to $38.02 per ounce of gold. At the same time that the dollar was being devalued by about 8%, the surplus countries saw their currencies revalued upward. After the change in official currency values the system was to operate with fixed exchange rates under which the central banks would buy and sell their currencies to maintain the exchange rate within 2.25% of the stated parity. Although the realignment of currency values provided by the Smithsonian agreement allowed a temporary respite from foreign exchange crises, the calm was short-lived. Speculative flows of capital began to put downward pressure on the pound and lira. In June 1972, the pound began to float according to supply and demand conditions. The countries experiencing large inflows of speculative capital, such as Germany and Switzerland, applied legal controls to slow further movements of money into their countries.

Although the gold value of the dollar had been officially changed, the dollar was still inconvertible into gold, and thus the major significance of the dollar devaluation was with respect to the foreign exchange value of the dollar, not to official gold movements. The speculative capital flows of 1972 and early 1973 led to a further devaluation of the dollar in February 1973, when the official price of an ounce of gold rose from $38 to $42.22. Still, the speculative capital flows persisted from the weak to the strong currencies. Finally, in March 1973, the major currencies began to float.

INTERNATIONAL RESERVE CURRENCIES

International reserves are the means of settling international debts. Under the gold standard, gold was the major component of international reserves. Following World War II, we had a gold exchange standard in which international reserves included both gold and a reserve currency, the US dollar. The reserve currency country was to hold gold as backing for the outstanding balances of the currency held by foreigners. These foreign holders of the currency were then free to convert the currency into gold if they wished. However, as we observed with the dollar, once the convertibility of the currency becomes suspect, or once large amounts of the currency are presented for gold, the system tends to fall apart.

At the end of World War II, and throughout the 1950s, the world demanded dollars for use as an international reserve. During this time, US balance of payments deficits provided the world with a much-needed source of growth for international reserves. As the rest of the world developed and matured, over time US liabilities to foreigners greatly exceeded the gold reserve backing these liabilities. Yet as long as the increase in demand for these dollar reserves equaled the supply, the lack of gold backing was irrelevant. Through the late 1960s, US political and economic events began to cause problems for the dollar's international standing, and the continuing US deficits were not matched by a growing demand, so that pressure to convert dollars into gold resulted in the dollar being declared officially no longer exchangeable for gold in August 1971.

Table 2.2 illustrates the diversification of the currency composition of foreign exchange reserves since the mid-1970s. The table shows a falling share of international reserves devoted to dollars until the beginning of the 1990s. The mark and yen gained larger shares of the international reserve portfolio from the mid-1970s to mid-1990s. In the 2000s the

Table 2.2 Share of national currencies in total identified official holdings of foreign exchange (in %)

	1977	1985	1993	2001	2006	2011	2015
All countries							
US Dollar	80.3	65.1	55.6	68.3	65.5	62.2	64.1
Pound Sterling	1.8	3.2	2.9	4.0	4.4	3.8	3.9
Deutshe Mark	9.3	15.5	14.0	–	–	–	–
French Franc	1.3	1.2	2.2	–	–	–	–
Swiss Franc	2.3	2.4	1.1	0.7	0.1	0.1	0.3
Netherlands Guilder	0.9	1.0	0.6	–	–	–	–
Japanese Yen	2.5	7.6	7.7	4.9	3.1	3.5	4.2
Other currencies	1.6	3.9	7.3	9.0	1.8	5.3	6.8
ECU's	–	–	8.6	–	–	–	–
Euro	–	–	–	13.0	25.1	25.0	20.7
Industrial countries							
US Dollar	89.4	63.2	49.9	74.5	68.1	66.3	64.5
Pound Sterling	0.9	2.0	2.0	1.8	3.2	2.5	3.1
Deutshe Mark	5.5	19.2	16.2	–	–	–	–
French Franc	0.3	0.5	2.5	–	–	–	–
Swiss Franc	0.8	1.8	0.3	0.4	0.1	0.2	0.4
Netherlands Guilder	0.6	1.0	0.4	–	–	–	–
Japanese Yen	1.8	8.5	7.7	5.5	4.2	4.2	4.7
Other currencies	0.7	3.9	5.8	8.1	1.9	3.9	5.7
ECU's	–	–	15.2	–	–	–	–
Euro	–	–	–	9.7	22.2	22.9	21.5
Developing countries							
US Dollar	70.9	67.5	63.1	64.1	61.5	57.6	63.6
Pound Sterling	2.8	4.7	4.0	5.5	6.0	5.3	5.0
Deutshe Mark	13.3	10.9	11.1	–	–	–	–
French Franc	2.3	2.1	1.9	–	–	–	–
Swiss Franc	3.9	3.1	2.2	0.9	0.1	0.1	0.1
Netherlands Guilder	1.2	1.1	0.9	–	–	–	–
Japanese Yen	3.2	6.5	7.6	4.5	1.4	2.7	3.4
Other currencies	2.5	4.0	9.3	9.6	1.6	6.9	8.3
Euro	–	–	–	15.3	29.4	27.4	19.6

Source: IMF, Currency Compilation of Official Foreign Reserves (COFER), September, 2015; Data for 2015 is first quarter data.

dollar share once again increased. Although the share of the dollar in 2015 is not as high as in the mid–1970s, it still exceeds 60% of the international reserves. Furthermore, the euro has a substantial share of reserves, at 20.7%, but it has not threatened the dominance of the dollar.

At first glance, it may appear very desirable to be the reserve currency and have other countries accept your balance of payments deficits as a necessary means of financing world trade. The difference between the cost of creating new balances and the real resources acquired with the new balances is called *seigniorage*. Seigniorage is a financial reward accruing to the issuer of currency. The central bank's seigniorage is the difference between the cost of money creation and the return to the assets it acquires. In addition to such central bank seigniorage, a reserve currency country also receives additional seigniorage when foreign countries demand the currency issued and put those in its vaults, as this reduces the inflationary pressure that money creation causes.

Table 2.2 indicates that the dollar is still, by far, the dominant reserve currency. Since the US international position has been somewhat eroded in the past few decades, the question arises as to why we did not see the Japanese yen, or Swiss franc emerge as the dominant reserve currency. Although the yen and Swiss franc have been popular currencies, the respective governments in each country have resisted a greater international role for their monies. Besides the apparently low additional seigniorage return to the dominant international money, there is another reason for these countries to resist. The dominant money producer (country) finds that international shifts in the demand for its money may have repercussions on domestic operations. For a country the size of the United States, domestic economic activity is large relative to international activity, so international capital flows of any given magnitude have a much smaller potential to disrupt US markets than would be the case for Japanese, or Swiss markets, where foreign operations are much more important. In this sense, it is clear why these countries have withstood the movement of the yen and franc to reserve currency status. Over time, we may find that the euro emerges as a dominant reserve currency as the combined economies of the euro-area countries provide a very large base of economic activity. However, Table 2.2 shows that the euro still only accounts for 20.7% of total international reserves, so it is not close to the 64.1% share taken by the dollar. In addition, the euro share seems to have stabilized at around 21–22% of the reserve holdings. Most of the growth in the euro reserve holdings has come at the expense of other currencies than the dollar, effectively creating a dual currency reserve system with the dollar and the euro dominating the international reserves.

FAQ: How Big Is the Foreign Reserve Buildup in China?

The Chinese central bank, the People's Bank of China, has been adding foreign exchange reserves at a very rapid pace in the 2000s. The growth in reserves has been so large, that China is by far the largest foreign reserve holder. The following chart shows the rapid addition of reserves in China.

Note in the chart that Chinese reserve holdings were small in the late 1990s, but have since grown to a tremendous amount of foreign exchange reserves. The reserve peaked in 2014 at nearly four trillion dollars, and in 2015 the reserves fell about 600 billion to slightly over 3.3 trillion dollars. Most of those assets are US dollar assets, implying that the central bank holds a tremendous amount of dollar assets.

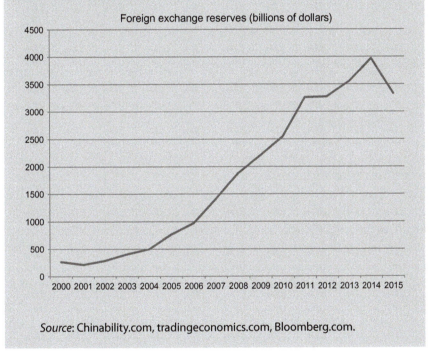

Foreign exchange reserves (billions of dollars)

Source: Chinability.com, tradingeconomics.com, Bloomberg.com.

In domestic monetary theory, economists often identify three roles of money. Money is said to serve as (1) a unit of account, (2) a medium of exchange, and (3) a store of value. Likewise, in an international context we can explain the choice of a reserve currency according to criteria relevant for each role. Table 2.3 summarizes the roles of a reserve currency. First, the role of the international unit of account results from information costs. We find that primary goods like coffee, tin, or rubber are quoted in terms of dollars worldwide. Since these goods are homogeneous, at

Table 2.3 Roles of a reserve currency

	Function	Resulting from private role	Official role
1. International unit of account	Information costs	Invoicing currency	Pegging currency
2. International medium of exchange	Transaction costs	Vehicle currency	Intervention currency
3. International store of value	Stable value	Banking currency	Reserve currency

least relative to manufactured goods, information regarding their value is conveyed more quickly when prices are quoted in terms of one currency worldwide. The private use as an invoicing currency in international trade contracts arises from the reserve currency's informational advantage over other currencies. Besides being a unit of account for private contracts, the reserve currency also serves as a base currency to which other currencies peg exchange rates.

A currency's role as an international medium of exchange is the result of transaction costs. In the case of the US dollar, the dollar is so widely traded that it is often cheaper to go from currency A to dollars to currency B, than directly from currency A to currency B. Thus, it is efficient to use the dollar as an international medium of exchange, and the dollar serves as the vehicle for buying and selling nondollar currencies. The private (mainly interbank) role as a vehicle currency means that the dollar (or the dominant reserve currency) will also be used by central banks in foreign exchange market intervention aimed at achieving target levels for exchange rates.

Finally, a currency's role as an international store of value results from the stability of its value. In other words, certainty of future value enhances a currency's role as a store of purchasing power. The US dollar's role in this area was diminished in the 1970s, and it seems likely that further instability in US monetary policy would contribute to a further fall. The private market use of the dollar for denominating international loans and deposits indicates the role of the dominant reserve currency in banking. In addition, countries will choose to hold their official reserves largely in the dominant reserve currency.

Fig. 2.3 shows the sharp growth in foreign reserves that has occurred in the last decade. During the Bretton Woods period the size of the

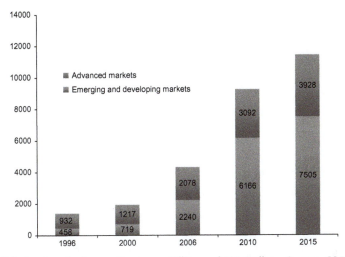

Figure 2.3 Foreign Exchange Reserves, Billions of US Dollars. *Source: COFER Data Report, IMF, 2015. Note that 2015 refers to 1st Quarter data.*

foreign reserves was a topic of interest, but became less important in the 1970s and 1980s. This topic has rebounded again as foreign reserve hold-ings have grown enormously in the 2000s. In particular emerging econ-omies, dominated by China, have added tremendous amounts of foreign exchange reserves. This sharp growth has been accompanied by sharp imbalances in trade balances, which will be a topic in the next chapter. However, before we can address the question of trade imbalances, we need to explore how exchange rate systems changed once the Bretton Woods agreement collapsed.

POST BRETTON WOODS: 1973 TO THE PRESENT

Although we refer to the exchange rate system in existence since 1973 as a floating rate system, few countries completely allow the market to define the exchange rate. In such a case we would call the exchange rate system a "purely floating" one. Instead, a multitude of methods to partly or com-pletely control the exchange rate has emerged. This choice of exchange rate system also dictates limitations on the ability of the central bank to conduct its monetary policy. Fig. 2.4 illustrates the major categories of exchange rate arrangements and the effect that such arrangements have on the monetary policy independence of a country. The types of exchange rate systems, in Fig. 2.4, range from (1), "dollarization" where the central

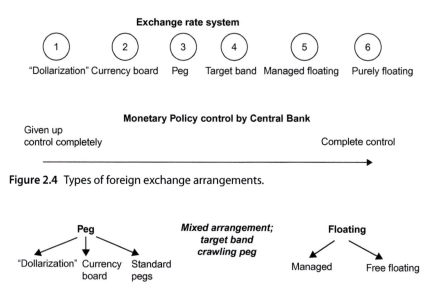

Figure 2.4 Types of foreign exchange arrangements.

Figure 2.5 Broad categories of exchange rate arrangements.

bank of the country has completely given up control of the money supply to adopt some other country's currency, to the other extreme of (6), purely floating, where the central bank retains domestic control over the currency in the country. In between, the central bank has some degree of control over the money supply.

The above categories can be summarized under three headings: peg, mixed, and floating, as shown in Fig. 2.5. All pegs involve a fixed rate that is selected by the government, whereas all the floating rates are to some degree market determined. The target bands and crawling pegs are exchange rate systems, somewhere in between the peg and floating, sharing some features of each. For example the target bands allow the exchange rate to be market determined within some range, but the rate is not allowed to go outside a range that is predetermined by the government.

We provide a brief description of each of the types of foreign exchange arrangements, starting with the exchange rate system with the most independent monetary policy to the one with the least independent monetary policy:

Free floating—The exchange rate is market determined, and any intervention is aimed at moderating fluctuations rather than determining the level of the exchange rate.

Managed floating—The monetary authority (usually the central bank) influences the exchange rate periodically through active foreign exchange market intervention with no preannounced path for the exchange rate.

Horizontal bands or *Target Bands*—The exchange rate fluctuates within an upper and lower band around a fixed central target rate. Such target bands allow for a moderate amount of exchange rate fluctuation while tying the currency to the target central rate.

Crawling pegs—The exchange rate is adjusted periodically in small amounts at a fixed, preannounced rate or in response to certain indicators (such as inflation differentials against major trading partners).

Crawling bands—The exchange rate is maintained within certain fluctuation margins around a central rate that is periodically adjusted at a fixed, preannounced rate or in response to certain indicators.

Fixed peg or *Conventional Peg*—The exchange rate is fixed against a major currency or some basket of currencies. Active intervention may be required to maintain the target pegged rate.

Currency board—A fixed exchange rate is established by a legislative commitment to exchange domestic currency for a specified foreign currency at a fixed exchange rate. New issues of domestic currency are typically backed in some fixed ratio (like one-to-one) by additional holdings of the key foreign currency.

"Dollarization" or *No separate legal tender*—Another country's currency is unilaterally adopted as the legal tender.

In Appendix A specific country examples of each of the above currency arrangements are provided.

THE CHOICE OF AN EXCHANGE RATE SYSTEM

Perfectly fixed or pegged exchange rates would work much as a gold standard does. All currencies would fix their exchange rate in terms of another currency, say, the dollar, and thereby would fix their rate relative to every other currency. Under such an arrangement each country would have to follow the monetary policy of the key currency in order to experience the same inflation rate and keep the exchange rate fixed.

Flexible or floating exchange rates occur when the exchange rate is determined by the market forces of supply and demand. As the demand for a currency increases relative to supply, that currency will appreciate, whereas currencies in which the quantity supplied exceeds the quantity demanded will depreciate.

Economists do not all agree on the advantages and disadvantages of a floating as opposed to a pegged exchange rate system. For instance, some would argue that a major advantage of flexible rates is that each country can follow domestic macroeconomic policies independent of the policies of other countries. To maintain fixed exchange rates, countries have to share a common inflation experience, which was often a source of problems under the post–World War II system of fixed exchange rates. If the dollar, which was the key currency for the system, was inflating at a rate faster than, say, Japan desired, then the lower inflation rate followed by the Japanese led to pressure for an appreciation of the yen relative to the dollar. Thus the existing pegged rate could not be maintained. Yet with flexible rates, each country can choose a desired rate of inflation and the exchange rate will adjust accordingly. Thus, if the United States chooses 8% inflation and Japan chooses 3%, there will be a steady depreciation of the dollar relative to the yen (absent any relative price movements). Given the different political environment and cultural heritage existing in each country, it is reasonable to expect different countries to follow different monetary policies. Floating exchange rates allow for an orderly adjustment to these differing inflation rates.

Still there are those economists who argue that the ability of each country to choose an inflation rate is an undesirable aspect of floating exchange rates. These proponents of fixed rates indicate that fixed rates are useful in providing an international discipline on the inflationary policies of countries. Fixed rates provide an anchor for countries with inflationary tendencies. By maintaining a fixed rate of exchange to the dollar (or some other currency), each country's inflation rate is "anchored" to the dollar, and thus will follow the policy established for the dollar.

Critics of flexible exchange rates have also argued that flexible exchange rates would be subject to destabilizing speculation. By *destabilizing speculation* we mean that speculators in the foreign exchange market will cause exchange rate fluctuations to be wider than they would be in the absence of such speculation. The logic suggests that, if speculators expect a currency to depreciate, they will take positions in the foreign exchange market that will cause the depreciation as a sort of self-fulfilling prophecy. But speculators should lose money when they guess wrong, so that only successful speculators will remain in the market, and the successful players serve a useful role by "evening out" swings in the exchange rate. For instance, if we expect a currency to depreciate or decrease in value next month, we could sell the currency now, which would result in a current depreciation. This will lead to a smaller future depreciation than would occur otherwise. The speculator then spreads the exchange rate change more evenly through time and tends to even out big jumps in the exchange rate. If the speculator had bet on the future depreciation by selling the currency now and the currency appreciates instead of depreciates, then the speculator loses and will eventually be eliminated from the market if such mistakes are repeated.

Research has shown that there are systematic differences between countries choosing to peg their exchange rates and those choosing floating rates. One very important characteristic is country size in terms of economic activity or GDP. Large countries tend to be more independent and less willing to subjugate domestic policies with a view toward maintaining a fixed rate of exchange with foreign currencies. Since foreign trade tends to constitute a smaller fraction of GDP the larger the country is, it is perhaps understandable that larger countries are less attuned to foreign exchange rate concerns than are smaller countries.

The openness of the economy is another important factor. By openness, we mean the degree to which the country depends on international trade. The greater the fraction of tradable (i.e., internationally tradable) goods in GDP, the more open the economy will be. A country with little or no international trade is referred to as a *closed economy*. As previously mentioned, openness is related to size. The more open the economy, the greater the weight of tradable goods prices in the overall national price level, and therefore the greater the impact of exchange rate changes on the national price level. To minimize such foreign-related shocks to the domestic price level, the more open economy tends to follow a pegged exchange rate.

Countries that choose higher rates of inflation than their trading partners will have difficulty maintaining an exchange rate peg. We find, in fact, that countries whose inflation experiences are different from the average follow floating rates, or a crawling-peg-type system in which the exchange rate is adjusted at short intervals to compensate for the inflation differentials.

Countries that trade largely with a single foreign country tend to peg their exchange rate to that country's currency. For instance, since the United States accounts for the majority of Barbados trade, by pegging to the US dollar, Barbados imparts to its exports and imports a degree of

Table 2.4 Characteristics associated with countries choosing to peg or float

Peggers	Floaters
Small size	Large size
Open economy	Closed economy
Harmonious inflation rate	Divergent inflation rate
Concentrated trade	Diversified trade

stability that would otherwise be missing. By maintaining a pegged rate between the Barbados dollar and the US dollar, Barbados is not unlike another state of the United States as far as pricing goods and services in United States–Barbados trade. Countries with diversified trading patterns will not find exchange rate pegging so desirable.

The evidence from previous studies indicates quite convincingly the systematic differences between peggers and floaters, which is summarized in Table 2.4. But there are exceptions to these generalities because neither all peggers nor all floaters have the same characteristics. We can safely say that, in general, the larger the country is, the more likely it is to float its exchange rate; the more closed the economy is, the more likely the country will float; and so on. The point is that economic phenomena, and not just political maneuvering, ultimately influence foreign exchange rate practices.

There is also concern about how the choice of an exchange rate system affects the stability of the economy. If the domestic policy authorities seek to minimize unexpected fluctuations in the domestic price level, then they will choose an exchange rate system that best minimizes such fluctuations. For instance, the greater the foreign tradable goods price fluctuations are, the more likely there will be a float, since the floating exchange rate helps to insulate the domestic economy from foreign price disturbances. The greater the domestic money supply fluctuations are, the more likely there will be a peg, since international money flows serve as shock absorbers that reduce the domestic price impact of domestic money supply fluctuations. With a fixed exchange rate, an excess supply of domestic money will cause a capital outflow because some of this excess supply is eliminated via a balance of payments deficit. With floating rates, the excess supply of money is contained at home and reflected in a higher domestic price level and depreciating domestic currency. Once again, the empirical evidence supports the notion that real-world exchange rate practices are determined by such economic phenomena.

CURRENCY BOARDS AND "DOLLARIZATION"

Developing countries with a long history of unstable exchange rates often find it difficult to convince the public that government policy will maintain stable exchange rates in the future. This lack of credibility on the part of a government can be overcome if some sort of constraint is placed on the discretionary policy-making ability of the authorities with control over monetary and exchange rate policy. One such form of constraint is a *currency board*. This form became the prototype for successful exchange rate pegging in the 1990s with the success of Argentina and Hong Kong in maintaining their currency value. However, the failure of the Argentinian currency board in 2001 led to a search for a new way to solve the credibility problem. With both Ecuador and El Salvador becoming "dollarized" to solve the credibility problem, this section also discusses the potential for solving the credibility problem by adopting another currency unilaterally.

The typical demise of a fixed exchange rate system comes when the central bank runs out of foreign currency to exchange for domestic currency and ends up devaluing the domestic currency. Currency boards achieve a credible fixed exchange rate by holding a stock of the foreign currency equal to 100% of the outstanding currency supply of the nation. As a result of such foreign currency holdings, people believe that the board will always have an adequate supply of foreign currency to exchange for domestic currency at the fixed rate of exchange. Critics of currency boards point to such reserve holdings as a cost of operating a currency board. However, since the board holds largely short-term, interest-bearing securities denominated in the foreign currency rather than actual noninterest-bearing currency to back its own currency, these interest earnings tend to make currency boards profitable.

During the Asian financial crisis in 1997–1998, the debate over currency boards was heightened by a proposed currency board for Indonesia. The Indonesian government wanted to introduce a currency board to buy credibility for the rupiah and halt a rapid rupiah depreciation. Critics emphasized several potential problems with a currency board that eventually led to the abandonment of the Indonesian plan. Critics emphasized that a currency board can only succeed if a sustainable fixed rate of exchange between the domestic currency and the US dollar is chosen. An obvious problem is what exchange rate is correct? If the exchange rate overvalues the domestic currency, then the currency board would be "attacked" by speculators exchanging domestic currency for dollars, betting on a devaluation of the domestic currency. Because the currency board has a finite supply of dollars, an exchange rate fixed at unsustainable levels would eventually lead to a large loss of dollar reserves so that the currency board collapses and the exchange rate is eventually devalued. Another problem related to a currency board is that the requirement to maintain foreign currency backing for the domestic currency would constrain the central bank from responding to a domestic financial crisis where the central bank might act as a "lender of last resort" to financial institutions. Because the central bank cannot create domestic currency to lend to domestic institutions facing a "credit crunch," the financial crisis could potentially erupt into a national economic crisis with a serious recession.

It is important to remember that boards do not engage in the monetary policy actions typical of central banks like the Federal Reserve in the United States. Their sole function is to provide for a fixed exchange rate between the domestic currency and some major currency like the US dollar. To promote public confidence in the banking system, some currency board countries also have central banks that simultaneously provide supervision of the domestic banking system and act as lenders of last resort to troubled banks. However, such central banks have no discretionary authority to influence the exchange rate; if they did, the public would likely doubt the government's commitment to maintaining the fixed exchange rate.

Appendix A shows that there are a substantial number of countries with currency boards. The ECCU member countries, Djibouti and Hong Kong, use the US dollar as the pegged currency for their currency boards. Some other countries, such as Bosnia-Herzegovina and Bulgaria, have chosen to peg the euro using a currency board. The choice of fixed versus floating exchange rates is often a difficult one for governments. In the case of developing countries that have made a choice for fixed rates, but face a skeptical public due to past policy mistakes, a currency board may be a reasonable way to establish a credible exchange rate system. Hong Kong has had a long successful currency board that even survived the Asian financial crisis. However, the recent experience of Argentina shows that a currency board is no guarantee of success.

For a decade, Argentina maintained a currency board arrangement that supported an exchange rate of 1 peso per US dollar. However, large fiscal deficits resulted in the essential insolvency of the government. At the same time that the government amassed large debts denominated in US dollars, economic fundamentals were consistent with peso devaluation. The fixed exchange rate of the currency board was no longer consistent with the economic realities created by the expansionary fiscal policy, and an economic crisis erupted in late 2001 and early 2002 that resulted in a run on dollars as people tried to exchange pesos for dollars at the obviously overvalued exchange rate of 1 peso per dollar. The crisis in Argentina saw rioting in the streets, the resignations of two presidents in quick succession, a freeze on bank deposit withdrawals, and a break with the fixed exchange rate. Once the currency board arrangement was ended, the peso quickly fell in value from one-to-one parity with the US dollar to a level of 3 pesos per dollar. The Argentine case serves as a warning that currency boards are not a guarantee of forever-fixed exchange rates. If government policy is inconsistent with the fixed exchange rate, the currency board cannot last.

Appendix A shows that there are thirteen countries that have "dollarized." Eight of the "dollarized" countries are using the US dollar as the official currency, three use the euro, and two use the Australian dollar. One major advantage of a "dollarized" economy is that there is no possibility of speculative attacks. In addition, the inflation rate comes from the adopted currency, generally leading to lower inflation rates for the "dollarized" economy. Finally, trade between the "dollarized" economy and other countries using the target currency becomes transparent, without any need to convert currencies or prices.

However, there are some drawbacks also with "dollarization." The central bank of a "dollarized" economy does not perform in the usual way. They do not engage in the monetary policy actions typical of central banks. The central bank of Ecuador, for example, does not have any influence over the money supply in Ecuador. This means that the central bank loses its ability to serve as a lender of last resort to troubled banks. In addition, it loses all seigniorage benefits. As the bank no longer issues currency, it cannot collect any seigniorage revenue. Even in the currency board case some seigniorage revenue exists, although it is tied to the foreign currency returns rather than domestic currency. However, in a "dollarized" economy the seigniorage return goes to the issuer of the currency rather than the "dollarized" country.

Most "dollarized" countries are small in geographic size. For example, the Republic of San Marino is a small country, with about 30,000 inhabitants, surrounded by Italy. Because of its small size and geographic position, it is not surprising that the Republic of San Marino has chosen the euro as its currency. Note that even though the Republic of San Marino uses the euro, it is not part of the European Monetary Union and cannot vote in the European Central Bank (ECB). It has adopted the euro on its own, rather than apply for admission to the euro system. Because many of the traditional "dollarized" countries are small, the success or failure of using "dollarization" as a solution for developing countries is still debated. However, recently countries such as Ecuador and El Salvador have "dollarized." In time these larger countries will provide more information about the applicability of "dollarization" to major developing economies.

OPTIMUM CURRENCY AREAS

The *optimum currency area* can be defined as the geographical area that would maximize economic benefits by keeping the exchange rate fixed within the area. Looking at the real world, we might suggest that North America and Western Europe appear to be likely currency areas given the geographic proximity of Canada, Mexico, and the United States, as well as the geographic position of the Western European nations. Since exchange rates between US and Canadian dollars and the Mexican peso seem closely linked (certainly the peso and the US dollar had a long history of fixed exchange rates), we might expect these three countries to maintain pegged exchange rates with each other and to float versus the rest of the world. Europeans, in fact, have explicitly adopted such a regional optimum currency area arrangement with the euro.

One necessary criterion for an optimum currency area is that the region should have relatively costless mobility of the factors of production (labor and capital). As an illustration of this theory, suppose we have two countries, A and B, producing computers and cotton, respectively. Suddenly there is a change in tastes resulting in a shift of demand from computers to cotton. Country A will tend to run a deficit balance of trade and have an excess supply of labor and capital since the demand for computers has fallen, whereas country B will run a surplus and have an excess demand for labor and capital because of the increase in demand for its cotton.

To correct the balance of trade deficit, factors of production could move from A to B and thereby establish new equilibrium wages and prices in each region. If factors can freely and cheaply migrate from an area lacking jobs to an area where labor is in demand, then the mobility will restore equilibrium. This is because the unemployment in one area is remedied by migration. Thus, fixed exchange rates within the area will be appropriate.

If factors are immobile, then the equilibrium will have to be restored solely through a relative price change. Such a relative price change could take place, if A and B have different currencies. Therefore a geographic area that does not have free movement of factors of production would likely benefit from dividing the geographic area into two or more flexible exchange rate zones.

THE EUROPEAN MONETARY SYSTEM AND THE EURO

The optimum currency area literature suggests that in a regional setting like Western Europe a system of fixed exchange rates might be appropriate. While the establishment of the common euro currency may be viewed as a kind of permanently fixed exchange rate, prior to the euro, a system to link currencies and limit exchange rate flexibility had been in place since the late 1970s. The European Monetary System (EMS) was established in March 1979. The EMS committed the member countries to maintaining small exchange rate fluctuations among themselves, while allowing for large fluctuations against outside currencies. The EMS worked quite well through the 1980s and led to optimism that the member nations eventually could evolve into a system with one ECB and one currency. It was in this spirit that the Maastricht Treaty was signed in December 1991 and a timetable for the evolution of the system was spelled out. The treaty called for:

- The immediate removal of restrictions on European flows of capital and greater coordination of monetary and fiscal policy.
- The establishment of a European Monetary Institute (EMI) in January 1994 to coordinate monetary policies of the individual central banks and make technical preparations for a single monetary policy.
- The irrevocable fixing of exchange rates among all member countries, with a common currency and a ECB in January 1997, at the earliest, and by January 1999, at the latest.

This last step did not occur until January 1999. The countries that moved to this last step of monetary union required their macroeconomic policy to converge to that of the other EMS countries. Convergence was defined as occurring when (a) the country's inflation rate did not exceed the average of the lowest three member country rates by more than 1.5%

points; (b) its interest rate on long-term government bonds did not exceed those of the three lowest-inflation members by more than 2% points; and (c) the country's government budget deficit did not exceed 3% of GDP, and outstanding government debt did not exceed 60% of GDP.

The new European currency, the euro, made its debut on January 1,1999. The symbol is €, and the ISO code is EUR. Euro notes and coins began to circulate on January 1, 2002. In the transition years of 1999–2001, people used the euro as a unit of account, denominating financial asset values and transactions in euro amounts. Bank accounts were available in euros and credit transactions were denominated in euros. However, actual cash transactions were not made with euros until euro cash started circulating in 2002.

Prior to the beginning of the euro, the value of each of the "legacy currencies" of the euro-area countries was fixed in terms of the euro. Table 2.5 shows the exchange rates at which each of the old currencies was fixed in terms of the euro. For instance, 1 euro is equal to 40.3399 Belgian francs or 1.95583 German marks. Of course, the prior monies of each of the Eurozone countries no longer are used, having been replaced by the euro.

One currency requires one central bank, and the euro is no exception. The ECB began operations on June 1, 1998, in Frankfurt, Germany, and now conducts monetary policy for the Eurozone countries. The national central banks like the Bank of Italy or the German Bundesbank are still operating and perform many of the functions they had prior to the ECB, such as regulating and supervising banks and facilitating payments

Table 2.5 Exchange rates of old national currencies replaced by the euro

Former currency	1 Euro
Belgian franc	BEF40.3399
German mark	DEM1.95583
Spanish peseta	ESP166.386
Finnish markka	FIM5.94753
French franc	FRF6.55957
Greek drachma	GRD340.750
Irish pound	IEP0.787564
Italian lira	ITL1936.27
Luxembourg franc	LUF40.3399
Netherlands guilder	NLG2.20371
Austrian schilling	ATS13.7603
Portuguese escudo	PTE200.482

systems in each nation. In some sense they are like the regional banks of the Federal Reserve System in the United States. Monetary policy for the euro-area countries is conducted by the ECB in Frankfurt just as monetary policy for the United States is conducted by the Federal Reserve in Washington, D.C. Yet the national central banks of the euro-area play an important role in each of the respective countries. The entire network of national central banks and the ECB are called the *European System of Central Banks.* Monetary policy for the euro-area is determined by the *Governing Council* of the ECB. This council is comprised of the heads of the national central banks of the euro-area countries plus the members of the ECB *Executive Board.* The board is made up of the ECB president and vice-president and four others chosen by the heads of the governments of the euro-area nations.

The original 11 countries, that adopted the euro, were: Belgium, Germany, Ireland, Spain, France, Italy, Luxembourg, The Netherlands, Austria, Portugal, and Finland. The original 11 became 12, before the euro cash even circulated, when Greece joined in 2001. Recently several new member countries have been added. The EU members that have been added are: Cyprus, Estonia, Malta, Slovakia, Slovenia, Latvia, and Lithuania. That makes it 19 eurozone members as of May, 2016. In addition, small countries that are not part of the EU have unilaterally adopted the euro, for example, Monaco, San Marino and the Vatican. In contrast, three member countries of the European Union in 1999 that were eligible have not adopted the euro and still maintain their own currencies and monetary policies. These three countries are Denmark, Sweden, and the United Kingdom. It remains to be seen when, and if, these countries will ever become part of the Eurozone.

SUMMARY

1. During the gold standard (1880–1914), currencies were convertible into gold at fixed exchange rates.
2. Fixed exchange rates broke down during the Interwar period (1918–1939). Many governments allowed their currencies to float as they suffered rapid inflation.
3. The Bretton Woods system (1944–1970) was an adjustable peg system, with every country fixing their currencies to an anchor currency (the US dollar) and the value of the anchor currency was fixed to gold. It is also called the "gold exchange standard" system.

4. The International Monetary Fund (IMF) was created in 1944 to monitor the operations of the Bretton Woods system.

5. The Bretton Woods system was ended in 1973. Since then the major developed nations began floating their exchange rates.

6. SDR is a special currency issued by the IMF to use as international reserves and settle international accounts between central banks.

7. Reserve currencies serve as an international unit of account, a medium of exchange, and a store of value.

8. The current exchange rate arrangements range from peg (such as dollarization, currency board, and standard peg) to floating (such as managed floating and free floating).

9. Countries with a floating exchange rate tend to have large, closed economies, with inflation rates that differ from those of their trading partners, and trade diversified across many countries.

10. The optimum currency area is the geographical region that could gain economic efficiency by fixing exchange rates within a group and floating exchange rates with the rest of the world. An example of an optimum currency area arrangement is the euro.

11. One of the necessary conditions for the optimal currency area is perfect mobility of the factors of production.

12. The EMS was established in March 1979 to maintain small exchange rate fluctuations among member countries, while allowing for floating against outside currencies. The EMS has evolved into a system with one currency, the euro, and one ECB in 1999.

EXERCISES

1. What type of exchange rate system was the gold standard? Explain how it is operated.

2. How does the gold standard eliminate the possibility of continuous balance of payments disequilibria?

3. How did the Bretton Woods system differ from the gold standard? What was the primary purpose of the IMF under the Bretton Woods? Why did the Bretton Woods system finally collapse?

4. What is seigniorage? Does the United State possess an unfair advantage in world commerce due to seigniorage?

5. What is the difference between "dollarization" and a currency board?

6. What is the difference between managed floating and free floating exchange rates?

7. Discuss the common economic reasons for why a country should adopt a fixed exchange rate arrangement.

8. Explain and graphically illustrate how speculators can attack a currency under the fixed exchange rate system.

9. How can a target zone help create a more stable exchange rate? Explain.

10. In what way is the Euro system of central banks similar to the Federal Reserve System?

FURTHER READING

Alesina, A., Barro, R.J., 2001. Currency Unions. Hoover Institution Press, Stanford.

Bordo, M.D., 1982. The classical gold standard: lessons from the past. In: Connolly, M.B. (Ed.), Int. Monet. Syst.: Choices for the Future, Praeger, New York.

Edison, H.J., Melvin, M., 1990. The determinants and implications of the choice of an exchange rate system. In: Haraf, W.S., Willett, T.D. (Eds.) Monet. Policy for a Volatile Glob. Econ, The AEI Press, Washington, D.C.

Edwards, S., Magendzo, I., 2006. Strict dollarization and economic performance: an empirical investigation. J. Money Credit Bank 38 (1), 269–282.

Edwards, S., Yeyati, E.L., 2005. Flexible exchange rates as shock absorbers. Eur. Econ. Rev. 49 (8), 2079–2105.

Levin, J.H., 2002. A Guide to the Euro. Houghton Mifflin, Boston.

Masson, P.R., Taylor, M.P., 1993. Policy Issu. in the Oper. of Currency Unions. Cambridge University Press, Cambridge.

McKinnon, R.I., 1963. Optimum currency areas. Am. Econ. Rev. September.

Mundell, R.A., 1961. A theory of optimum currency areas. Am. Econ. Rev. 51 (4), 657–665.

Pollard, P., 2001. The creation of the euro and the role of the dollar in international markets. Fed. Rev. St. Louis Rev 83 (5), 17–36.

Savvides, A., 1990. Real exchange rate variability and the choice of exchange rate regime by developing countries. J. Int. Money Finance.

APPENDIX A CURRENT EXCHANGE RATE ARRANGEMENTS

Table A.1 lists the exchange rate arrangements of the IMF member countries. In addition, information about the type of monetary policy framework that is used in the member countries is provided.

Table A.1 Exchange rate framework, 2014

Exchange rate arrangement (number of countries)	Monetary policy framework						
	Exchange rate anchor				Monetary aggregate target (25)	Inflation-targeting framework (34)	Other (43)
	US dollar (43)	Euro (26)	Composite (12)	Other (8)			
No separate legal tender (13)	Ecuador El Salvador Marshall Islands Micronesia Palau Panama Timor-Leste Zimbabwe	Kosovo Montenegro San Marino		Kiribati Tuvalu			
Currency board (12)	Djibouti Hong Kong SAR ECCU Antigua and Barbuda Dominica Grenada St. Kitts and Nevis St. Lucia St. Vincent and the Grenadines	Bosnia and Herzegovina Bulgaria Lithuania		Brunei Darussalam			
Conventional peg (44)	Aruba The Bahamas Bahrain Barbados Belize Curaçao and Sint Maarten Eritrea Jordan Oman Qatar Saudi Arabia South Sudan Turkmenistan United Arab Emirates Venezuela	Cabo Verde Comoros Denmark São Tomé and Principe WAEMU Benin Burkina Faso Côte d'Ivoire Guinea-Bissau Mali Niger Senegal Togo CEMAC Cameroon Central African Rep. Chad Rep. of Congo Equatorial Guinea Gabon	Fiji Kuwait Libya Morocco Samoa	Bhutan Lesotho Namibia Nepal Swaziland			Solomon Islands

Stabilized arrangement (21)	Guyana Iraq Kazakhstan Lebanon	Maldives Suriname Trinidad and Tobago	FYR Macedonia	Singapore Vietnam	Bangladesh Burundi Democratic Rep. of the Congo Guinea Sri Lanka Tajikistan Yemen		Angola Azerbaijan Bolivia Egypt
Crawling peg (2) Crawl-like arrangement (15)	Nicaragua Honduras Jamaica		Croatia	Botswana	China Ethiopia Uzbekistan	Armenia Dominican Republic Guatemala	Argentina Belarus Haiti Lao P.D.R. Switzerland Tunisia
Pegged exchange rate within horizontal bands (1)				Tonga			
Other managed arrangement (18)	Cambodia Liberia			Algeria Iran Syria	The Gambia Myanmar Nigeria Rwanda	Czech Rep.	Costa Rica Kyrgyz Rep. Malaysia Mauritania Pakistan Russia Sudan Vanuatu

(Continued)

Table A.1 Exchange rate framework, 2014 (Continued)

Exchange rate arrangement (number of countries)	Monetary policy framework						
	Exchange rate anchor				Monetary aggregate target (25)	Inflation-targeting framework (34)	Other (43)
	US dollar (43)	Euro (26)	Composite (12)	Other (8)			
Floating (36)					Afghanistan	Albania	India
					Kenya	Brazil	Mauritius
					Madagascar	Colombia	Mongolia
					Malawi	Georgia	Zambia
					Mozambique	Ghana	
					Papua New Guinea	Hungary	
					Seychelles	Iceland	
					Sierra Leone	Indonesia	
					Tanzania	Israel	
					Ukraine	Korea	
					Uruguay	Moldova	
						New Zealand	
						Paraguay	
						Peru	
						Philippines	
						Romania	
						Serbia	
						South Africa	
						Thailand	
						Turkey	
						Uganda	

Free floating (29)	Australia	Somalia
	Canada	United States
	Chile	EMU
	Japan	Austria
	Mexico	Belgium
	Norway	Cyprus
	Poland	Estonia
	Sweden	Finland
	United Kingdom	France
		Germany
		Greece
		Ireland
		Italy
		Latvia
		Luxembourg
		Malta
		Netherlands
		Portugal
		Slovak Rep.
		Slovenia
		Spain

Source: Annual exchange rate arrangements and restrictions, October 2014, from IMF.org, 2015.

CHAPTER 3

The Balance of Payments

Contents

We have all heard of the balance of payments. Unfortunately, common usage does not allow us to discuss *the* balance of payments because there are several ways to measure the balance, and the press often blurs the distinctions among these various measures. In general, the *balance of payments* records a country's trade in goods, services, and financial assets with the rest of the world. Such trade is divided into useful categories that provide summaries of a nation's trade.

In June 2014, the US Bureau of Economic Analysis released comprehensively restructured international economic accounts. The restructuring was done to closer align with the latest revision of the International Monetary Fund's (IMF) *Balance of Payments and International Investment Position Manual, 6th edition.* Most countries in the world have followed the IMF update, resulting in international economic accounting that is almost identical across countries. Therefore the following discussion applies equally to the United States as well as other countries. Fig. 3.1 presents the general categories of the balance of payments for the United States. This figure uses the general categories to make it easier to identify the popular summary measures of the balance of payments. Table 3A in the appendix presents the detailed balance of payments for a country, in this case for Brazil. Because most countries follow the IMF directive for balance of

Line		1970	1985	2000	2005	2010	2015
	Current account						
1	**Exports of goods and services and income receipts (credits)**	68.4	394.1	1,471.5	1,896.0	2,630.8	3,138.7
2	Exports of goods and services	56.6	289.1	1,075.3	1,286.0	1,853.6	2,223.6
3	Goods	42.5	215.9	784.9	913.0	1,290.3	1,513.5
4	Services	14.2	73.2	290.4	373.0	563.3	710.2
5	Primary income receipts	11.7	105.0	358.8	544.0	684.9	783.1
6	Investment income	11.7	105.0	354.4	539.2	679.0	776.0
7	Compensation of employees	—	—	4.4	4.8	5.9	7.0
8	Secondary income (current transfer) receipts	—	—	37.4	66.0	92.3	132.0
9	**Imports of goods and services and income payments (debits)**	66.1	512.3	1,882.3	2,641.4	3,072.8	3,622.8
10	Imports of goods and services	54.4	411.0	1,447.8	2,000.3	2,348.3	2,763.4
11	Goods	39.9	338.1	1,231.7	1,695.8	1,939.0	2,272.8
12	Services	14.5	72.9	216.1	304.4	409.3	490.6
13	Primary income payments	5.5	79.3	339.6	476.3	507.3	591.8
14	Investment income	5.5	79.3	328.7	460.4	493.3	574.5
15	Compensation of employees	—	—	11.0	15.9	14.0	17.3
16	Secondary income (current transfer) payments	6.2	22.0	94.8	164.8	217.2	267.7
	Financial account						
19	**Net US acquisition of financial assets excluding financial derivatives (net increase in assets/financial outflow (+))**	9.3	47.1	589.3	572.3	963.4	242.2
20	Direct investment assets	7.6	21.2	188.0	61.9	354.6	345.1
21	Portfolio investment assets	1.1	3.0	159.7	267.3	199.6	186.3
22	Other investment assets	3.2	19.0	241.3	257.2	407.4	−282.9
23	Reserve assets	−2.5	3.9	0.3	−14.1	1.8	−6.3
24	**Net US incurrence of liabilities excluding financial derivatives (net increase in liabilities/financial inflow (+))**	7.2	146.5	1,067.0	1,273.0	1,386.3	426.0
25	Direct investment liabilities	1.5	22.1	350.1	138.3	259.3	409.9
26	Portfolio investment liabilities	11.7	68.0	442.0	832.0	820.4	263.4
27	Other investment liabilities	−5.9	56.5	275.0	302.7	306.6	−247.2
28	Financial derivatives other than reserves, net transactions	n.a.	n.a.	n.a.	n.a.	−14.1	−25.4
	Statistical discrepancy						
29	**Statistical discrepancy**	−0.2	18.7	−66.9	31.6	5.1	274.9
	Balances						
30	**Balance on current account (line 1 less line 9)**	2.3	−118.2	−410.8	−745.4	−442.0	−484.1
31	Balance on goods and services (line 2 less line 10)	2.3	−121.9	−372.5	−714.2	−494.7	−539.8
32	Balance on goods (line 3 less line 11)	2.6	−122.2	−446.8	−782.8	−648.7	−759.3
33	Balance on services (line 4 less line 12)	−0.3	0.3	74.3	68.6	154.0	219.6
34	Balance on primary income (line 5 less line 13)	6.2	25.7	19.2	67.6	177.7	191.3
35	Balance on secondary income (line 8 less line 16)	−6.2	−22.0	−57.4	−98.8	−125.0	−135.6

Figure 3.1 US international transactions in billions of dollars. Note that the capital account has been removed to simplify the table. The capital account balance is negligible. *Bureau of Economic Analysis, International Transactions, March 17, 2016.*

payments, the particular country does not matter. In this chapter we will discuss several summary measures of the balance of payments, pointing out their uses as well as their drawbacks.

The balance of payments is an accounting statement based on double-entry bookkeeping. Every transaction is entered on both sides of the balance sheet, as a credit and as a debit. Credit entries are those entries that will bring foreign exchange into the country, whereas debit entries record items that would mean a loss of foreign exchange. In Fig. 3.1, debit entries enter the balance of payments as a negative value. For instance, suppose we record the sale of a machine from a US manufacturer to a French importer and the manufacturer allows the buyer 90 days credit to pay. The machinery export is recorded as a credit in the merchandise account, whereas the credit extended to the foreigner is a debit to the financial account. Thus, credit extended belongs in the same broad account with stocks, bonds, and other financial instruments of a short-term nature.

If, for any particular account, the value of the credit entries exceeds the debits, we say that a *surplus* exists. On the other hand, where the debits exceed the credits, then a *deficit* exists. Note that a surplus or deficit can apply only to a particular area of the balance of payments, since the sum of the credits and debits on all accounts will always be equal; in other words, the balance of payments always balances. This will become apparent in the following discussion. Let us consider some of the popular summary measures of the balance of payments.

CURRENT ACCOUNT

The *current account* deals primarily with trade in goods and services, and is defined as including the value of trade in merchandise, services, primary income, and secondary income. *Merchandise* is the export and import in tangible commodities. The *services* category refers to trade in the services of factors of production: land, labor, and capital. Included in this category are travel, tourism, royalties, transportation costs, and insurance premiums. The *primary income* account (formerly known as *investment income*) reflects investment income and compensation to employees. The payment for the services of capital, or the return on investments, is recorded as investment income. The amounts of interest and dividends paid internationally are large and are growing rapidly as the world financial markets become more integrated. The final component of the current account is labeled *secondary income* (formerly known as *unilateral transfers*). This category includes items that are transferred in one direction, e.g., US foreign aid, gifts, and retirement pensions. The United States usually records a large deficit on these items.

Summing up the debits and credits shows the balance on a subsection of the international transactions. The balance of payments entries in Fig. 3.1 actually end at line 29. Lines 30–35 are summaries drawn from lines 1 to 28. The summaries come from drawing lines in the balance of payments at different places. A line is drawn in the balance of payments schedule and then the debit and credit items above such a line are summed. For example, if we draw a line at the current account balance items ending with secondary income (line 16) and sum all credit and debit entries above, this would give us the current account surplus/deficit. A current account deficit implies that a country is running a net surplus below the line and that the country is a net borrower from the rest of the world.

Returning to Fig. 3.1, line 30 shows that there was a current account surplus of $2.3 billion in 1970 and a deficit of $484.1 billion in 2015. The $484.1 billion current account deficit of 2015 is the sum of a $759.3 billion merchandise trade deficit, a $219.6 billion services surplus, a $191.3 billion primary income surplus, and a $135.6 billion secondary income deficit. In 1970, the United States ran a merchandise trade surplus of $2.6 billion. Following a $2 billion deficit in 1971, the merchandise account has been in deficit every year since, except 1973 and 1975.

Fig. 3.2 illustrates how the current account has changed over time. The current account is shown as a fraction of GDP, to control for inflation and the growth of the US economy over the time period. The current account

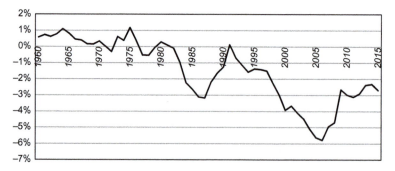

Figure 3.2 Current account as a fraction of GDP. *Federal Reserve of St. Louis FRED 2 database, authors' calculation.*

deficit growth of the 1980s was unprecedented at the time, but has since been dwarfed by the deficits of recent years. The current account deficit peaked in 2005–2006 with the current account fraction of GDP exceeding 6%, and has settled at 2.5–3.0% in recent years.

The current account excludes financial account transactions—purchases and sales of financial assets. Since the items below the line of the current account must be equal in value (but opposite in sign) to the current account balance, we can see how the current account balance indicates financial activity (below the line) as well as the value of trade in merchandise, services, primary and secondary income that are recorded above the line. In a period (year or quarter) during which a current account deficit is recorded, the country must borrow from abroad an amount sufficient to finance the deficit.

Since the balance of payments always balances, the massive current account deficits of recent years are matched by massive financial account surpluses. This means that foreign investment in US assets, such as securities, has been at very high levels. Some analysts have expressed concern over the growing foreign indebtedness of the United States. The end of the chapter reviews the issue.

FAQ: How big is the US current account deficit compared to other countries?

The US current account deficit is the largest in the world in absolute size. However, the dollar amount of the current account deficit can be deceiving, because the United States is the largest economy in the world. A better comparison is to compare the size of the current account deficit/surplus to a country's GDP. By doing this we put the deficit in comparable terms across countries. The following figure shows the current account deficit/surplus for selected countries in 2015. The figure shows that the United States does not have the largest current account deficit as a fraction of GDP. The United Kingdom has one of the largest current account deficits with a 5.2% of GDP. That is almost twice the US current account deficit. In contrast, some other European countries have very large current account surpluses. The Netherlands and Germany have gigantic surpluses due to the weak Euro, and Norway and Sweden also have large surpluses. Note that China has a much more reasonable surplus at 2.7%.

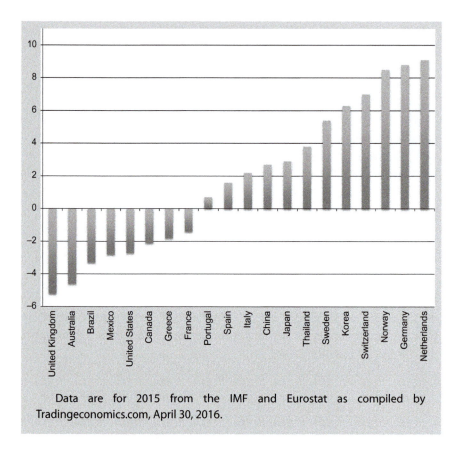

Data are for 2015 from the IMF and Eurostat as compiled by Tradingeconomics.com, April 30, 2016.

FINANCING THE CURRENT ACCOUNT

The offsetting financial account is named the *Financial Account* (formerly called Capital Account).[1] Large current account deficits imply large financial account surpluses. The financial account transactions are recorded below the current account items in the balance of payments. Referring back to Fig. 3.1, lines 19–28 record financial account transactions. We see that financial account transactions include both official and private transactions.

For ease of understanding, Table 3.1 provides a summary of US financial account transactions from 2003 to 2015. In this table, the debit and

[1]Technically the Capital Account still exists, but now refers to transactions not related to production, such as debt forgiveness and other transfers not related to production. These transactions were formerly reported in Unilateral Transfers and are fairly minor. Because of the small amounts we do not include the Capital Account in Fig. 3.1.

Table 3.1 US financial account transactions (flows, in billions of dollars)

Year	Direct Investment		Portfolio Investment		Other Investment		Reserve Foreign Official	
	Assets	Liabilities	Assets	Liabilities	Assets	Liabilities	Assets	Liabilities
2003	197.2	111.3	133.1	301.1	44.3	215.4	−1.5	278.1
2004	378.1	207.9	192.0	496.5	495.5	493.0	−2.8	397.8
2005	61.9	138.3	267.3	597.2	257.2	278.2	−14.1	259.3
2006	296.1	294.3	493.4	682.7	549.8	651.3	−2.4	487.9
2007	532.9	340.1	380.8	714.7	658.6	647.7	0.1	481.0
2008	351.7	332.7	−284.3	−53.2	−381.8	−380.1	4.8	554.6
2009	313.7	153.8	375.9	−95.5	−609.7	−220.2	52.3	480.2
2010	354.6	259.3	199.6	424.7	407.4	305.1	1.8	397.2
2011	440.4	257.4	85.4	117.7	−45.3	358.6	15.9	243.3
2012	377.9	232.0	238.8	358.0	−453.7	−371.3	4.5	397.1
2013	399.2	287.2	476.2	254.4	−228.4	191.0	−3.1	309.5
2014	357.2	131.8	538.1	613.7	−99.5	131.5	−3.6	100.4
2015	345.1	409.9	186.3	493.7	−282.9	−367.6	−6.3	−109.9

Source: BEA, March 17, 2016 release, Tables 1.1 and 9.1; authors' calculation.

credit items are entered separately so that we can identify the sources of changes in net financial flows (financial inflows less financial outflows). For instance, in 2015 we see that US private portfolio investment purchases abroad totaled $186.3 billion. This is a financial account debit entry because it involves foreign exchange leaving the United States. Note that this corresponds to the line 21 in Fig. 3.1. Table 3.1 indicates that private portfolio investment purchases in the United States by foreigners totaled $493.7 billion in 2015. This is a credit item in the financial account since it brings foreign exchange to the United States. Note that this is different from line 26 in Fig. 3.1, because the liabilities in the financial account include both private and official liabilities. In Table 3.1 the private and official liabilities have been separated.

Before interpreting the recent history of US international financial flows, we will consider the definitions of each of the individual financial account items.

- *Direct investment*: Private financial transactions that result in the ownership of 10% or more of a business firm.
- *Portfolio investment*: Private sector net purchases of equity (stock) and debt securities.
- *Other investment*: Currency, deposits, loans, insurance technical reserves, trade credit, and advances.
- *Reserve assets*: Changes in US official reserve assets (gold, SDRs, foreign currency holdings, and reserve position in the IMF).
- *Foreign official liabilities*: Net purchases of US government securities, obligations of US government corporations and agencies, securities of US state and local governments, and changes in liabilities to foreign official agencies reported by US banks.

Some financial account transactions are a direct result of trade in merchandise and services. For instance, many goods are sold using trade credit. The exporter allows the importer a period of time—typically 30, 60, or 90 days—before payment is due. This sort of financing will generally be reflected in *other investment assets*, because such transactions are handled by the exporter's bank. Portfolio management by international investors would result in changes to the portfolio investment account. Official transactions involve governments and are motivated by a host of economic and political considerations.

The recent financial account transactions are very interesting from an economic viewpoint. In general, one can see that globalization is evident in the sharp increases in the overall size of the transactions. In most years the US direct investment abroad has exceeded the direct investment by foreigners in the United States. Note also that even throughout the recent banking crisis, the direct investment continued. However, the portfolio investment account tells a different story. In the 2000s, the foreign purchases of US securities have far outweighed the US purchases of foreign securities. In 2008 during the "Great Recession" the portfolio investment turned negative for both US residents and foreign residents. Fortunately it has since recovered. Similarly, the foreign official purchases of US assets far outpace the US government's purchases of foreign assets. Thus, foreign central banks are increasing their holdings of US assets at a rapid pace.

Table 3.1 also provides an interesting account of the US financial crisis in 2008. Before the crisis one can see substantial purchases of US securities, both by foreign central banks and by private citizens. Note that in 2005–2007 private purchases of US liabilities averaged around $660 billion dollars, and approximately an additional $400 billion was purchased annually by official sources. Thus, over a trillion dollars was added to the US economy annually from 2005 to 2007, providing ample supply of investment capital in the United States. In 2008 this source of funds completely disappeared from foreign private sources, with only official purchases remaining. However, US purchases abroad also became negative, indicating that US investors sold foreign securities to bring home almost $300 billion in liquidity. Similarly, both US and foreign international investors sold other investment assets, with both entries taking on substantial negative values. The negative values in other investment assets continued through 2015, implying that banking assets were still sensitive a long time after the 2008 crash. Note also that direct investment stayed steady throughout and after the Great Recession of 2008. Thus, the volatility from year to year in the financial accounts comes primarily from other investment assets and liabilities.

ADDITIONAL SUMMARY MEASURES

So far we have focused primarily on the current account of the balance of payments. In terms of practical importance to economists, government policymakers, and business firms, this emphasis on the current account is warranted. However, there are other summary measures of balance of payments phenomena. Within the current account categories, the balance on merchandise trade is often cited in the popular press (because it is reported on a monthly basis by the United States). The *balance of trade* (line 3 less line 11 in Fig. 3.1) records a surplus when merchandise exports exceed imports. Domestic business firms and labor unions often use the balance of trade to justify a need to protect the domestic market from foreign competition. When a country is running a large balance of trade deficit, local industries that are being hurt by import competition will argue that the trade balance reflects the harm done to the economy. Because of the political sensitivity of the balance of trade, it is a popularly cited measure.

The *official settlements balance* measures changes in financial assets held by foreign monetary agencies and official reserve asset transactions. The official settlements balance serves as a measure of potential foreign exchange pressure on the dollar, in that official institutions may not want to hold increasing stocks of dollars but would rather sell them, which would drive down the foreign exchange value of the dollar. Yet if there is a demand for the dollar, official stocks of dollars may build without any foreign exchange pressure. Furthermore, in the modern world it is not always clear whether official holdings are what they seem to be, since (as we will see in a later chapter) the Eurodollar market allows central banks to turn official claims against the United States into private claims. Still, monetary economists have found the official settlements account to be useful because changes in international reserves are one element on which the nation's money supply depends.

Because it is hard to distinguish official and private liabilities, the Bureau of Economic Analysis only reports the combination in Fig. 3.1. In Table 3.1 the *foreign official liabilities* have been calculated so that an official settlements balance can be computed. The official settlements balance in Table 3.1 is the difference between the last two columns. In the 2000s and 2010s the official settlements balance has been substantially negative, but the foreign official liabilities have been reduced in 2014 and even turned negative in 2015, as the dollar strengthened.

The foreign monetary agency holdings of the liabilities of most countries are trivial, so that the official settlements balance essentially measures international reserve changes. In the case of the United States, the official settlements balance primarily records changes in short-term US liabilities held by foreign monetary agencies. This demand for dollar-denominated short-term debt by foreign central banks is what allows the United States to finance current account deficits largely with dollars. Other countries must finance deficits by selling foreign currency, and, as a result, they face a greater constraint on their ability to run deficits as they eventually deplete their stocks of foreign currency.

TRANSACTIONS CLASSIFICATIONS

So far we have defined the important summary measures of the balance of payments and have developed an understanding of the various categories included in a nation's international transactions. The actual classification of transactions is often confusing to those first considering such issues. To aid in understanding these classification problems, we will analyze six transactions and their placement in a simplified US balance of payments.

First, we must remember that the balance of payments is a balance sheet, so, at the bottom line, total credits equal total debits. This means that we use double-entry bookkeeping—every item involves two entries, a credit and a debit, to the balance sheet. The credits record items leading to inflows of payments. Such items are associated with a greater demand for domestic currency or supply of foreign currency to the foreign exchange market. The debits record items that lead to payments outflows. These are associated with a greater supply of domestic currency or demand for foreign currency in the foreign exchange market. Now consider the following six hypothetical transactions and their corresponding entries in Table 3.2.

1. A US bank makes a loan of $1 million to a Romanian food processor. The loan is funded by creating a $1 million deposit for the Romanian firm in the US bank. The loan represents a private financial outflow and is recorded as a debit to private financial. The new deposit is recorded as a credit to the private financial account, since an increase in foreign-owned bank deposits in US banks is treated as a financial inflow.

Table 3.2 Balance of payments

	Credit (+)	Debit (−)	Net balance
Merchandise	$1,000,000 (2) 100,000 (5)		
Services		$10,000 (4)	
Primary income	10,000 (3)		
Secondary income		100,000 (5)	
Current account			*$1,000,000*
Official financial	$50,000,000 (6)	$50,000,000 (6)	
Private financial	1,000,000 (1) $10,000 (4)	1,000,000 (1) 1,000,000 (2) $10,000 (3)	
Financial account			*−$1,000,000*
Total	$52,120,000	$52,120,000	

Note: The numbers in parentheses refer to the six transactions we have analyzed.

2. A US firm sells $1 million worth of wheat to the Romanian firm. The wheat is paid for with the bank account created in (1). The wheat export represents a merchandise export of $1 million, and thus we credit merchandise $1 million. Payment using the deposit results in the decrease of foreign-owned deposits in US banks; this is treated as a financial outflow, leading to a $1 million debit to the private financial account.

3. A US resident receives $10,000 in interest from German bonds she owns. The $10,000 is deposited in a German bank. Earnings on international foreign investments represent a credit to the primary income account. The increase in US-owned foreign bank deposits is considered a financial outflow and is recorded by debiting the private financial account in the amount of $10,000.

4. A US tourist travels to Europe and spends the $10,000 German deposit. Tourist spending is recorded in the services account. The US tourist spending abroad is recorded as a $10,000 debit to the services account. The decrease in US-owned foreign deposits is considered a private financial inflow and is recorded by a $10,000 credit to the private financial account.

5. The US government gives $100,000 worth of grain to Nicaragua. The grain export is recorded as a $100,000 credit to the merchandise account. Since the grain was a gift, the balancing entry is secondary income; in this case, there is a debit of $100,000 to secondary income.

6. The Treasury Department of the government of Japan buys $50 million worth of US government bonds paid for with a deposit in a US bank. Foreign government purchases of US government securities are recorded as an official financial inflow so we credit the official financial account $50 million. The reduction in foreign-owned deposits in US banks is treated as a financial outflow; but, since the deposit was owned by a foreign government, there is a $50 million debit to the official financial account.

Note that the current account balance is the sum of the merchandise, services, primary income and secondary income accounts. Summing the credits and debits, we find that the credits sum to $1,110,000, whereas the debits sum to $110,000, so that there is a positive, or credit, balance of $1 million on the current account.

The financial entries are typically the most confusing, particularly those relating to changes in bank deposits. For instance, the third transaction we analyzed recorded the deposit of $10,000 in a German bank as a debit to the private financial account of the United States. The fourth transaction recorded the US tourist's spending of the $10,000 German bank deposit as a credit to the private financial account of the United States. This may seem confusing because early in the chapter it was suggested that credit items are items that bring foreign exchange into a country, while debit items involve foreign exchange leaving the country. But neither of these transactions affected bank deposits in the United States, just foreign deposits. The key is to think of the deposit of $10,000 in a German bank as money that had come from a US bank account. Increases in US-owned deposits in foreign banks are debits whether or not the money was ever in the United States. What matters is not whether the money is ever physically in the United States, but the country of residence of the owner. Similarly, decreases in US-owned foreign deposits are recorded as a credit to private financial, whether or not the money is actually brought from abroad to the United States.

The item called "statistical discrepancy" (line 29) in Fig. 3.1 is not the result of not knowing where to classify some transactions. The international transactions that are recorded are simply difficult to measure accurately. Taking the numbers from customs records and surveys of business firms will not capture all of the trade actually occurring. Some of this may be due to illegal or underground activity, but in the modern dynamic economy we would expect sizable measurement errors even with no illegal activity. It is simply impossible to observe every transaction, so we must rely on a statistically valid sampling of international transactions.

CURRENT ACCOUNT DISEQUILIBRIA

So far in this chapter we have studied the accounting procedures and definitions of the balance of payments. Now we want to consider the reasons for why a country would be in a current account surplus or deficit. Using some national income and product accounting (NIPA), we can see what must be true about the domestic economy for the country to be in a current account deficit or surplus.

Let us derive a relationship between the current account and domestic variables. Starting with the definition of GDP:

$$Y = C + I + G + (X - M)$$

where Y is GDP, C is our domestic consumption, I is our domestic private investment, G is the government's consumption, X is our exports, and M is our imports. Our current account is then the net exports, $(X - M)$, in the above relationship. Add the national income relationship:

$$Y = C + S + T$$

where S is the private saving and T are the taxes paid. The national income relationship says that individuals will spend their earnings Y on consumption and taxes, and save the remainder.

Now, set the two equations equal to each other and cancel out the C, and after some rearranging you will be left with:

$$(S - I) + (T - G) = (X - M)$$

In other words, the current account balance depends on the private saving/investment relationship, $(S - I)$, and the government's fiscal surplus/deficit, $(T - G)$. A current account deficit could come from a fiscal deficit and/or that private investment exceeding private saving, whereas a current account surplus implies a fiscal surplus and/or private saving exceeding private investment. We will look at $(S - I)$ and $(T - G)$ in the case of the US current account deficit.

If the US current account deficit comes primarily from the fiscal deficit then we should see an increase in the current account deficit at the same time that the fiscal deficit increases. Economists have dubbed this case the "twin deficit" explanation. In Fig. 3.3 we can see that the US current account deficit and the US fiscal deficit sometimes move together, but often the two move apart. For example, in the early 1980s, the large fiscal deficit during the Reagan era seems to have been transmitted to the current account also. Interestingly, economists in the 1980s worried about

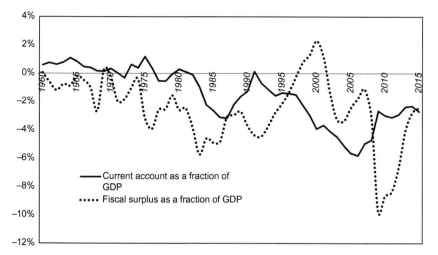

Figure 3.3 Current account and fiscal surplus/deficit as a fraction of GDP. *Federal Reserve of St. Louis FRED 2 database, authors' calculation.*

the US current account deficits as unsustainable. However, as we can see the United States has continued to grow with even larger current account deficits than those in the 1980s.

The second explanation focuses on the investment and saving relationship. If there are interesting investment opportunities in the United States and the private saving is insufficient then a current account deficit is necessary to allow foreigners to supply funds that can be used for investment purposes. In Fig. 3.4 we can see that personal saving has decreased from about 8% during the 1960s and 1970s to a low of 2% in the middle of the 2000s. All else equal the United States would need to cut private investment dramatically due to the slowdown in saving. However, Fig. 3.4 shows that especially after 1990 the current account deficit and the private saving have moved together. This implies that foreign saving is being used to finance US private investment through the current account deficit.

The evidence in Figs. 3.3 and 3.4 indicates that both the fiscal imbalance and the private saving/investment imbalance are likely to have been the cause of the US current account deficit at different times. Similarly one can look at these two channels to see the cause of a current account surplus. In the case of a surplus a country must have a fiscal surplus and/or have domestic saving that exceed private investment. For example, if a country has a current account surplus and a balanced fiscal budget, then private saving must exceed private investment. In other words the country

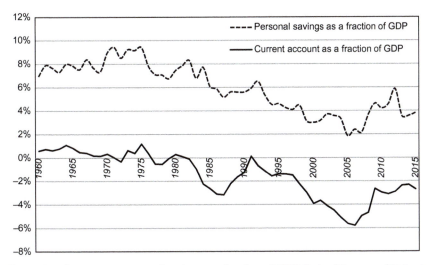

Figure 3.4 Current account and saving as a fraction of GDP. *Federal Reserve of St. Louis FRED 2 database, authors' calculation.*

does not have enough opportunities for investment so saving flows abroad. In the next section we study the implications of a current account imbalance and how current account imbalances can be remedied.

BALANCE OF PAYMENTS EQUILIBRIUM AND ADJUSTMENT

Let us consider the economic implications of the balance of payments. For instance, since merchandise exports earn foreign exchange while imports involve outflows of foreign exchange, we often hear arguments for policy aimed at maximizing the trade or current account surplus. Is this in fact desirable? First, it must be realized that, because one country's export is another's import, it is impossible for everyone to have surpluses. On a worldwide basis, the total value of exports equals the total value of imports—i.e., there is globally balanced trade. Actually, the manner in which trade data are collected imparts a surplus bias to trade balances. Exports are recorded when goods are shipped, while imports are recorded upon receipt. Because there are always goods in transit from the exporter to the importer, if we sum the balance of trade for all nations we would expect a global trade surplus. However, the global current account balance has summed to a deficit in recent years. The problem seems to involve the difficulty of accurately measuring international financial transactions. Merchandise trade can be measured fairly accurately, and the global sum of trade balances is roughly zero; but, service transactions are more difficult to observe, and investment income flows seem to be the major source of global current account discrepancies. The problem arises because countries receiving financial inflows (the debtors) more accurately record the value received than the resident countries of the creditors. For instance, if an investor in Singapore bought shares of stock in Mexico, the government of Mexico is more likely to observe accurately the transaction than is the government of Singapore. Yet even with these bookkeeping problems facing government statisticians, the essential economic point of one country's deficit being another's surplus is still true.

Since one country must always have a trade deficit if another has a trade surplus, is it necessarily true that surpluses are good and deficits bad and that one country benefits at another's expense? In one sense, it would seem that imports should be preferred to exports. In terms of current consumption, merchandise exports represent goods that will be consumed by foreign importers and is no longer available for domestic consumption. As we learn from studying international trade theory, the benefits of free international trade are more efficient production and increased consumption. Imports allow countries to realize a higher living standard than they could by just having domestic production. Children have more toys at Christmas because of imports from China. Bananas and pineapples are readily available due to trade with tropical countries. If trade between nations is voluntary, then it is difficult to argue that deficit countries are harmed while surplus countries benefit by trade.

In general, it is not obvious whether a country is better or worse off if it runs payments surpluses rather than deficits. Consider the following simple example of a world with two countries, A and B. Country A is a wealthy creditor country that has extended loans to poor country B. In order for country B to repay these loans, B must run trade surpluses with A to earn the foreign exchange required for repayment. Would you rather live in rich country A and experience trade deficits or in poor country B and experience trade surpluses? Although this is indeed a simplistic example, there are real-world analogues of rich creditor countries with trade deficits and poor debtor nations with trade surpluses. The point here is that you cannot analyze the balance of payments apart from other economic considerations. Deficits are not inherently bad, nor are surpluses necessarily good.

Balance of payments equilibrium is often thought of as a condition in which exports equal imports or credits equal debits on some particular subaccount, like the current account or the official settlements account. In fact, countries can have an equilibrium balance on the current account that is positive, negative, or zero, depending upon what circumstances are sustainable over time. For instance, a current account deficit will be the equilibrium for the United States if the rest of the world wants to accumulate US financial assets. This involves a US financial account surplus as US financial assets are sold to foreign buyers, which will be matched by a current account deficit. So equilibrium need not be a zero balance. However, to simplify the next analysis, let us assume that equilibrium is associated with a zero balance. In this sense, if we had a current account equilibrium, then the nation would find its net creditor or debtor position unchanging since there is no need for any net financing—the current account export items are just balanced by the current account import items. Equilibrium on the official settlements basis would mean no change in short-term financial assets held by foreign monetary agencies and reserve assets. For most countries, this would simply mean that their stocks of international reserves would be unchanging.

What happens if there is a disequilibrium in the balance of payments—say the official settlements basis? Now there will be reserve asset losses from deficit countries and reserve accumulation by surplus countries. International reserve assets comprise gold, IMF *special drawing rights* (SDR) (recall from Chapter 2, International Monetary Arrangements, that this is a credit issued by the IMF and allocated to countries on the basis of their level of financial support for the IMF), and foreign exchange. To simplify matters (although this is essentially the case for most countries), let us consider foreign exchange alone. The concept of balance of payments equilibrium is linked to the supply and demand diagram presented in this Chapter 1 and Chapter 2, International Monetary Arrangements. In the case of *flexible exchange rates*, where the exchange rate is determined by free market supply and demand, balance of payments equilibrium is restored by the operation of the free market. Therefore, the official settlements account will be zero. In contrast, as we have learned in Chapter 2, International Monetary Arrangements, exchange rates are not always free to adjust to changing market conditions. With *fixed exchange rates*, central banks set exchange rates at a particular level. When the exchange rate is fixed the dollar can be overvalued or undervalued and the central banks must now finance the trade imbalance by international reserve flows. Specifically, in the case of a trade deficit, the Federal Reserve sells foreign currency for dollars. In this case, the US trade deficit could continue only as long as the stock of foreign currency lasts and the official settlements balance will show such an intervention.

Besides these methods of adjusting a balance of payments disequilibrium, countries sometimes use direct controls on international trade, such as government-mandated quotas or prices, to shift the supply and demand curves and induce balance of payments equilibrium. Such policies are particularly popular in developing countries where chronic shortages of international reserves do not permit financing the free-market-determined trade disequilibrium at the government-supported exchange rate.

The mechanism of adjustment to balance of payments equilibrium is one of the most important practical problems in international economics. The discussion here is but an introduction; much of the analysis of Chapters 12, Determinants of the Balance of Trade, 13, The IS–LM–BP Approach, 14, The Monetary Approach, and 15, Extensions and Challenges to the Monetary Approach, is related to this issue as well.

THE US FOREIGN DEBT

One implication of financial account transactions, in Table 3.1, is the net creditor or debtor status of a nation. A *net debtor* owes more to the rest of the world than it is owed, while a *net creditor* is owed more than it owes. The United States became a net international debtor in 1986 for the first time since World War I. The high current account deficits of the 1980s were matched by high financial account surpluses. This rapid buildup of foreign direct investment and purchases of US securities led to a rapid drop in the net creditor position of the United States in 1982 to a net debtor status by 1986. Ever since the United States has remained a debtor nation and has gradually increased its debtor position year after year.

The detailed net international investment position is provided in Table 3.3. One can think of Table 3.3 as a sum of Table 3.1, reflecting the net position of the United States vis-à-vis the rest of the world at any given time. In contrast, Table 3.1 provides the flow of goods and service during a particular year. Line 19 in Table 3.3 provides the cumulative net investment position for the United States. It shows that the United States was the largest creditor in the world in the early 1980s, but in the mid-1980s the net position started to deteriorate, and the United States became the biggest debtor nation in the world with a net position in the end of 2015 of −$7,356.8 billion. Thus, foreigners have more than $7 trillion in claims on US assets in excess of the US claims on foreign assets. The detailed accounts are also of interest. There is an enormous amount of claims on foreign assets held by US residents. Over $23 trillion worth of claims on foreign assets are held by US residents, whereas foreigners hold almost $31 trillion in claims. In comparison, the US GDP is estimated to be around 18 trillion in 2015. So the international asset holdings far exceed the US GDP.

Recall from Table 3.1 that the current account deficit results in foreigners adding more claims on US assets. The US net international investment position is a sum of all the past current account deficits and surpluses. Thus, the current account is a useful measure because it summarizes the trend with regard to the net debtor position of a country. For this reason, international bankers focus on the current account trend as one of the crucial variables to consider when evaluating loans to foreign countries.

Table 3.3 US net international investment position (billions of dollars, March 31, 2016)

Line	Type of investment	1980	1985	1990	1995	2000	2005	2010	2015
1	**US assets**	**839.1**	**1,392.1**	**2,415.7**	**4,094.4**	**7,641.7**	**13,357.0**	**21,767.8**	**23,208.3**
2	Assets excluding financial derivatives (sum of lines 5, 6, 8, and 9)	839.1	1,392.1	2,415.7	4,094.4	7,641.7	12,167.0	18,115.5	20,810.6
3	Financial derivatives other than reserves, gross positive fair value (line 7)	n.a.	n.a.	n.a.	n.a.	n.a.	1,190.0	3,652.3	2,397.6
4	**By functional category**								
5	Direct investment at market value	297.3	475.7	853.3	1,493.6	2,934.6	4,047.2	5,486.4	6,907.9
6	Portfolio investment	78.0	138.7	425.5	1,278.7	2,556.2	4,629.0	7,160.4	9,534.4
7	Financial derivatives other than reserves, gross positive fair value	n.a.	n.a.	n.a.	n.a.	n.a.	1,190.0	3,652.3	2,397.6
8	Other investment	292.3	659.7	962.1	1,146.0	2,022.6	3,302.8	4,980.1	3,984.7
9	Reserve assets	171.4	117.9	174.7	176.1	128.4	188.0	488.7	383.6
10	**US liabilities**	**542.2**	**1,287.8**	**2,565.2**	**4,371.9**	**9,178.6**	**15,214.9**	**24,279.6**	**30,565.1**
11	Liabilities excluding financial derivatives (sum of lines 14, 15, and 18)	542.2	1,287.8	2,565.2	4,371.9	9,178.6	14,082.8	20,737.7	28,224.5
12	Financial derivatives other than reserves, gross negative fair value (line 16)	n.a.	n.a.	n.a.	n.a.	n.a.	1,132.1	3,541.9	2,340.5
13	**By functional category**								
14	Direct investment at market value	99.9	309.3	661.2	1,135.5	3,023.8	3,227.1	4,099.1	6,513.1
15	Portfolio investment	242.6	473.7	946.8	1,901.0	4,008.5	7,337.8	11,869.3	16,666.2
16	Financial derivatives other than reserves, gross negative fair value	n.a.	n.a.	n.a.	n.a.	n.a.	1,132.1	3,541.9	2,340.5
17	Other investment	199.7	504.7	957.2	1,335.5	2,146.3	3,517.8	4,769.3	5,045.2
18	**US net international investment position (line 1 less line 10)**	**296.9**	**104.3**	**−149.5**	**−277.6**	**−1,536.8**	**−1,857.9**	**−2,511.8**	**−7,356.8**

Source: Bureau of Economic Analysis.

HOW SERIOUS IS THE US FOREIGN DEBT?

In the last section we concluded that the United States owes $7.4 trillion more than it has in receivables from the rest of the world. How serious is this? We hear a lot about the US federal debt, but rarely about the US international debt situation. Although the net amount sounds enormous, the detailed accounts in Table 3.1 bring some comfort about the debt situation. The types of assets that United States acquires differ from the type of foreign liabilities that the United States has. For example, if we examine the last decade of assets and liabilities we can see from Table 3.1 that the United States acquired in excess of $3.7 trillion in foreign direct investment, whereas direct investment by foreigners in the United States was only about $2.7 trillion. In contrast, foreign central banks acquired $3.3 trillion of US assets while the US reserves almost did not change in the 10-year period. Thus, the United States invests in high-yield assets while much of foreign assets are low yielding. The composition of asset holdings causes the return to assets held by foreigners in the United States to be low relative to the return for US residents' investments abroad.

In addition to the composition of assets and liabilities, the depreciation of the dollar in the last decade has resulted in a particularly favorable outcome for the US investment income. Gourinchas and Rey (2005) point out that almost all US foreign liabilities are in dollars. In contrast, 70% of US assets are in foreign currency. Therefore a depreciation of the dollar increases the value US-owned foreign assets while keeping the value of the foreign liabilities the same.

In fact, although the United States owes $7.4 trillion more than it has in receivables from the rest of the world, the return on US investment is so much higher that the total net income from assets held by US residents in other countries exceeds the return of US assets held by foreigners. We can see this by looking back at the income receipts and payments in Fig. 3.1. The income receipts in 2015 were $776 billion, line 6, and the payments were $575, line 14. Thus, the United States generated a net income surplus of $201 billion even though the asset base was much smaller for the United States. In conclusion, the international debt is not yet a burden for the United States.

SUMMARY

1. The balance of payments records a country's international transactions: payments and receipts that cross the country's border.
2. The balance of payments uses the double-entry bookkeeping method. Each transaction has a debit and a credit entry.

3. If the value of the credit items on a particular balance of payments account exceeds (is less than) that of the debit items, a surplus (deficit) exists.
4. The current account is the sum of the merchandise, services, primary income, and secondary income accounts.
5. Current account deficits are offset by financial account surpluses.
6. The balance of trade is the merchandise exports minus the merchandise imports.
7. The official settlements balance is equal to changes in financial assets held by foreign monetary agencies and official reserve asset transactions.
8. An increase (decrease) in US-owned deposits in foreign banks is a debit (credit) to the US financial account. While an increase (decrease) in foreign-owned deposits in US banks is a credit (debit) to the US financial account.
9. The United States became a net international debtor in 1986.
10. Deficits are not necessarily bad, nor are surpluses necessarily good.
11. With floating exchange rates, the equilibrium in the balance of payments can be restored by exchange rate changes.
12. With fixed exchange rates, the balance of payments will not be automatically restored. Thus, central banks must either intervene to finance current account deficits or impose trade restrictions to restore the equilibrium.

EXERCISES

1. Explain the principles of double-entry bookkeeping in the balance of payments. In terms of international transactions, what do we count as a debit and a credit?
2. Classify the following transactions and enter them into the US balance of payments.
   a. An American tourist travels to Frankfurt and spends $1000 on hotel, bratwurst, and beer. He pays with a check drawn on a Tulsa, Oklahoma, bank.
   b. Mercedes-Benz in Germany sells $400,000 of its cars to a US distributor, allowing for 90-day trade credit until payment is due.
   c. Herr Schmidt in Germany receives a $100 check, drawn on a US bank, from his grandson in New York as a birthday gift.
   d. A resident in Sun City, Arizona, receives a $2000 dividend check from a German company. The check is from a German bank.
   e. The US government donates $100,000 worth of wheat to Germany.

3. What is the current account balance in question 2?

4. If a country has a current account deficit, will it be a net lender or borrower to the rest of the world?

5. Should the country be concerned about its current account deficit? Discuss.

FURTHER READING

Bergin, P., 2000. Should we worry about the large U.S. current account deficit? Fed. Rev. Bank San Francisco Econ. Lett December 22.

Clift, J., June 2015. Agent provocateur. Finan. Dev.

Coughlin, C.C., Pakko, M.R., Poole, W., 2006. How dangerous is the U.S. current account deficit? Fed. Rev. Bank St. Louis. Reg. Econ. April.

Freund, C. and Warnock F., 2006. Current account deficits in industrial countries: the bigger they are, the harder they fall. NBER Working Paper No. 11823. December.

Glick, R., 1986. The largest debtor nation. Fed. Rev. Bank San Franc. Wkly Lett. February 14.

Gonelli, A., 1993. The basics of foreign trade and exchange. Fed. Rev. Bank N.Y.

Gourinchas, P., Rey, H., 2007. From World Banker to World Venture Capitalist: U.S. External Adjustment and Exorbitant Privilege. In: Clarida, R.H. (Ed.), G7 Current Account Imbalances: Sustainability and Adjustment, University of Chicago Press, Chicago, IL.

Marquez, J., Workman, L., 2000. Modeling the IMF's statistical discrepancy in the global current account. Fed. Rev. Board. Int. Finan. Div. July.

Motala, J., 1997. Statistical discrepancies in the world current account. Finan. Dev., 24–25. March.

Table 3A Detailed international transactions for Brazil (US dollar millions)

	2015		
	Aug	**Sep**	**Oct**
Current account	**−2,606**	**−3,066**	**−4,166**
Balance on goods and services	−264	−273	−920
Balance on goods	2,362	2,641	1,879
Services	−2,626	−2,914	−2,799
Manufacturing services on physical inputs owned by others	−0	0	−0
Maintenance and repair services n.i.e.	7	23	23
Transport	−346	−398	−435
Travel	−827	−774	−549
Business	−110	−93	−52
Personal	−717	−681	−497
Health-related	0	0	−0
Education-related	−70	−69	−47
Other, including tourism	−648	−612	−449
Construction	6	9	2
Insurance and pension services	−78	−38	−13
Financial services	−21	23	−8
Charges for the use of intellectual property n.i.e.	−425	−488	−281
Telecommunications, computer, and information services	−172	−151	−177
Operating leasing services	−1,380	−1,696	−1,971
Other business services, including architecture and engineering	728	681	761
Personal, cultural, and recreational services	−32	−25	−29
Government goods and services n.i.e.	−86	−81	−122
Primary income	−2,570	−3,000	−3,523
Compensation of employees	26	30	23
Investment income	−2,596	−3,030	−3,546
Other primary income	−	−	−
Secondary income	228	207	277
General government	12	−25	−37
Financial corporations, nonfinancial corporations, households, and NPISHs	216	232	314
Capital account	**64**	**30**	**13**
Financial account: Net lending (+)/net borrowing (−)	**−2,178**	**−2,646**	**−3,581**
Direct investment	−4,942	−7,267	−6,713
Net acquisition of financial assets	308	−1,231	−0
Net incurrence of liabilities	5,250	6,037	6,712
Portfolio investment	1,509	1,868	3,502
Net acquisition of financial assets	−81	68	369
Net incurrence of liabilities	−1,590	−1,800	−3,133
Financial derivatives (other than reserves) and employee stock options	397	403	−386
Net acquisition of financial assets	−1,861	−2,707	−1,832
Net incurrence of liabilities	−2,258	−3,111	−1,446

Table 3A Detailed international transactions for Brazil (US dollar millions) (Continued)

	2015		
	Aug	**Sep**	**Oct**
Other investment	455	8 903	335
Net acquisition of financial assets	3,735	11,148	2,616
Net incurrence of liabilities	3,280	2,245	2,281
Other equity	–	–	–
Currency and deposits	1,211	9,579	−1,539
Loans	−1,544	−436	165
Insurance, pension, and standardized guarantee schemes	−4	−5	−7
Trade credit and advances	868	−177	1,719
Other accounts receivable/payable	−76	−58	−3
Special drawing rights (Net incurrence of liabilities)	–	–	–
Reserve assets	403	−6,553	−318
Monetary gold	–	–	–
Special drawing rights	−0	−0	0
Reserve position in the IMF	65	−144	−0
Other reserve assets	338	−6,409	−319
Net errors and omissions	**364**	**391**	**572**

Source: Banco Central Do Brazil, December 2015, authors' calculation.

PART II

International Parity Conditions

CHAPTER 4

Forward-Looking Market Instruments

Contents

In Chapter 1, The Foreign Exchange Market, we considered the problem of a US importer buying Swiss watches. Since the exporter requires payment in Swiss francs, the transaction requires an exchange of US dollars for francs. In the discussion in Chapter 1, The Foreign Exchange Market, it was assumed that the payment was done immediately, thus the chapter discussed the *spot market*—exchanging dollars for francs today at the current spot exchange rate. In the real world payments are not immediate. Instead the purchaser is usually granted 30, 60, or 90 days to pay for the purchase. Thus, the transaction requires the purchaser and the seller to try to predict the future foreign currency value. This chapter deals with instruments that help cover the risk of a foreign currency value becoming too high when the importer has a foreign currency liability, or too low when the exporter has a foreign currency receivable.

Suppose we return to the example of the US watch importer. Earlier, the importer purchased francs in the spot market to settle a contract payable now. Yet much international trade is contracted in advance of delivery and payment. It would not be unusual for the importer to place an order for Swiss watches for delivery at a future date. For instance, suppose the order calls for delivery of the goods and payment of the invoice in 3 months. Specifically, let's say that the order is for CHF100,000.

What options does the importer have with respect to payment? One option is to wait 3 months and then buy the francs. A disadvantage of this strategy is that the exchange rate could change over the next 3 months in a way that makes the deal unprofitable. Looking at Fig. 4.1, we see that the current spot rate is CHF0.9937 per $1, or CHF100,000 = $100,634 (100,000/0.9937). But there is no guarantee that this exchange rate (and the consequent dollar value of the contract) will prevail in the future. If the dollar were to *depreciate* against the franc, then it would take more dollars to buy any given quantity of francs. For instance, suppose that 3 months later the future spot rate (which is currently unknown) is CHF0.75 = $1. Then it would take $133,333 to purchase CHF100,000, and the watch purchase would not be as profitable for the importer. Of course, if the dollar were to *appreciate* against the franc, then the profits would be larger. As a result of this uncertainty regarding the dollar/franc exchange rate in the future, the importer may not want to choose the strategy of waiting 3 months to buy francs.

An alternative is to buy the francs now and hold or invest them for 3 months. This alternative has the advantage that the importer knows exactly how many dollars are needed now to buy CHF100,000. But the importer is faced with a new problem of coming up with cash now and investing the francs for 3 months. Another alternative that ensures a certain dollar price of francs is using the *forward exchange market*. As will be shown in Chapter 6, Exchange Rates, Interest Rates, and Interest Parity, there is a close relationship between the forward market and the former alternative of buying francs now and investing them for 3 months. For now, we will focus on the operation of the forward market.

Country	Closing mid-point spot rate	3 Month forward	One year forward
Argentina (Peso)	8.4645	9.335	11.981
Australia (Australian $)	1.2220	1.2301	1.2035
Brazil (Real)	2.6582	2.7261	2.9417
Canada (Canadian $)	1.1583	1.1606	1.1671
India (Indian Rupee)	63.1225	64.3525	67.4425
Indonesia (Rupiah)	12385.0	12590.0	13235.0
Japan (Yen)	119.895	119.792	119.174
Sweden (Krona)	7.8283	7.8256	7.8015
Switzerland (Franc)	0.9937	0.9919	0.9840
UK (Pound)	0.6413	0.6418	0.6426
Euro (Euro)	0.8264	0.8257	0.8220

Figure 4.1 Selected currency spot and forward exchange rates. *Source: Financial Times, Dec. 31, 2014. All rates are in foreign currency per dollar.*

FORWARD RATES

The forward exchange market refers to buying and selling currencies to be delivered at a future date. Fig. 4.1 includes forward exchange rates for the major traded currencies, including the Swiss franc. Most countries in the world have forward markets and maturities and amounts are set in each transaction. Thus, this figure only represents a small selection of the available quotes. Note in the figure that the 3-month or 90-day forward rate on the Swiss franc is CHF0.9919 = $1. Note that Fig. 4.1 also shows 1-year forwards. Often 1-month and 6-month forward rates are also quoted, as these are also commonly traded maturities.

The advantage of the forward market is that we have established a set exchange rate between the dollar and the franc and do not have to buy the francs until they are needed in 90 days. This may be preferred to the option of buying francs now and investing them for 3 months, because it is neither necessary to part with any funds now nor to have knowledge of investment opportunities in francs. (However, the selling bank may require that the importer hold "compensating balances" or "margin" until the 90-day period is up—that is, leave funds in an account at the bank, allowing the bank to use the money until the forward date.) With a forward rate of $1.00817 = CHF1 (1/0.9919), CHF100,000 will sell for $100,817. The importer now knows with certainty how many dollars the watches will cost in 90 days. In addition, note that the importer only pays a small amount above the spot exchange rate for this forward contract. Instead of paying $100,634 for 100,000 Swiss franc in the spot market, the importer can pay an additional $183 for a contract that delivers the CHF100,000 in 90 days.

If the forward exchange price of a currency exceeds the current spot price, that currency is said to be selling at a *forward premium*. A currency is selling at a *forward discount* when the forward rate is less than the current spot rate. The forward rates in Fig. 4.1 indicate that the British pound is selling at a discount against the dollar, but the Japanese yen is selling at a premium. A forward premium or discount is expressed in annualized percent terms to make it comparable to interest rates. In the above case of the Swiss franc, the franc has a forward premium of 0.725 percent. To compute this we find the expected percent change $[(F_t - S_t)/S_t] \ast 100$ and then multiply it by 4 to annualize the results. Note that the result will indicate a negative result, but that refers to the dollar, because the exchange rates in Table 4.1 are in terms of foreign currency per dollar. Thus there is a discount of 0.725 percent on the dollar and a premium of 0.725 percent on the Swiss franc. The implications of a currency selling at a discount or premium will be explored in coming chapters. In the event that the spot and forward rates are equal, the currency is said to be *flat*.

SWAPS

A *foreign exchange swap* is an arrangement where there is a simultaneous exchange of two currencies on a specific date at a rate agreed at the time of the contract, and a reverse exchange of the same two currencies at a date further in the future at a rate agreed at the time of the contract. Swaps are an efficient way to meet the firm's need for foreign currencies because they combine two separate transactions into one, thus cutting transactions costs in half. The firm avoids any foreign exchange risk by matching the liability created by borrowing foreign currencies with the asset created by lending domestic currency, both to be repaid at the known future exchange rate. This is known as *hedging* the foreign exchange risk.

For example, suppose Citibank wants pounds now, and wants to hold the pounds for 3 months. Instead of borrowing the pounds, Citibank could enter into a swap agreement wherein they trade dollars for pounds now and pounds for dollars in 3 months. The terms of the arrangement are obviously closely related to conditions in the forward market, since the swap rates will be determined by the discounts or premiums in the forward exchange market.

Suppose Citibank wants pounds for 3 months and works a swap with HSBC. Citibank will trade dollars to HSBC and in return will receive pounds. In 3 months the trade is reversed. Citibank will payout pounds to HSBC and receive dollars (of course, there is nothing special about the 3-month period used here—swaps could be for any period). Suppose the spot rate is $/£ = $2.00 and the 3-month forward rate is $/£ = $2.10, so that there is a $0.10 premium on the pound. These premiums or discounts are actually quoted in basis points when serving as swap rates (a *basis point* is 1/100%, or 0.0001). Thus the $0.10 premium converts into a swap rate of 1000 points, which is all the swap participants are interested in; they do not care about the actual spot or forward rate since only the difference between them matters for a swap.

Swap rates are usefully converted into percent per annum terms to make them comparable to other borrowing and lending rates (remember a swap is the same as borrowing one currency while lending another currency for the duration of the swap period). The swap rate of 1000 points or 0.1000 was for a 3-month period. To convert this into annual terms, we find the percentage return for the swap period and then multiply this by the reciprocal of the fraction of the year for which the swap exists. The percentage return for the swap period is equal to the

$$\text{Premium(discount)}/\text{spot rate} = 0.10/\$2.00 = 0.05$$

The fraction of a year for which the swap exists is

$$3 \text{ months}/12 \text{ months} \Rightarrow 1/4 \text{ of the year}$$

And the reciprocal of the fraction is

$$1/(1/4) = 4$$

Thus, the percent per annum premium (discount) or swap rate is

$$\text{Annualized percentage swap rate} = 0.05 \times 4 = 20\%$$

This swap, then, yields a return of 20% per annum, which can be compared to the other opportunities open to the bank.

An alternative swap agreement is a *currency swap*. A currency swap is a contract in which two counterparties exchange streams of interest payments in different currencies for an agreed period of time and then exchange principal amounts in the respective currencies at an agreed exchange rate at maturity. Currency swaps allow firms to obtain long-term foreign currency financing at lower cost than they can by borrowing directly. Suppose a Canadian firm wants to receive Japanese yen today with repayment in 5 years. If the Canadian firm is not well known to Japanese banks, the firm will pay a higher interest rate than firms that actively participate in Japanese financial markets. The Canadian firm may approach a bank to arrange a currency swap that will reduce its borrowing costs. The bank will find a Japanese firm desiring Canadian dollars. The Canadian firm is able to borrow Canadian dollars more cheaply than the Japanese firm, and the Japanese firm is able to borrow yen more cheaply than the Canadian firm. The intermediary bank will arrange for each firm to borrow its domestic currency and then swap the domestic currency for the desired foreign currency. The interest rates paid on the two currencies will reflect the forward premium in existence at the time the swap is executed. When the swap agreement matures, the original principal amounts are traded back to the source firms. Both firms benefit by having access to foreign funds at a lower cost than they could obtain directly.

FAQ: What Is a Credit Default Swap?

It is difficult to keep up with all the terminology, but the financial crisis in 2008–2009 highlighted hedging instruments that were not well known to the public. *Credit Default Swaps* (CDS) had become a huge international market in the 2000s. A CDS is a type of insurance scheme that protects the buyer from a default in the payments. The buyer of the CDS pays a fee to the seller during the term of the CDS. The seller of the CDS will then receive a fee for taking on the risk of a default of the payments by the party that is making a payment.

For example, assume that a Japanese company has borrowed money by issuing a bond and has agreed to pay a periodic amount twice a year to the bond holders (the lenders). A bond holder may then purchase a CDS to cover the risk of the Japanese firm defaulting on their payments. The bond holder buys such a CDS from a financial institution like AIG. Note that the bond holder (lender) now has hedged the default risk of the Japanese firm, but still has a risk that the seller of the CDS, in this case AIG, defaults and does not honor their commitment to pay off in the case of default. This was not seen as an issue until the financial crisis showed that the sellers of CDSs were vulnerable. AIG adopts the risk that the Japanese firm will continue to make its payments. As long as the Japanese borrower makes payments on time, AIG just collects the 'premium' or price of the CDS from the bond holder and incurs no costs to payout since there is no default. In the financial crisis, 'counterparty risk' became a very important issue as some of the largest financial institutions in the world were in danger of defaulting on obligations such as credit default swaps since the probability of a large volume of defaults increased dramatically.

Credit Default Swaps
(USD trillions)

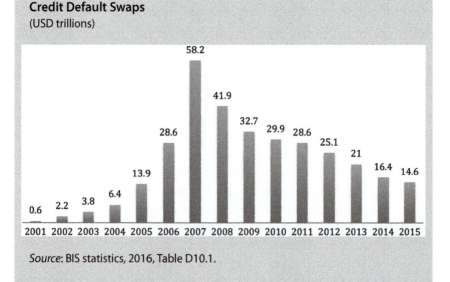

Source: BIS statistics, 2016, Table D10.1.

As can be seen in the figure above the CDS market had grown tremendously in the beginning of the 2000s peaking before the great recession. In 2007, 58.2 trillion outstanding CDS existed, as compared to 2.2 trillion 5 years earlier. After the Great Recession the CDS market has slowed down, but it still plays an important role in prudent risk management of financial obligations.

Table 4.1 Foreign exchange market turnover
Average daily turnover (billions of US dollars)

Instrument	2001	2004	2007	2010	2013	2016
Spot transactions	386	631	1,005	1,488	2,046	1,654
Outright forwards	130	209	362	475	679	700
Foreign exchange swaps	656	954	1,714	1,759	2,239	2,383
Currency swaps	7	21	31	43	54	96
FX options and other products	60	119	212	207	337	254
Total foreign exchange instruments	**1,239**	**1,934**	**3,324**	**3,971**	**5,355**	**5,087**

Source: Bank for International Settlements, Triennial Central Bank Survey, September 2016.

Table 4.1 presents data on the volume of activity in the foreign exchange market. In 2016 about 33% of the transactions reported by the banks surveyed are spot transactions. Foreign exchange swaps constitute 47% of the business, while currency swaps are quite small. Outright forwards account for around 14%. Thus, foreign exchange swaps have more than three times the volume of outright forwards. Foreign exchange options are relatively small at about 5%.

In foreign exchange trading, the ultimate buyers and sellers of currency do not always trade directly with one another but often use someone in the middle—a *broker*. If a bank wants to buy a particular currency, several other banks could be contacted for quotes, or the bank representative could input an order with an electronic broker where many banks participate and the best price at the current time among the participating banks is revealed. While trading in the broker's market is in progress, the names of the banks making bids and offers are not known until a deal is reached. This anonymity may be very important to the trading banks, because it allows banks of different sizes and market positions to trade on an equal footing.

In the electronic brokers market, computer programs take offers to buy and sell from different agents and match them. In addition to the electronic brokers, there are electronic dealing systems. Rather than talking directly over the telephone dealer-to-dealer, computer networks allow for trades to be executed electronically. The use of electronic broker systems varies greatly across countries. Approximately 54% of trading in the United States goes through such networks, compared to 66% in the United Kingdom and 48% in Japan.

FUTURES

The foreign exchange market we have discussed (spot, forward, and swap transactions) is a global market. Commercial banks, business firms, and governments in various locations buy and sell foreign exchange using telephone and computer systems with no centralized geographical market location. However, additional institutions exist that have not yet been covered, one of which is the foreign exchange futures market. The *futures market* is a market where foreign currencies may be bought and sold for delivery at a future date. The futures market differs from the forward market in that only a few currencies are traded; moreover, trading occurs in standardized contracts and in a specific geographic location. Note that futures contracts are traded on organized exchanges, such as the International Monetary Market (IMM) of the Chicago Mercantile Exchange (CME), which is the largest currency futures market. An exchange facilitates buying and selling and guarantees that all commitments are honored. CME futures are traded on the British pound, Canadian dollar, Japanese yen, Swiss franc, Australian dollar, Mexican peso, and euro. The contracts involve a specific amount of currency to be delivered at specific maturity dates. Contracts mature on the third Wednesday of March, June, September, and December. In the forward market, contracts are typically 30, 90, or 180 days long, but can be for any term agreed by the parties, and are maturing every day of the year. Forward market contracts are written for any amount agreed upon by the parties involved. In the CME futures market the contracts are written for fixed amounts: GBP62,500, CAD100,000, JPY12,500,000, CHF125,000, MXN500,000, and EUR125,000.

The futures table shows the dollar prices quoted for each unit of the contract. In Fig. 4.2 the columns for each contract are:

Month – Month that the contract matures

Open – The price that contract had at the beginning of the trading day

14-Sep-15	Month	Open	High	Low	Settle	Lifetime High	Lifetime Low	Open Int
British Pound (CME)-£62,500; $ per £								
	Sep-15	1.5432	1.5470	1.5384	1.5394	1.5924	1.4591	58,483
	Dec-15	1.5421	1.5463	1.5365	1.5427	1.5892	1.4625	1,45,236
	Mar-16	1.5425	1.5446	1.5368	1.5422	1.5789	1.4687	116
	Jun-16	1.5404	1.5404	1.5404	1.5418	1.5758	1.4903	236
	Sep-16	1.5368	1.5402	1.5368	1.5415	1.5854	1.4896	9
	Dec-16	1.5380	1.5380	1.5380	1.5418	1.5380	1.5150	6
	Mar-17	1.5399	1.5405	1.5399	1.5421	1.5405	1.5399	4
Swiss Franc (CME)-CHF 125,000; $ per CHF								
	Sep-15	1.0318	1.0343	1.0290	1.0293	1.1855	0.9849	23,339
	Dec-15	1.0354	1.0378	1.0322	1.0356	1.1912	1.0020	36,009
	Mar-16	1.0250	1.0341	1.0250	1.0396	1.1984	0.9954	24
	Jun-16	1.0475	1.0475	1.0475	1.0440	1.2047	1.0107	7
	Sep-16	1.0295	1.0500	1.0295	1.0492	1.0500	1.0295	3

Figure 4.2 Futures market. *Source: Wall Street Journal, Market data Center, September 14, 2015.*

High – The highest price the contract reached during the day

Low – The lowest price the contract reached during the day

Settle – The price the contract had at closing of the day

Lifetime High – The highest price the contract has reached at any point during the contract life

Lifetime Low – The lowest price the contract has reached at any point during the contract life

Open Int – The volume traded for a particular contract

The futures markets provide a hedging facility for firms involved in international trade, as well as a speculative opportunity. Speculators will profit when they accurately forecast a future price for a currency that differs significantly (by more than the transaction cost) from the current contract price. For instance, if we believe that in September the pound will sell for $1.70, and the September futures contract is currently priced at $1.5415 (the settle price), we would buy a September contract. To buy a British pound contract we need to pay 1.5415 × 62,500 = $96,343.75. However, we are only obligated to pay that when the contract matures in September. Since the futures exchange guarantees the settlement of all contracts, they request that participants deposit cash to help ensure that the contract will be honored (in forward contracts the bank will know the participants and might not require any security). For example, the exchange might ask for 10% of the contract value, or $9634.38 as a security or *margin*. The margin is a cushion for potential losses that you may incur on the contract, to make sure you will honor your contract.

Each day the futures market will quote the September contract that we now own, until the maturity date, so the value of the contract changes on a daily basis. At maturity each pound will cost $1.5415, but the contract does not have to be kept until maturity. For example, assume that the price of the pound contract goes to $1.65 in August. We can now sell our contract for $1.65 × 62,500 = $103,125 for a profit of $6,781.25 (less transactions costs), or we can wait and hope that the September rate will be even more favorable. Note also that the security deposit is returned to us if we sell the contract. In contrast, a fall in the value of the pound in August will hurt our financial position. If the pound falls to $1.50 then our pound position is only worth $93,750. If we still believe that the pound price will go up in September then it makes sense to wait and hold onto the contract. In cases when the negative position becomes serious, the seller might be worried that we will not be able to honor the position in September. Therefore, they might ask for more security, for example an extra $2,593.75 to make the total margin $12,228.13. This is called a *margin call*.

As the preceding examples show, a futures contract may not be held to maturity by the initial purchaser. Only the last holder of the contract has to take delivery of the foreign exchange. Thus, the futures market can be used to hedge risk, but can also be used by speculators. The speculators can take ownership of a fairly large contract with a small initial investment. Thus, speculators can be highly leveraged and have futures contracts worth lots more than the net worth of the individual. This is how Nick Leeson caused Barings Bank to collapse. In a 3-month period Nick bought 20,000 futures contracts worth about 180,000 pounds each. He was speculating that the contracts would increase in value, but instead the contracts lost almost $1 billion (*see* www.nickleeson.com, for more details.).

In comparing the types of participants in the futures market and forward markets, we have already concluded that futures markets can be used for speculation as well as hedging. In addition, the futures contracts are for smaller amounts of currency than are forward contracts, and therefore serve as a useful hedging vehicle for relatively small firms. Forward contracts are within the realm of wholesale banking activity and are typically used only by large financial institutions and other large business firms that deal in very large amounts of foreign exchange.

The financial crisis of 2008 highlighted another important difference between forwards and futures. When one trades a forward, the counterparty is a bank. As became evident with the failure of Lehman Brothers in 2008, banks are subject to credit risk. If the bank that is the counterparty to your forward contract fails during the life of the contract, then the contract will not be honored, leaving you with a foreign exchange risk exposure. In contrast, futures contracts are traded on an exchange and the exchange guarantees the performance of each contract. So to the extent that bank credit risk is important, futures may be attractive relative to forwards.

OPTIONS

Besides forward and future contracts, there is an additional market where future foreign currency assets and liabilities may be hedged; it is called the *options market*. A foreign currency option is a contract that provides the right to buy or sell a given amount of currency at a fixed exchange rate on or before the maturity date (these are known as "American" options; "European" options may be exercised only at maturity). A *call option* gives the right to buy currency and a *put option* gives the right to sell. The price at which currency can be bought or sold is called the *strike price* or *exercise price*.

The use of options for hedging purposes is straightforward. Suppose a US importer is buying equipment from a Swiss manufacturer, with a CHF1 million payment due in September. The importer can hedge against a franc appreciation by buying a call option that confers the right to purchase francs until the September maturity, at a specified price. To find the right contract, the US importer has a large choice of strike prices to choose from. Fig. 4.3 shows the options prices for a CHF125,000 contract. Note that contracts are in fixed amounts with fixed maturity dates, just like the futures contracts on organized exchanges like the Philadelphia Exchange. However, large multinational firms often buy options directly from banks. Such custom options may be for any size or date agreed to and therefore provide greater flexibility than is possible on organized exchanges.

Fig. 4.3 shows the options quotes for the Swiss franc contract that matures in September, 2016. The quotes are from July 8, 2016 when the spot Swiss franc value was $1.0212. The first column in the figure shows

Option size:	125,000
Swiss franc:	1.0212
Latest options:	08-07-2016
Options expiration:	09-09-2016

Strike price	Call	Put
0.980	0.0429	0.0017
0.985	0.0384	0.0022
0.985	0.0341	0.0029
0.995	0.0300	0.0038
1.000	0.0262	0.0050
1.005	0.0226	0.0065
1.010	0.0194	0.0083
1.015	0.0166	0.0104
1.020	0.0141	0.0129
1.025	0.0119	0.0157
1.030	0.0100	0.0188
1.035	0.0084	0.0222
1.040	0.0071	0.0259
1.045	0.0060	0.0298
1.050	0.0050	0.0338
1.055	0.0043	0.0380
1.060	0.0036	0.0424

Figure 4.3 Option prices for the Swiss franc.
Source: Barchart.com using data from CME Group.

the strike prices available. Each strike price has a cost in terms of dollars per Swiss franc for a call or put option in the remaining columns. For example, a put option would be quoted in the third column.

Returning to our trader who has a payment of CHF1 million in September, the liability in September is presently costing the company $1,021,200 (CHF1 million @ $1.0212). If the franc appreciated to $1.10 over the next 3 months, then using the spot market in 3 months would change the value of the imports to $1,100,000 (CHF1,000,000 × $1.1), an increase in the cost of the imports of $78,800. A call option will provide insurance against such change. But there are many options to choose from. If we are only interested in a substantial increase in the value of the Swiss franc, we should choose a higher strike price because it is cheaper. If we cannot tolerate much movement at all, we would pick a lower strike price, but be willing to pay a higher upfront cost. For example, if we choose to protect ourselves against a substantial movement in the Swiss franc we might choose 1.060 as a strike price. This strike price would give us the right to buy Swiss francs at $1.06. It will cost us $0.0036 per Swiss franc. Thus, the CHF125,000 contract would cost us $450 (0.0036 ×125,000). However, we need eight contracts to cover our liability so the total cost for the option cover is $3,600.

With the options contract, we can now avoid any increase in the cost of the currency above 1.06, and at the same time take advantage of any reduction in the cost of the Swiss franc. For example, if the Swiss franc next month falls in value to $1.00, we can let the option expire and buy Swiss francs on the spot market at a cost of $1,000,000, a savings of $21,200 from our initial liability. But having the option not to exercise the trade comes at a cost. Even if we do not exercise the option contract, we still have to pay the full amount of the option premium of $3,600.

An option is said to be *in the money* when the strike price is less than the current spot rate for a call option, or greater than the current spot rate for a put option. Returning to our example of the US importer buying CHF1 million of equipment to be paid for in September, the current spot rate is $1.0212 per CHF. If the importer buys a September call option with a strike price of 1.010, then this contract can already be exercised to buy cheap currency. By exercising the option the importer can already buy Swiss francs at $1.01, and could then turn around and sell them on the spot market for $1.0212. This type of contract is "in the money" and would cost more than a contract that is not "in the money." Similarly a strike price that is above the current spot rate would be "in the money" for a put option.

If we knew with certainty what the future exchange rate would be, there would be no market for options, futures, or forward contracts. In an uncertain world, risk-averse traders willingly pay to avoid the potential loss associated with adverse movements in exchange rates. An advantage of options over futures or forwards is greater flexibility. A futures or forward contract is an obligation to buy or sell at a set exchange rate. An option offers the right to buy or sell if desired in the future and is not an obligation.

OTHER FORWARD-LOOKING INSTRUMENTS

The growth of options contracts since the early 1980s has stimulated the development of new products and techniques for managing foreign exchange assets and liabilities. One recent development combines the features of a forward contract and an option contract. Terms such as *break forward*, *participating forward*, or *FOX* (forward with option exit) refer to forward contracts with an option to break out of the contract at a future date. In this case, the forward exchange rate price includes an option premium for the right to break the forward contract. The incentive for such a contract comes from the desire of customers to have the insurance provided by a forward contract when the exchange rate moves against them and yet not lose the potential for profit available with favorable exchange rate movements.

One might first wonder whether a break–forward hedge could not be achieved more simply by using a straight option contract. There are several attractive features of the break-forward contract that do not exist with an option. For one thing, an option requires an upfront premium payment. The corporate treasurer may not have a budget for option premiums or may not have management approval for using options. The break forward hides the option premium in the forward rate. Since the price at which the forward contract is broken is fixed in advance, the break forward may be treated as a simple forward contract for tax and accounting purposes, whether the contract is broken or not.

One of the more difficult problems in hedging foreign exchange risk arises in bidding on contracts. The bidder submits a proposal to perform some task for the firm or government agency that will award a contract to the successful bidder. Since there may be many other bidders, the bidding firms face the foreign exchange risk associated with the contract only if they are, in fact, awarded the contract. Suppose a particular bidder assesses that it has only a 20% chance of winning the contract. Should that bidder buy a forward contract or option today to hedge the foreign exchange risk it faces in the event it is the successful bidder? If substantial foreign exchange risk is involved for the successful bidder, then not only the bidders but also the contract awarder face a dilemma.

The bids will not be as competitive in light of the outstanding foreign exchange risk as they would be if the exchange rate uncertainty were hedged.

One approach to this problem is the *Scout* contract. Midland Bank developed the Scout (share currency option under tender) as an option that is sold to the contract awarder, who then sells it to the successful bidder. The awarding agency now receives more competitive, and perhaps a greater number of, bids because the bidders now know that the foreign exchange hedge is arranged.

Over time, we should expect a proliferation of new financial market products aimed at dealing with future transactions involving foreign exchange. If there is a corporate interest in customizing an option or a forward arrangement to a specific type of transaction, an innovative bank will step in and offer a product. The small sample of new products discussed in this section is intended to suggest the practical use of these financial innovations.

SUMMARY

1. Many international transactions involve future delivery of goods and payments, subjecting traders to uncertainty about future exchange rate fluctuations at the time of delivery. Therefore, several forward-looking market instruments exist to reduce traders' currency risk.
2. The forward exchange market is composed of commercial banks buying and selling foreign currencies to be delivered at a future date.
3. When the forward price of a currency is greater than (less than) the spot price, the currency is said to sell at a forward premium (discount). When the forward price is equal to the spot price, a currency is sold at a forward flat.
4. The advantage of the forward exchange market is that a specified exchange rate between currencies has been established and no buying/selling of the currency is needed until a specified date in the future.
5. The forward exchange swap is a combination of spot and forward transactions of the same amount of the currency delivered in two different dates. The two steps are executed in one single step.
6. The currency swap is a contract between two parties to exchange the principal and interest payments of a loan in one currency to the equivalent term of loan in another currency. Both parties benefit from

having access to a long-term foreign currency financing at a lower cost than they could obtain directly.

7. Foreign currency futures are standardized contracts traded on established exchanges for delivery of currencies at a specified future date.

8. The futures market differs from the forward market in that only a few currencies are traded; each currency has a standardized contract of a fixed amount and predetermined dates; and contracts are traded only in a specific location. The participants in the futures market also include speculators, since the future contracts can be bought and sold before the contracts mature.

9. Foreign currency options are contracts that give the buyer the right to buy (call option) or sell (put option) currencies at a specified price within a specific period of time. The strike price is the price at which the owner of the contract has the right to transact.

EXERCISES

1. Use Fig. 4.1 to determine whether each of the currencies listed here is selling at a 3-month forward premium or discount against the dollar:
   a. Pound
   b. Swiss franc
   c. Yen
   d. Canadian dollar

2. Calculate the per annum premium (discount) of a 3-month forward contract on Canadian dollars based on the information in Fig. 4.1.

3. List at least three ways in which a futures contract differs from a forward contract.

4. Assume US corporation XYZ needs to arrange to have £10,000 in 90 days. Discuss the alternatives available to the corporation in meeting this obligation. What factors are important in determining which strategy is best?

5. Suppose you are the treasurer of a large US multinational firm that wants to hedge the foreign exchange risk associated with a payable of 1,000,000 UK pound due in 90 days. How many futures contracts would cover your risk?

6. Suppose you are the treasurer of a US multinational firm that wants to hedge the foreign exchange risk associated with your firm's sale of equipment to a Swiss firm worth CHF1,000,000. The receivable is due in 6 months. You want to ensure that Swiss francs are worth at least

$0.90 when the francs are received so you want a strike price of $0.90. How many options contracts do you need to hedge this risk? Do you want a call or put on Swiss francs? What has to happen to the spot rate in 6 months for you to let the option expire?

FURTHER READING

Baba, N., Packer, F., Nagano, T., 2008. The spillover of money market turbulence to FX swap and cross-country swap market. BIS Q. Rev., 73–86.

Broll, U., Zilcha, I., 1992. Exchange rate uncertainty, futures markets and the multinational firm Eur. Econ. Rev.

Géczy, C., Minton, B.A., Schrand, C., 1997. Why firms use currency derivatives. J. Finance, 1323–1354.

Lien, D., Wang, K.P., 2004. Optimal bidding and hedging in international markets. J. Int. Money Finance 23, 785–787.

Mengle, D., 2007. Credit derivatives: an overview. Fed. Rev. Bank Atlanta Econ. Rev., 1–24. Fourth Quarter.

CHAPTER 5

Eurocurrency Markets and the LIBOR

Contents

The foreign exchange market is a market in which monies are traded. Money serves as a means of paying for goods and services, and the foreign exchange market exists to facilitate international payments. Just as there is a need for international money payments, there also is a need for international credit or deposits and loans denominated in different currencies. The international deposit and loan market is often called the *Eurocurrency market*, and banks that accept these deposits and make loans are often called *Eurobanks*.

The use of the prefix *Euro*, as in Eurocurrency or Eurobank, is misleading, since the activity described is related to *offshore banking* (providing foreign currency borrowing and lending services) in general and is in no way limited to Europe. For instance, the Eurodollar market originally referred to dollar banking outside the United States. But now a type of Eurodollar banking also occurs in the United States. The Euroyen market involves yen-denominated bank deposits and loans outside Japan. Similarly there are Euroeuros (the name for euro-denominated bank deposits) and Eurosterling (the name for the UK pound denominated bank deposits).

International Money and Finance.

105

The distinguishing feature of the Eurocurrency market is that the currency used in the banking transaction generally differs from the domestic currency of the country in which the bank is located. However, this is not strictly the case, as some international banking activity in domestic currency may exist. Where such international banking occurs, it is segregated from other domestic currency banking activities in regard to regulations applied to such transactions. As we learn in the next section, offshore banking activities have grown rapidly because of a lack of regulation, which allows greater efficiency in providing banking services.

REASONS FOR OFFSHORE BANKING

The Eurodollar market began in the late 1950s. Why and how the market originated have been subjects of debate, but there is agreement upon certain elements. Given the reserve currency status of the dollar, it was only reasonable that the first external money market to develop would be for dollars. Some argue that the Communist countries were the source of early dollar balances held in Europe, since these countries needed dollars from time to time but did not want to hold these dollars in US banks for fear of reprisal should hostilities flare up. Thus the dollar deposits in UK and French banks owned by the Communists would represent the first Eurodollar deposits.

Aside from political considerations, the Eurobanks developed as a result of profit considerations. Since costly regulations are imposed on US banks, banks located outside the United States could offer higher interest rates on deposits and lower interest rates on loans than their US competitors. For instance, US banks are forced to hold a fraction of their deposits in the form of noninterest-bearing reserves. Because Eurobanks are essentially unregulated and hold much smaller reserves than their US counterparts, they can offer narrower spreads on dollars. The *spread* is the difference between the deposit and loan interest rate. Besides lower reserve requirements, Eurobanks also benefit from having no government-mandated interest rate controls, no deposit insurance, no government-mandated credit allocations, no restrictions on entry of new banks (thus encouraging greater competition and efficiency), and low taxes. This does not mean that the countries hosting the Eurobanks do not use such regulations. What we observe in these countries are two sets of banking rules: various regulations and restrictions apply to banking in the domestic currency, whereas offshore banking activities in foreign currencies go largely unregulated.

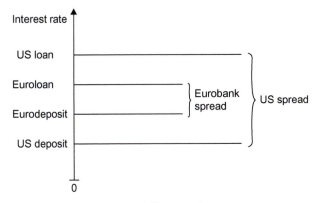

Figure 5.1 Comparison of US and Eurodollar spreads.

Fig. 5.1 portrays the standard relationship between the US domestic loan and deposit rates and the Euroloan and Eurodeposit rates. The figure shows that US spreads exceed Eurobank spreads. Eurobanks are able to offer a lower rate on dollar loans and a higher rate on dollar deposits than their US competitors. Without these differences the Eurodollar market would likely not exist, since Eurodollar transactions, lacking deposit insurance and government supervision, are considered to be riskier than are domestic dollar transactions in the United States. This means that with respect to the supply of deposits to Eurobanks, the US deposit rate provides an interest rate floor for the Eurodeposit rate, since the supply of deposits to Eurobanks is perfectly elastic at the US deposit rate (this means that if the Eurodeposit rate fell below this rate, Eurobanks would have no dollar deposits). With respect to the demand for loans from Eurobanks, US loan rates provide a ceiling for Euroloan rates because the demand for dollar loans from Eurobanks is perfectly elastic at the US loan rate (any Eurobank charging more than this would find the demand for its loans falling to zero).

INTEREST RATE SPREADS AND RISK

Interest rates on a particular currency might be constrained by capital controls. Controls on international capital flows could include quotas on foreign lending and deposits or taxes on international capital flows. For instance, if Switzerland limits inflows of foreign money, then we could have a situation where the domestic Swiss deposit interest rate exceeds the external rate on Swiss franc deposits in other nations. Although foreigners would prefer to have their Swiss franc deposits in Swiss banks in order to earn the higher interest, the legal restrictions on capital flows might prohibit such a response.

It is also possible that a perceived threat to private property rights could lead to seemingly perverse interest rate relations. If the United States threatens to confiscate foreign deposits, the funds would tend to leave the United States and shift to the external dollar market. This could result in the Eurodollar deposit rate falling below the US deposit rate.

In general risk contributes to the domestic spread exceeding the external spread. In domestic markets government agencies help ensure the sound performance of domestic financial institutions, whereas the Eurocurrency markets are largely unregulated, with no central bank ready to come to the rescue. There is an additional risk in international transactions in that investment funds are subject to control by the country of currency denomination (when it is time for repayment) as well as the country of the deposit bank. For instance, suppose a US firm has a US dollar bank deposit in Hong Kong. When the firm wants to withdraw those dollars—say, to pay a debt in Taiwan—not only is the transaction subject to control in Hong Kong (the government may not let foreign exchange leave the country freely), but the United States may control outflows of dollars from the United States, so that the Hong Kong bank may have difficulty paying back the dollars. It should be recognized that even though domestic and external deposit and loan rates differ, primarily because of risk, all interest rates tend to move together. When the domestic dollar interest rate is rising, the external rate will also tend to rise.

The growth of the Eurodollar market is the result of the narrower spreads offered by Eurobanks. We have seen the size of the Eurodollar market grow as the total demand for dollar-denominated credit has increased and as dollar banking has moved from the United States to the external market. The shift of dollar intermediation has occurred as the Eurodollar spread has narrowed relative to the domestic spread or as individual responsiveness to the spread differential has changed.

Over time important external markets have developed for the other major international currencies (euro, pound, yen, Canadian dollar, and Swiss franc). But the value of activity in Eurodollars (which refers to offshore banking in US dollars) dwarfs the rest. In the end of 2015, the Bank for International Settlements estimated the currency composition of the Eurocurrency market to be: US dollar, 58%; euro, 26%; yen, 3%; British pound, 6%; with other currencies taking the remainder.

Fig. 5.2 illustrates the foreign assets held by banks of different nations. The major role of the United Kingdom and the United States in international banking is obvious. Note that the figure distinguishes between bank assets, including interbank claims and credit extended to nonbanks. Interbank claims are deposits held in banks in other countries. If we want to know the actual amount of credit extended to nonbank borrowers, we must remove the interbank activity. Fig. 5.2 illustrates the huge size of the interbank market in international finance. An example of interbank deposits versus credit extended to nonbanks is provided later in this chapter.

INTERNATIONAL BANKING FACILITIES

In December 1981 the Federal Reserve permitted US banks to engage in Eurobanking activity on US soil. Prior to this time, US banks engaged in international banking by processing loans and deposits through their offshore branches. Many "shell" bank branches in places like the Cayman Islands or the Bahamas really amounted to nothing more than a small office and a telephone. Yet by using these locations for booking loans and deposits, US banks could avoid the reserve requirements and interest rate regulations that applied to normal US banking.

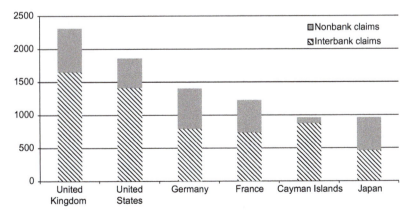

Figure 5.2 Bank's cross-border positions in USD billions. *BIS Statistical Bulletin, March 2016.*

In December 1981 international banking facilities, or *IBFs*, were legalized in the US. IBFs did not involve any new physical presence in US bank offices. Instead they simply required a different set of books for an existing bank office to record the deposits and loans permitted under the IBF proposal. IBFs are allowed to receive deposits from, and make loans to, nonresidents of the United States or other IBFs. These loans and deposits are kept separate from the rest of the bank's business because IBFs are not subject to reserve requirements, interest rate regulations, or Federal Deposit Insurance Corporation deposit insurance premiums applicable to normal US banking.

The goal of the IBF plan is to allow banking offices in the United States to compete with offshore banks without having to use an offshore banking office. The location of IBFs reflects the location of banking activity in general. It is not surprising that New York State, as the financial center of the country, has over 75% of IBF deposits. Aside from New York, California and Illinois are the only states with a significant IBF business. After IBFs were permitted, several states encouraged their formation by granting low or no taxes on IBF business. The volume of IBF business that resulted mirrored the preexisting volume of international banking activity, with New York dominating the level of activity found in other states.

Since IBFs grew very rapidly following their creation, we may ask where the growth came from. Rather than new business that was stimulated by the existence of IBFs, it appears that much of the growth was a result of shifting business from Caribbean shell branches to IBFs. After the first month of IBF operation, $29.1 billion in claims on foreign residents existed. During this same period, the claims existing at Caribbean branches of US banks fell $23.3 billion. Since this time IBF growth has continued with growth of Eurodollar banking in general. As of June 2011 the IBFs surpassed the $700 billion mark, almost entirely as interbank claims.

OFFSHORE BANKING PRACTICES

The Eurocurrency market handles a tremendous volume of funds. Because of the importance of interbank transactions, the gross measure overstates the actual amount of activity regarding total intermediation of funds between nonbank savers and nonbank borrowers, as Fig. 5.2 shows. To measure the amount of credit actually extended through the Eurobanks, we use the net size of the market—subtracting interbank activity from total deposits or total loans existing. To understand the difference between the gross and net volume of Eurodollar activity, consider the following example.

Suppose that a US firm, IBM in New York, shifts $1 million from its US bank to a Eurobank, Eurobank A, to receive a higher return on its deposits. Table 5.1 shows the T-accounts recording this transaction. The US bank now has a liability (recorded on the right-hand side of its balance sheet) of $1 million owed to Eurobank A, since the ownership of the $1 million deposit has shifted from IBM to Eurobank A. Eurobank A records the transaction as a $1 million asset in the form of a deposit it owns in the US bank, plus a $1 million liability from the deposit it has accepted from IBM. Now suppose that Eurobank A does not have a borrower waiting for $1 million (US), but another Eurobank, Eurobank B, does have a borrower. Eurobank A will deposit the $1 million with Eurobank B, earning a fraction of a percent more than it must pay IBM for the $1 million.

Table 5.2 shows that after Eurobank A deposits in Eurobank B, the US bank now owes the US dollar deposit to Eurobank B, which is shown as

Table 5.1
IBM-New York Deposits $1 Million in Eurobank A.

US Bank	
Assets	*Liabilities*
	$1 million due Eurobank A

Eurobank A	
Assets	*Liabilities*
$1 million deposit in US Bank	$1 million Eurodollar deposit due IBM

Table 5.2
Eurobank A Deposits $1 Million in Eurobank B.

US Bank	
Assets	*Liabilities*
	$1 million due Eurobank B

Eurobank A	
Assets	*Liabilities*
$1 million Eurodollar deposit in Eurobank B	$1 million Eurodollar deposit due IBM

Eurobank B	
Assets	*Liabilities*
$1 million deposit in US Bank	$1 million Eurodollar deposit due Eurobank A

Table 5.3
Eurobank B Loans $1 Million to BMW.

US Bank	
Assets	*Liabilities*
	$1 million due BMW

Eurobank A	
Assets	*Liabilities*
$1 million Eurodollar deposit in Eurobank B	$1 million Eurodollar deposit due IBM

Eurobank B	
Assets	*Liabilities*
$1 million loan to BMW	$1 million Eurodollar deposit due Eurobank A

BMW-Munich	
Assets	*Liabilities*
$1 million deposit in US Bank	$1 million loan owed to Eurobank B

an asset of Eurobank B, matched by the deposit liability of $1 million from Eurobank B to Eurobank A.

Finally in Table 5.3, Eurobank B makes a loan to BMW in Munich. Now the US bank has transferred the ownership of its deposit liability to BMW (Whenever dollars are actually spent following a Eurodollar transaction, the actual dollars must come from the United States—only the United States creates US dollars; the Eurodollar banks simply act as intermediaries.). The gross size of the market is measured as total deposits in Eurobanks, or $2 million ($1 million in Eurobank A and $1 million in Eurobank B). The net size of the market is found by subtracting interbank deposits, and thus is a measure of the actual credit extended to nonbank users of dollars. In the example, Eurobank A deposited $1 million in Eurobank B. If we subtract this interbank deposit of $1 million from the total Eurobank deposits of $2 million, we find the net size of the market to be $1 million. This $1 million is the value of credit actually intermediated to nonbank borrowers.

Since the Eurodollar market deals with such large magnitudes, it is understandable that economists and politicians are concerned about the effects the Eurodollar market can have on domestic markets. In the United States,

Eurodollar deposits are counted in the M3 definition of the money supply. Measures of the US money supply are used by economists to evaluate the resources available to the public for spending. Eurodollars are not spendable money but, instead, are money substitutes like time deposits in a domestic bank. Because Eurodollars do not serve as a means of payment, Eurobanks are not able to create money as banks can in a domestic setting. Eurobanks are essentially intermediaries; they accept deposits and then loan these deposits.

Even though Eurodollars do not provide a means of payment, they still may have implications for domestic monetary practice. For countries without efficient money markets, access to the very efficient and competitive Eurodollar market may reduce the demand for domestic money, because the domestic company need not use domestic currency for its transactions anymore.

All banks are interested in maximizing the spread between their deposit and loan interest rates. In this regard, Eurobanks are no different from domestic banks. All banks are also concerned with managing risk, the risk associated with their assets and liabilities. Like all intermediaries, Eurobanks tend to borrow short term and lend long term. Thus if the deposit liabilities were reduced greatly, we would see deposit interest rates rise very rapidly in the short run. The advantage of matching the term structures of deposits and loans is that deposits and loans are maturing at the same time, so that the bank is better able to respond to a change in demand for deposits or loans.

Deposits in the Eurocurrency market are for fixed terms, ranging from days to years, although most are for less than 6 months. Certificates of deposit are considered to be the closest domestic counterpart to a Eurocurrency deposit. Loans in the Eurocurrency market can range up to 10 or more years. The interest rate on a Eurocurrency loan is usually stated as some spread over LIBOR (London Interbank Offered Rate) and is adjusted at fixed intervals, like every 3 months. These adjustable interest rates serve to minimize the interest rate risk to the bank.

Large loans are generally made by *syndicates* of Eurobanks. Syndicates of banks are an organized group of banks. The syndicate will be headed by a lead or managing bank; other banks wishing to participate in the loan will join the syndicate and help fund the loan. By allowing banks to reduce their level of participation in any loan, syndicates can participate in more loans. Thus each individual bank reduces their risk by having a diversified loan portfolio.

LIBOR

As of the end of 2010 the NYSE market capitalization was slightly over $13 trillion dollars, and we hear news every day of what happened to the stock market. The LIBOR affects financial assets worth at least 25 times more, but rarely receives any press. *LIBOR* stands for *London Interbank Offered Rate* and is the interest rate at which a group of large London banks could borrow from each other each morning. Loans of $10 trillion and Swaps worth about $350 trillion around the world are directly tied to the LIBOR, according to the British Bankers Association. For example, approximately half of the United States adjustable mortgages are estimated to be tied to the LIBOR.

THE BBA LIBOR

In February 2014 the LIBOR changed from the BBA LIBOR to the ICE LIBOR. To understand the reasons for this we are first going to discuss the way the LIBOR was traditionally computed and then compare it to today's methodology. The BBA LIBOR was collected by the British Bankers' Association (BBA). The LIBOR established a value each day at 11:00 a.m. London time for each major currency. LIBOR is the key rate for fixing interest rates around the world. For instance a variable interest rate loan in some currency may be priced at 2% points above LIBOR and adjusted annually. Once a year the interest rate on the loan would be adjusted to the currency value of LIBOR plus 2% points.

LIBOR was fixed daily for the following 10 currencies: the British pound (GBP), Canadian dollar (CAD), Danish krone (DKK), euro (EUR), US dollar (USD), Australian dollar (AUD), Japanese yen (JPY), New Zealand dollar (NZD), Swedish krona (SKR), and Swiss franc (CHF). There were 15 maturities for which LIBOR was set each day, from an overnight rate all the way up to 12 months. Thus a total of 150 rates were set each day.

The daily value of LIBOR was drawn from a panel of contributing banks chosen based upon their reputation, level of activity in the London market, and perceived expertise in the currency concerned. For example, for the US dollar 16 different respected banks submitted quotes, and the four highest and four lowest quotes were eliminated. The borrowing costs for the remaining eight banks were averaged into the LIBOR rate. Shortly before 11:00 a.m. each business day, each bank reported the rate at which it could borrow funds of a reasonable market size by accepting interbank offers from banks other than the LIBOR panel of contributing banks.

Recently an investigation has begun into a possible collusion between banks to set the LIBOR. It has been alleged that there have been significant departures from the actual costs of borrowing by a number of banks. The potential misreporting can pay off greatly for banks. According to Snider and Youle (2010) a collusion among the banks to change the LIBOR by 0.25% could earn a single bank as much as $3.37 billion in a single quarter. Thus the incentive to quote incorrect rates or to collude exists.

LIBOR RIGGING

Traders at many influential banks were accused of rigging the LIBOR rate, during 2006–2010. A large number of banks that have been accused of receiving excess profits from LIBOR rigging have agreed to pay large fines. Table 5.4 shows that banks have already agreed to pay almost $9 billion in fines related to LIBOR rigging, as of July, 2016.

In addition to fining banks, prosecutors have also charged individual traders with rigging the LIBOR. One such trader at UBS and Citigroup,

Table 5.4 Fines Paid by Banks for LIBOR Cheating

Bank	Date	Amount (in millions of US dollars)
UBS	May 20, 2015	$203
Deutsche Bank	April 23, 2015	$2,500
Lloyds TSB Bank	July 28, 2014	$380
Citigroup	December 04, 2013	$95
Deutsche Bank	December 04, 2013	$984
JP Morgan	December 04, 2013	$108
Royal Bank of Scotland	December 04, 2013	$530
Societe Generale	December 04, 2013	$600
Rabo Bank	October 29, 2013	$1,066
JP Morgan	October 21, 2013	$92
ICAP	September 25, 2013	$87
Royal Bank of Scotland	February 06, 2013	$612
UBS	December 19, 2012	$1,500
Barclays Bank	June 27, 2012	$450

Source: Nytimes.com, March 23, 2016; ft.com, December 04, 2013.

Tom Hayes, was accused of setting up a network of brokers and traders to rig the LIBOR rate to create huge profit for the banks. On August 3, 2015 Tom Hayes was convicted of conspiring to rig the LIBOR rate, and sentenced to 14 years in jail later reduced to 11 years and a $1.2 million fine. In November, 2015 two Rabobank traders were convicted of LIBOR rigging, followed by three Barclays traders that were convicted in July, 2016.[1] Many other people have been also charged and are awaiting trials or have pleaded guilty already.

With such massive cheating the LIBOR rate needed to be overhauled. In February 2014 the new ICE LIBOR was introduced that remedied certain weakness of the BBA LIBOR.

THE ICE LIBOR

The LIBOR was published by the British Bankers Association from January, 1986 until January, 2014. In February, 2014 the LIBOR continued to be published by an organization called the ICE Benchmark Administration. This organization has refined the process of submitting quotes and reduced the number of currencies and maturities. The reduction in currencies and maturities happened, because some maturities were thinly traded and some currencies less popular resulting in more volatility in the LIBOR and more of a temptation to fix rates. Therefore LIBOR is currently limited to five currencies: USD, GBP, EUR, JPY, and CHF, with seven maturities from overnight to 12 months.

In addition to removing thin maturities, the new LIBOR has a much stronger oversight over the rates that are submitted by banks. The structure of the ICE LIBOR has independent directors overseeing the survey with participation from the Federal Reserve System, Swiss National Bank and Bank of England. The new LIBOR focuses on accountability of the banks. The senior manager from the bank that submits rate has to be able to provide evidence to support the rate submitted, and the manager is held personally liable. In this way a manager can be prosecuted for entering a false rate. In addition, analysts have been hired to examine statistical evidence to detect if any discrepancy in the submissions can be found.

The ICE LIBOR is published on a daily basis, except for certain holidays. Table 5.5 shows the rates on July 7, 2016 for all currencies and

[1] Source: Reuters Business News, August 3, 2015; Blomberg.com, July 4, 2016.

Table 5.5 LIBOR rates as of July 7, 2016

Maturity	Currencies				
	US Dollar	Pound Sterling	Swiss Franc	Japanese Yen	Euro
Spot Next/Overnight	0.4127	0.4787	−0.7988	−0.0677	−0.4013
1 Week	0.4378	0.4862	−0.8258	−0.0703	−0.3871
1 Month	0.4743	0.4772	−0.8166	−0.0529	−0.3617
2 Month	0.5552	0.4915	−0.7916	−0.0309	−0.3289
3 Month	0.6646	0.5187	−0.7802	−0.0285	−0.3037
6 Month	0.9349	0.6106	−0.7066	−0.0254	−0.1917
1 Year	1.2465	0.8449	−0.5910	0.0625	−0.0693

Source: https://www.theice.com/marketdata/reports/170.

maturities. For all currencies the longer maturities have higher rates. Across currencies rates are grouped in two groups. The dollar and pound are very similar with positive rates. The other three currencies have negative rates, with the Swiss franc being strongly negative, the euro substantially negative and the yen slightly negative.

SUMMARY

1. The Eurocurrency market is the offshore banking market where commercial banks accept deposits and extend loans in a currency other than the domestic currency.
2. The Eurodollar, the US dollar-denominated deposits and loans outside the US, has the highest value of activity among other currency offshore banking.
3. Compared to domestic banks, the Eurobanks have lower operating costs and are less regulated. Therefore they are able to offer narrower spread than domestic banks.
4. Because of fewer regulations, the Eurobanking has gained more popularity among investors and grown rapidly.
5. The Eurocurrency market improves efficiency of international finances. Efficiency comes from access to low-cost borrowing, lack of government regulations, and strong competition among the Eurobanks.
6. LIBOR is an important interest rate that the Eurodollar market uses as a benchmark interest rate to set its loan rates.
7. The LIBOR is collected by the ICE Benchmark Administration since February 2014.
8. International banking facilities (IBFs) are departments of US banks that are permitted to engage in Eurocurrency banking.
9. The net size of the Eurodollar market measures the amount of credit actually extended to nonbanks.
10. Large Eurocurrency loans are made by bank syndicates.

EXERCISES

1. Why must Eurobanks operate with narrower spreads than domestic banks? What would happen if the spreads were equal in both markets?
2. Use T-accounts to explain the difference between the gross and net size of the Eurodollar market.

3. Create an example of $10 million being deposited in the Eurodollar market by a US manufacturing firm, Motorola. Your example should include at least one interbank transaction before the dollars are borrowed by a French public utility firm, Paris Electric. How is the gross size of the Eurodollar market affected by your example? What about the net size?

4. Discuss how the Eurobanks can survive when they operate with such a small spread.

5. What could be the risks for depositors if they decide to use the Eurocurrency market for their deposits?

6. What are the IBFs? Why did the Federal Reserve authorize the establishment of the IBFs? Explain.

FURTHER READING

Apergis, N., 1997. Domestic and eurocurrency yields: any exchange rate link? evidence from a VAR model. J. Policy Model 19 (10), 41–49.

Bremnes, H., Gjerde, O., Saettem, F., 1997. A multivariate cointegration analysis of interest rates in the eurocurrency market. J. Int. Money Financ. 16 (5), 767–778.

Snider, C., Youle, T., 2010. Does the LIBOR Reflect the Banks' Borrowing Costs? Working Paper. University of Minnesota. April.

Snider, C., Youle, T., 2014. The Fix is in, Detecting Portfolio Driven Manipulation of the LIBOR. Dartmouth College. October.

Hsieh, N.C.T., Lin, A., Swanson, P.E., 1999. Global money market interrelationships. Int. Rev. Econ. Financ 8, 71–85.

Key, S.J., 1982. International banking facilities. Fed. Reserve Bull. 68, 565–576. October

MacKenzie, D., 2008. What's in a number? The importance of LIBOR. Real-world Econ. Rev. 47, 237–242.

CHAPTER 6

Exchange Rates, Interest Rates, and Interest Parity

Contents

International trade occurs in both goods and financial assets. Exchange rates change in a manner to accommodate this trade. In this chapter, we study the relationship between interest rates and exchange rates, and consider how exchange rates adjust to achieve equilibrium in financial markets.

INTEREST RATE PARITY

The *interest rate parity* explains the relationship between returns to bond investments between two countries. Interest rate parity results from profit-seeking arbitrage activity, specifically *covered interest rate arbitrage*. Let us go through an example of how covered interest arbitrage works. For expositional purposes

$i_\$$ = interest rate in the United States

$i_\pounds$ = interest rate in the United Kingdom

F = forward exchange rate (dollars per pound)

E = spot exchange rate (dollars per pound)

where the interest rates and the forward rate are for assets with the same term to maturity (e.g., 3 months or 1 year), the investor in the United States can earn $(1 + i_\$)$ at home by investing \$1 for 1 period (for instance, 1 year). Alternatively the US investor can invest in the United Kingdom by converting dollars to pounds and then investing the pounds. Here \$1 is equal to $1/E$ pounds (where E is the dollar price of pounds). Thus by investing in the United Kingdom, the US resident can earn $(1 + i_£)/E$. This is the quantity of pounds resulting from the \$1 invested. Remember \$1 buys $1/E$ pounds, and £1 will return $1 + i_£$ after 1 period. Thus $1/E$ pounds will return $(1 + i_£)/E$ after 1 period. Since the investor is a resident of the United States, the investment return will ultimately be converted into dollars. But since future spot exchange rates are not known with certainty, the investor can eliminate the uncertainty regarding the future dollar value of $(1 + i_£)/E$ by *covering* the £ currency investment with a forward contract. By selling $(1 + i_£)/E$ pounds to be received in a future period in the forward market today, the investor has guaranteed a certain dollar value of the pound investment opportunity. The *covered return* is equal to $(1 + i_£)F/E$ dollars. The US investor can earn either $1 + i_\$$ dollars by investing \$1 at home or $(1 + i_£)F/E$ dollars by investing the dollar in the United Kingdom. Arbitrage between the two investment opportunities results in

$$1 + i_\$ = (1 + i_£)F/E$$

which can be rewritten as:

$$1 + i_\$ / (1 + i_£)F/E \qquad (6.1)$$

Eq. (6.1) can be put in a more useful form by subtracting 1 from both sides, giving us the *exact interest rate parity* equation:

$$(i_\$ - i_£)/(1 + i_£) = (F - E)/E \qquad (6.2)$$

This equation can be approximated by noting that the denominator on the left side is almost one. Approximating by assuming that the denominator is equal to one results in the *approximate covered interest rate parity* equation:

$$(i_\$ - i_£) = (F - E)/E \qquad (6.3)$$

The smaller $i_£$, the better the approximation of Eqs. (6.3) to (6.2). Eq. (6.3) indicates that the interest differential between a comparable US and UK investment is equal to the forward premium or discount on the pound. (We must remember that, since interest rates are quoted at annual rates or percent per annum, the forward premiums or discounts must also be quoted at annual rates.) Now let us consider an example. Ignoring bid-ask spreads, we observe the following Eurocurrency market interest rates:

Euro $: 15%

Euro £: 10%

The exchange rate is quoted as the dollar price of pounds and is currently $E = 2.00$. Given the previous information, what do you expect the 12-month forward rate to be?

Using Eq. (6.3) we can plug in the known values for the interest rates and spot exchange rate and then solve for the forward rate:

$$0.15 - 0.10 = (F - 2.00)/2.00$$

which simplifies to

$$F = 2.00(0.15 - 0.10) + 2.00 - 2.10$$

Thus we would expect a 12-month forward rate of $2.10 to give a 12-month forward premium equal to the 0.05 interest differential.

Suppose a bank sets the 12-month forward rate at $2.15, instead of $2.10. This would lead to arbitrage opportunities. How would the arbitragers profit? They could buy pounds at the spot rate and then invest and sell the pounds forward for dollars, because the future price of pounds is higher than that implied by the interest parity relation. These actions would tend to increase the spot rate and lower the forward rate, thereby bringing the forward premium back in line with the interest differential. The interest rates could also move, because the movement of funds into pound investments would tend to depress the pound interest rate, whereas the shift out of dollar investments would tend to raise the dollar rate.

EFFECTIVE RETURN ON A FOREIGN INVESTMENT

The interest parity relationship can also be used to illustrate the concept of the *effective return on a foreign investment*. Eq. (6.3) can be rewritten so that the dollar interest rate is equal to the pound rate plus the forward premium. Thus the returns to investing in dollar assets and pound denominated assets are:

$$i_\$ = i_£ + (F - E)/E \qquad (6.4)$$

Covered interest parity ensures that Eq. (6.4) will hold. Note that the interest rate on the bond $i_£$ is not the relevant return measure by itself, since this is the return in pounds. Instead the effective return to a UK investment is composed of an interest rate return and an exchange rate return. But suppose we do not use the forward market, yet we are US residents who buy UK bonds. Even in this case the effective return would be composed of two parts. The first part would be the interest rate return and the second would be the expected change in the exchange rate, as we now need to take into account the expected spot rate in the future. In other words, the return on a UK investment, plus the expected change in the value of UK currency, is our expected return on a pound investment. If the forward exchange rate is equal to the expected future spot rate, then the forward premium is also the expected change in the exchange rate.

DEVIATIONS FROM COVERED INTEREST RATE PARITY

Even though foreign exchange traders quote forward rates based on interest differentials and current spot rates so that the forward rate will yield a forward premium equal to the interest differential, we may ask: How well does interest rate parity hold in the real world? Since deviations from interest rate parity would seem to present profitable arbitrage opportunities, we would expect profit-seeking arbitragers to eliminate any deviations. Still, careful studies of the data indicate that small deviations from interest rate parity do occur. There are several reasons why interest rate parity may not hold exactly, and yet we can earn no arbitrage profits from the situation. The most obvious reason is the transactions cost between markets. Because buying and selling foreign exchange and international securities involves a cost for each transaction, there may exist deviations from interest rate parity that are equal to, or smaller than, these transaction costs. In this case, speculators cannot profit from the deviations, since the price of buying and selling in the market would wipe out any apparent gain. Studies indicate that for comparable financial assets that differ only in terms of currency of denomination (e.g., dollar- and pound-denominated Eurodeposits in a German bank), 100% of the deviations from interest rate parity can be accounted for by transaction costs.

Besides transaction costs, there are other reasons why interest rate parity may not hold perfectly. One other reason, for small deviations from interest rate parity, is the potential difference in taxation of interest earnings and foreign exchange rate earnings. If these are differently taxed in a country then the effective return Eq. (6.4) might not hold since one side involves only interest earnings and the other interest earnings and foreign exchange earnings. Thus it may be misleading to simply consider pretax effective returns to decide if profitable arbitrage is possible.

Two more reasons for why interest rate parity might not hold perfectly are government controls and political risk. If government controls on financial capital flows exist, then an effective barrier between national markets is in place. If an individual cannot freely buy or sell the currency or securities of a country, then the free market forces that work in response to effective return differentials will not function. Indeed, even the threat of controls could affect the interest rate parity condition. Political risk is often mentioned in conjunction with government controls. The interest rate parity condition is not directly affected by political risk, such as a regime change. Instead it is the threat of the new regime imposing capital controls that affects the interest rate parity condition. We should note, however, that the external or Eurocurrency market often serves as a means of avoiding political risk, since an individual can borrow and lend foreign currencies outside the home country of each currency. For instance, the Eurodollar market provides a market for US dollar loans and deposits in major financial centers outside the United States, thereby avoiding any risk associated with US government actions.

INTEREST RATES AND INFLATION

To better understand the relationship between interest rates and exchange rates, we now consider how inflation can be related to both. To link exchange rates, interest rates, and inflation, we must first understand the role of inflation in interest rate determination. Economists distinguish between real and nominal rates of interest. The *nominal interest rate* is the rate actually observed in the market. The *real rate* is a concept that measures the return after adjusting for inflation. If you lend someone money and charge that person 5% interest on the loan, the real return on your loan is less when there is inflation. For instance, if the rate of inflation is 10%, then the debtor will pay back the loan with dollars that are worth less. In fact, so much less that you, the lender, end up with less purchasing power than you had when you initially made the loan.

This all means that the nominal rate of interest will tend to incorporate inflation expectations in order to provide lenders with a real return for the use of their money. The expected effect of inflation on the nominal

Table 6.1 Interest rates and inflation rates for selected countries

Country	Inflation rate (%)	Interest rate (%)
Portugal	−0.20	0.95
South Korea	1.30	2.00
United States	1.60	1.25
Turkey	8.90	10.75
Argentina	36.40	26.15

Source: CIA World Factbook, 2014; www.deposits.org, Sep. 2015.

interest rate is often called the *Fisher effect* (after Irving Fisher, a pioneer of the determinants of interest rates), and the relationship between inflation and interest rates is given by the *Fisher equation:*

$$i = r + \pi^e \tag{6.5}$$

where i is the nominal interest rate, r the real rate, and π^e the expected rate of inflation. Thus an increase in π^e will tend to increase i. For example, the fact that interest rates in the 1970s were much higher than in the 1960s is the result of higher inflationary expectations in the 1970s. Across countries, at a specific time, we should expect interest rates to vary with inflation. Table 6.1 shows that nominal interest rates tend to be higher in countries that have recently experienced higher rates of inflation.

EXCHANGE RATES, INTEREST RATES, AND INFLATION

If we combine the Fisher Eq. (6.5) and the interest parity Eq. (6.3), we can determine how interest rates, inflation, and exchange rates are all linked. First, consider the Fisher equation for the United States and the United Kingdom:

$$i_\$ = r_\$ + \pi^e_\$ \text{ for the United States,}$$

and

$$i_£ = r_£ + \pi^e_£ \text{ for the United States.}$$

Global investors now want to have as high as possible real returns from their investments. If global markets allow free flow of capital, one might expect that the real returns across countries equalize. If we assume that the real rate of interest is the same internationally, then $r_\$ = r_£$. In this case, the nominal interest rates, $i_\$$ and $i_\pounds$, differ solely by expected inflation, so we can write

$$i_\$ - i_\pounds = \pi_\$^e - \pi_\pounds^e \qquad (6.6)$$

The interest parity condition of Eq. (6.3) indicates that the interest differential is also equal to the forward premium, or

$$i_\$ - i_\pounds = \pi_\$^e - \pi_\pounds^e = (F - S)/E \qquad (6.7)$$

Eq. (6.7) summarizes the link among interest, inflation, and exchange rates.

In the real world the interrelationships summarized by Eq. (6.7) are determined simultaneously, because interest rates, inflation expectations, and exchange rates are jointly affected by new events and information. For instance, suppose we begin from a situation of equilibrium, where interest parity holds. Suddenly there is a change in US policy that leads to expectations of a higher US inflation rate. The increase in expected inflation will cause dollar interest rates to rise. At the same time exchange rates will adjust to maintain interest parity. If the expected future spot rate is changed, we would expect F to carry much of the adjustment burden. If the expected future spot rate is unchanged, the current spot rate would tend to carry the bulk of the adjustment burden. Finally if central bank intervention is pegging exchange rates at fixed levels by buying and selling to maintain the fixed rate, the domestic and foreign currency interest rates will have to adjust to parity levels. The fundamental point is that the initial US policy change led to changes in inflationary expectations, interest rates, and exchange rates simultaneously, since they all adjust to new equilibrium levels.

EXPECTED EXCHANGE RATES AND THE TERM STRUCTURE OF INTEREST RATES

There is no such thing as *the* interest rate for a country. Interest rates within a country vary for different investment opportunities and for different maturity dates on similar investment opportunities. The structure of interest rates existing on investment opportunities over time is known as the *term structure of interest rates*. For instance in the bond market we will observe 3-month, 6-month, 1-year, 3-year, and even longer-term bonds. If the interest rates rise with the term to maturity, then we observe a rising term structure. If the interest rates are the same regardless of term, then the term structure will be flat. We describe the term structure of interest rates by describing the slope of a line connecting the various points in time at which we observe interest rates.

There are several competing theories that explain the term structure of interest rates. We will discuss three theories:

1. *Expectations*: This theory suggests that the long-term interest rate tends to be equal to an average of short-term rates expected over the long-term holding period. In other words an investor could buy a long-term bond or a series of short-term bonds, so the expected return from the long-term bond will tend to be equal to the return generated from holding the series of short-term bonds.

2. *Liquidity premium*: Underlying this theory is the idea that long-term bonds incorporate a risk premium since risk-averse investors would prefer to lend short term. The premium on long-term bonds would tend to result in interest rates rising with the holding period of the bond.

3. *Preferred habitat*: This approach contends that the bond markets are segmented by maturities. In other words there is a separate market for short- and long-term bonds, and the interest rates are determined by supply and demand in each market. If the markets are segmented then the returns in the long-term bond market can be very different from the short-term bond market.

Although we could use these theories to explain the term structure of interest rates in any one currency, in international finance we use the term structures for different currencies to infer expected exchange rate changes. For instance if we compared Euro–dollar and Euro–euro deposit rates for different maturities, like 1-month and 3-month deposits, the difference between the two term structures should reflect expected exchange rate changes, as long as the expected future spot rate is equal to the forward rate. Of course, if there are capital controls, then the various national markets become isolated and there would not be any particular relationship between international interest rates.

Fig. 6.1 plots the Eurocurrency deposit rates at a particular time for 1- to 6-month terms. We know from the interest rate parity condition that when one country has higher interest rates than another, the high-interest-rate currency is expected to depreciate relative to the low-interest-rate currency. The only way an interest rate can be above another one is if the high-interest-rate currency is expected to depreciate; thus, the effective rate, $i + (F - E)/E$ (as shown in Eq. (6.4), with the forward rate used as a predictor of the future spot rate), is lower than the observed rate, i, because of the expected depreciation of the currency ($F < E$).

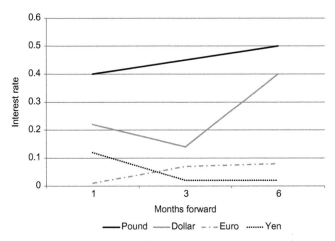

Figure 6.1 Eurocurrency interest rates for December 31, 2014. www.ft.com.

If the distance between two of the term structure lines is the same at each point, then the expected change in the exchange rate will be constant. To see this more clearly, let us once again consider the interest parity relation given by Eq. (6.3):

$$i_\$ - i_£ = (F - E)/E$$

This expression indicates that the difference between the interest rate in two countries will be equal to the forward premium or discount when the interest rates and the forward rate reflect the same term to maturity. If the forward rate is equal to the future spot rate, then we can say that the interest differential is also approximately equal to the expected change in the spot rate. This means that at each point in the term structure, the difference between the national interest rates should reflect the expected change in the exchange rate for the two currencies being compared. By examining the different points in the term structure, we can determine how the exchange rate expectations are changing through time. One implication of this is that even if we did not have a forward exchange market in a currency, the interest differential between that currency and other currencies would allow us to infer expected future exchange rates.

Now we can understand why a constant differential between two interest rates implies that future changes in the exchange rate are expected to occur at some constant rate. Thus if two of the term structure lines are parallel, then the exchange rate changes are expected to be constant (the currencies will appreciate or depreciate against each other at a constant rate). On the other hand, if two term structure lines are diverging, or moving farther apart from one another, then the high-interest-rate currency is expected to depreciate at an increasing rate over time. For term structure lines that are converging, or moving closer together, the high-interest-rate currency is expected to depreciate at a declining rate relative to the low-interest-rate currency.

To illustrate the exchange rate–term structure relationship, let us look at Fig. 6.1. In Fig. 6.1 the term structure line for the yen lies below that of the dollar. We should then expect the Japanese yen to appreciate against the US dollar and the yen should sell at a forward premium against the dollar. With regard to the slopes of the curves, the term structure line for Japan and the United States are diverging over time. The divergence of the US line from the Japanese line suggests that the yen is expected to appreciate against the dollar at a faster rate over time.

Looking at the other currencies in Fig. 6.1 we can see differences in the expected changes in the exchange rates. The term structure line for the pound lies above that of the dollar so we should expect the pound to depreciate in value against the dollar and sell at a forward discount against the dollar. The fact that the term structure of the euro lies below both the pound and dollar indicates that the euro is expected to appreciate against both of those currencies in the table. A particularly interesting case is the term structure for the euro and the yen, because these intersect. The yen is expected to depreciate or sell at a forward discount against the euro at 1-month maturity, but at the 3-month and 6-month maturities the yen sells at forward premium against the euro.

SUMMARY

1. The interest parity relationship indicates that the interest rate differential between investments in two currencies will equal to the forward premium or discount between the currencies.
2. The international investment is *covered* when investors use the forward contracts to cover or hedge themselves from risk of the unknown future spot exchange rates.
3. A currency is at a forward premium (discount) by as much as its interest rate is lower (higher) than the interest rate in the other country.
4. Covered interest parity links together four rates, which are the current spot exchange rate, the current forward exchange rate, and the

current interest rates in two countries. If one of these rates change, at least one of the others must also change to maintain the covered interest parity.

5. Covered interest arbitrage ensures interest parity.
6. Deviations from interest rate parity could be the result of transaction costs, differential taxation, government controls, or political risk.
7. The real interest rate is equal to the nominal interest rate minus the expected rate of inflation.
8. If real interest rates are equal in two countries, then the interest rate differential will equal to expected inflation rate differential, which in turn will equal to the forward premium or discount between two currencies.
9. The term structure of interest rates is the relationship between interest rates on various bonds with different terms to maturity.
10. Differences between the term structure of interest rates in two countries will reflect the expected exchange rate changes.

EXERCISES

1. Suppose you want to infer expected future exchange rates in a less developed country that has free-market-determined interest rates but does not have a forward exchange market. Is there any other way of inferring expected future exchange rates? Under what assumptions?
2. **a.** Show that there is a direct relationship between the forward premium and the "real" interest rate differential between two currencies.
   b. Under what conditions will the forward premium equal the expected "inflation" differential between two currencies?
3. Give four reasons why, when interest parity does not hold exactly, we are unable to take advantage of arbitrage to earn profits.
4. Suppose the 1-year interest rate on British pounds is 11%, the dollar interest rate is 6%, and the current $/£ spot rate is $1.80.
   a. What do you expect the spot rate to be in 1 year?
   b. Why can we not observe the expected future spot rate?
5. Assume that the 1-year interest rate in the United States is 2% and the 1-year interest rate in Sweden is 4%. Is there a premium or discount on the Swedish krona?
6. If two countries had identical term structures of interest rates, what is the expected future exchange rate change between the two currencies?

FURTHER READING

Choudhry, B., Titman, S., 2001. Why real interest rates, cost of capital and price/earnings ratios vary across countries. J. Int. Money Financ., 165–190. April.

Lothian, J.R., Wu, L., 2011. Uncovered interest rate parity over the last two centuries. J. Int. Money Financ. 30 (3), 448–473.

McKinnon, R.I., 1979. Money in International Exchange. Oxford, New York.

Pigott, C., 1993–1994. International interest rate convergence: a survey of the issues and evidence. Fed. Res. Bank N.Y. Q. Rev. Winter 18 (4), 24–38.

Solnik, B., 1978. International parity conditions and exchange risk. J. Bank Financ. 2, 281–293.

Throop, A.W., 1994. Linkages of national interest rates. FRBSF Wkly. Lett. 94, September 1–4.

Wainwright, K., Chiang, A.C., 2004. Fundamental Methods Mathematical Economics. McGraw-Hill, New York.

APPENDIX A WHAT ARE LOGARITHMS, AND WHY ARE THEY USED IN FINANCIAL RESEARCH?

Although this is not a course in mathematics, there are certain techniques that are so prevalent in modern financial research that not to use them would be a disservice to the student. Logarithms are a prime example. The most important reason for the use of logarithms is that they show the "true" percentage distance. In addition, they facilitate calculations in financial relationships.

What are Logarithms?

Logarithms are a way of transforming numbers to simplify mathematical analysis of a problem. One way to view a logarithm as the *power* to which some *base* must be raised to give a certain number. For example, we all know that the square of 10 is 100, or $10^2 = 100$. Therefore if 10 is our base, we know that 10 must be raised to the second power to equal 100. We could then say that the logarithm of 100 to the base 10 is 2. This is written as

$$\log_{10} 100 = 2$$

What then is the $\log_{10}$ of 1000? Of course, $\log_{10} 1000 = 3$, because

$$10 \times 10 \times 10 = 10^3 = 1000.$$

In general any number greater than 1 could serve as the base by which we could write all positive numbers. Picking any arbitrary number designated as a, where a is greater than 1, we could write any positive number b as

$$\log_a b = c$$

where c is the power to which a must be raised to equal b.

Rather than pick any arbitrary number for our base a, there is a particular number that arises naturally in economic phenomena. This number is approximately 2.71828, and it is called e. The value of e arises in the continuous compounding of interest. Specifically, $e = \lim_{n \to \infty}(1 + 1/n)n$, where n is the number of times interest is compounded per year. The value of some principal amount, P, in 1 year, compounded continuously at r percent interest, is $V = Pe^r$. If $r = 100\%$, then the amount of principal and interest after 1 year is $V = Pe$. Since e comes *naturally* out of continuous compounding, we refer to e as the base of the *natural logarithms*. Financial researchers utilize logarithms to the base e. Rather than write the log of some number b as $\log_e b = c$, it is common to express $\log_e$ as ln, so that we write

$$\ln b = c$$

In all uses of logarithms in this text, we assume log b is actually ln b or the natural logarithm; it is for convenience that we drop the e subscript and simply write log b rather than $\log_e b$.

Why Use Logarithms in Financial Research?

If the lesson so far has seemed rather esoteric and unrelated to your interests, here is the payoff.

A useful feature of logarithms is that the change in the logarithm of some variable is commonly used to measure the percentage change in the variable (the measure is precise for compound changes and approximate for simple rates of change). If we want to calculate the percentage change in the yen/\$ exchange rate (E) between today (period t) and yesterday (period $t - 1$), we could calculate $(E_t - E_{t-1})/E_{t-1}$. Alternatively we could calculate $\ln E_t - \ln E_{t-1}$.

For example, let us assume that the $E_{t-1} = 80$ for the yen/\$ in the past value and $E_t = 125$ for the yen/\$ in the current period. What is the percentage change in the value of the yen? If we use the formula $(E_t - E_{t-1})/E_{t-1}$ then the percentage change is 56.25%, but if we use the $\ln E_t - \ln E_{t-1} = 44.63\%$. The two values are near each other, but not quite the same. Now assume that the exchange rate was quoted in inverse form instead as \$/yen. The rates become $E_{t-1} = 0.0125$ for the yen/\$ and $E_t = 0.008$. Note that these are identical to the rates quoted above. What is the percentage change in the value of the yen? If we use the formula $(E_t - E_{t-1})/E_{t-1}$ then the percentage change is -36%, but if we use the $\ln E_t - \ln E_{t-1} = -44.63\%$. So when we use natural logarithms the percentage distance becomes identical no matter how currencies are quoted.

The fact that percentage distances are the same, whatever the base period value, is a very convenient feature of logarithms. In the Covered Interest Rate Parity concept, we need to be able to move back and forth in currencies, and using natural logarithms we know that this will equal the interest rate differentials.

Natural logarithms also have some convenient mathematical properties. Three extremely helpful properties of logarithms that are used frequently in international finance are:

1. The log of a product of two numbers is equal to the sum of the logs of the individual numbers:

$$\ln(MN) = \ln M + \ln N$$

2. The log of a quotient is equal to the difference of the logs of the individual numbers:

$$\ln(M/N) = \ln M - \ln N$$

3. The log of some number M raised to the N power is equal to N times the log of M:

$$\ln(M^N) = N(\ln M)$$

Since many relationships in financial research are products or ratios, by taking the logs of these relationships, we are able to analyze simple, linear, additive relationships rather than more complex phenomena involving products and quotients.

This appendix serves as a brief introduction or review of logarithms. Rather than provide more illustrations of the specific use of logarithms in international finance, at this point it is preferable to study the examples that arise in the context of the problems, as analyzed in subsequent chapters. More general examples of the use of logarithms may be found in Wainwright and Chiang (2004).

CHAPTER 7

Prices, Exchange Rates, and Purchasing Power Parity

Contents

Chapter 1, The Foreign Exchange Market, discussed the role of foreign exchange market arbitrage in keeping foreign exchange rates the same in different locations. If the dollar price of the yen is higher at Bank of America in San Francisco than at Citibank in New York, we would expect traders to buy yen from Citibank and simultaneously sell yen to Bank of America. This activity would raise the dollar/yen exchange rate quoted by Citibank and lower the rate at Bank of America until the exchange rate quotations are transaction costs close. Such arbitrage activity is not limited to the foreign exchange market. We would expect arbitrage to be present in any market where similar goods are traded in different locations. For instance, the price of gold is roughly the same worldwide at any point in time. If gold sold at a higher price in one location than in another, arbitragers would buy gold where it is cheap and sell where it is high until the prices are equal (allowing for transaction costs). Similarly we would expect the price of tractors or automobiles or sheet steel to be related across geographically disparate markets. However, there are good economic reasons why prices for some goods are more similar across countries than others.

This tendency for similar goods to sell for similar prices globally provides a link between prices and exchange rates. If we wanted to know why exchange rates change over time, one obvious answer is that, as prices change internationally, exchange rates must also change to keep the prices measured in a common currency equal across countries. In other words, exchange rates should adjust to offset differing inflation rates between countries. This relationship between the prices of goods and services and exchange rates is known as purchasing power parity (PPP). Although we are hesitant to refer to PPP as a theory of the exchange rate, for reasons that will be made apparent shortly, it is important to study the relationship between price levels and exchange rates in order to understand the role of goods markets (as distinct from financial asset markets) in international finance.

ABSOLUTE PURCHASING POWER PARITY

Our first view of purchasing power parity (PPP) is absolute PPP. Here we consider the exchange rate to be given by the ratio of price levels between countries. If E is the spot exchange rate (domestic currency units per foreign unit), P the domestic price index, and P^F the foreign price index, the absolute PPP relation is written as:

$$P/P^F = E \qquad (7.1)$$

For those readers who are not familiar with price indexes, P and P^F may be thought of as consumer price indexes or producer price indexes. A price index is supposed to measure average prices in an economy and therefore is subject to the criticism that, in fact, it measures the actual prices faced by no one. To construct such an index, we must first determine which prices to include—that is, which goods and services are to be monitored. Then these various items need to be assigned weights reflecting their importance in total spending. Thus the consumer price index would weight housing prices very heavily, but bread prices would have only a very small weight. The final index is a weighted average of the prices of the goods and services surveyed.

Phrased in terms of price indexes, absolute PPP, as given in Eq. (7.1), indicates that the exchange rate between any two currencies is equal to the ratio of their price indexes. Therefore the exchange rate is a *nominal* magnitude, dependent on prices. We should be careful when using real-world price index data that the various national price indexes are comparable in terms of goods and services covered as well as base year (the reference year used for comparisons over time). If changes in the world were only nominal, then we would expect PPP to hold if we had true price indexes. The significance of this last sentence will be illustrated soon.

Eq. (7.1) can be rewritten as

$$P = EP^F \tag{7.2}$$

so that the domestic price level is equal to the product of the domestic currency price of foreign currency and the foreign price level. Eq. (7.2) is called the *law of one price* and indicates that goods sell for the same price worldwide. For instance, we might observe a shirt selling for $10 in the United States and £4 in the United Kingdom. If the $/£ exchange rate is $2.50 per pound, then $P = EP^F = (2.50)(4) = 10$. Thus the price of the shirt in the United Kingdom is the same as the US price, once we use the exchange rate to convert the pound price into dollars and compare prices in a common currency.

Unfortunately, for this analysis, the world is more complex than the simple shirt example. The real world is characterized by differentiated products, costly information, and all sorts of impediments to the equalization of goods prices worldwide. Certainly the more homogeneous goods are, the more we expect the law of one price to hold. Some commodities, which retain essentially the same form worldwide, provide the best examples of the law of one price. Gold, for instance, is quoted in dollar prices internationally, and so we would be correct in stating that the law of one price holds quite closely for gold. However, shirts come in different styles, brand names, and prices, and we do not expect the law of one price to hold domestically for shirts, let alone internationally.

THE BIG MAC INDEX

Fig. 7.1 illustrates how a Big Mac is priced differently in different countries. The first column shows the price in local currency and the third column shows the implied price in dollars. The figure indicates the cost of a Big Mac varies drastically across countries. In China a Big Mac costs the equivalent of $2.74, much less than the $4.79 a Big Mac costs in the United States. In contrast a Big Mac costs the equivalent of $6.82 in Switzerland. If you have traveled extensively abroad you are aware that wide discrepancies exist between prices of similar products and services across countries.

Country	Local currency price	Exchange rate (Foreign currency/$)	Dollar cost
United States	4.79	1	4.79
Brazil	Real 13.50	3.15	4.28
Britain	Pound 2.89	0.64	4.51
Canada	C$ 5.85	1.29	4.54
China	Yuan 17.00	6.21	2.74
Japan	Yen 370	123.94	2.99
Norway	NKr 46	8.14	5.65
Sweden	SKr 43.70	8.52	5.13
Switzerland	SFr 6.50	0.95	6.82
Thailand	Baht 108.00	34.09	3.17

Figure 7.1 The Big Mac Index for selected countries. *The Economist, July, 2015.*

One might wonder why we would ever expect PPP to hold, since we know that international trade involves freight charges and tariffs. Given the costs associated with shipping goods, we would not expect PPP to hold for any particular good—so why would we anticipate the relationship phrased in terms of price indexes to hold as in Eq. (7.1)? Furthermore not all goods are traded internationally, yet the prices of these goods are captured in the national price indexes. As the prices of nontraded goods change, the price indexes change. But this does not affect exchange rates since the changing prices of nontraded goods does not give rise to international trade flows, and so no change in the supply and demand for currencies need result. Recently economists have added many refinements to the analysis of PPP that we need not consider here. The important lesson to be learned is the potential problem associated with using price indexes to explain exchange rate changes.

So far, we have emphasized variations in the exchange rate brought about by changing price indexes or nominal changes. However, it is reasonable to assume that much of the week-to-week change in exchange rates is the result of real rather than nominal events. Besides variations in the price level due to general inflation, we can also identify *relative price changes*. Inflation results in an increase in all prices, but relative price changes indicate that not all prices move together. Some prices increase faster than others, and some rise while others fall. An old analogy that students often find useful is to think of inflation as an elevator carrying a load of tennis balls, which represent the prices of individual goods. As the inflation continues, the balls are carried higher by the elevator, which means that all prices are rising. But as the inflation continues and the elevator rises, the balls, or individual prices, are bouncing up and down. So while the elevator raises all the balls inside, the balls do not bounce up and down together. The balls bouncing up have their prices rising relative to the balls going down.

If we think of different elevators as representing different countries, then if the balls were still while the elevators rose at the same rate, the exchange rate would be constant, as suggested by PPP. Moreover, if we looked at sufficiently long intervals, we could ignore the bouncing balls, since the large movements of the elevators would dominate the exchange rate movements. If, however, we observed very short intervals during which the elevators move only slightly, we would find that the bouncing balls, or relative price changes of individual goods, would largely determine the exchange rate.

RELATIVE PURCHASING POWER PARITY

There is an alternative view of PPP besides the absolute PPP just discussed. Relative PPP is said to hold when

$$\hat{E} = \hat{P} - \hat{P}^F \tag{7.3}$$

where a hat ($^$) over a variable denotes percentage change. So Eq. (7.3) says that the percentage change in the exchange rate $(\hat{E})$ is equal to the percentage change in the domestic price level $(\hat{P})$ minus the percentage change in the foreign price level $(\hat{P}^F)$ Therefore although absolute PPP states that the exchange rate is equal to the ratio of the price indexes, relative PPP deals with percentage changes in these variables.

We usually refer to the percentage change in the price level as the rate of inflation. So another way of stating the relative PPP relationship is by saying that the percentage change in the exchange rate is equal to the inflation differential between the domestic and foreign country. If we say that the percentage change in the exchange rate is equal to the inflation differential, then we can ignore the actual levels of E, P, and P^F and consider the changes, which is not so strong an assumption as absolute PPP.

It should be noted that, if absolute PPP holds, then relative PPP will also hold. But if absolute PPP does not hold, relative PPP still may. This is so because the level of E may not equal P/P^F, but the change in E could still equal the inflation differential.

Having observed in the preceding section how relative prices can determine exchange rates, we can, with reason, believe that over time these relative price changes will decrease in importance compared to inflation rates, so that in the long run inflation differentials will dominate exchange rate movements. The idea is that the real events that cause relative price movements are often random and short run in nature. By *random*, we mean they are unexpected and equally likely to raise or lower the exchange rate. Given this characterization, it follows that these random relative price movements will tend to cancel out over time (otherwise, we would not consider them equally likely to raise or lower E).

TIME, INFLATION, AND PPP

Several researchers have found that PPP holds better for high-inflation countries. When we say "holds better," we mean that the equalities stated in Eqs. (7.1) and (7.2) are more closely met by actual exchange rate and price level data observed over time in high-inflation countries compared to low-inflation countries. In high-inflation countries, changes in exchange rates are highly correlated with inflation differentials because the sheer magnitude of inflation overwhelms the relative price effects, whereas in low- or moderate-inflation countries the relative price effects dominate exchange rate movements and lead to discrepancies from PPP. In terms of our earlier example, when the elevator is moving faster (high inflation), the movement of the balls inside (relative prices) is less important; however, when the elevator is moving slowly (low inflation), the movement of the bouncing balls is quite important.

Besides the rate of inflation, the period of time analyzed has an effect on how well PPP holds. We expect PPP to hold better for annual data than for monthly data, since the longer time frame allows for more inflation. Thus random relative price effects are less important, and we find exchange rate changes closely related to inflation differentials. Using the elevator analogy, the longer the time frame analyzed, the farther the elevator moves, and the more the elevator moves, the less important will be the balls inside. This suggests that studies of PPP covering many years are more likely to yield evidence of PPP than studies based on a few years' data.

The literature on PPP is voluminous and tends to confirm the conclusions we have made. Researchers have presented evidence that relative price shifts can have an important role in the short run, but over time the random nature of the relative price changes reduces the importance of these unrelated events. Investigations over long periods of time (100 years, for instance) have concluded that PPP holds better in the long run.

DEVIATIONS FROM PPP

So far, the discussion has included several reasons why deviations from PPP occur. When discussing the role of arbitrage in goods markets, it was said that the law of one price would not apply to differentiated products or products that are not traded internationally. Furthermore since international trade involves shipping goods across national borders, prices may differ because of shipping costs or tariffs. Relative price changes can also be a reason why PPP would hold better in the long run than the short run. Such relative price changes result from real economic events, like changing tastes, bad weather, or government policy. The Appendix A provides further details on how relative prices can affect the PPP.

Since consumers in different countries consume different goods, price indexes are not directly comparable internationally. We know that evaluating PPP between the United States and Japan using the US and Japanese consumer price indexes is weakened by the fact that the typical Japanese consumer buys a different basket of goods than the typical US consumer. In this case the law of one price could hold perfectly for individual goods, yet we would observe deviations from PPP using the consumer price index for Japan and the United States.

It is important to realize that PPP is not a theory of exchange rate determination. In other words inflation differentials do not *cause* exchange rate change. PPP is an equilibrium relationship between two *endogenous* variables. When we say that prices and exchange rates are endogenous, we mean that they are simultaneously determined by other factors. The other factors are called *exogenous* variables. Exogenous variables may change independently, as with bad weather or government policy. Given a change in an exogenous variable, as with poor weather and a consequent poor harvest, both prices and exchange rates will change. Deviations in measured PPP will occur if prices and exchange rates change at different speeds. Evidence suggests that following some exogenous *shock*, changes in exchange rates precede changes in prices.

Such a finding can be explained by theorizing that the price indexes used for PPP calculations move slowly because commodity prices are not as flexible as financial asset prices (the exchange rate is the price of monies). We know that exchange rates vary throughout the day as the demand and supply for foreign exchange vary. But how often does the department store change the price of furniture, or how often does the auto parts store change the price of tires? Since the prices that enter into published price indexes are slower to adjust than are exchange rates, it is not surprising that exchange rate changes seem to lead price changes. Yet if exchange rates change faster than goods prices, then we have another reason why PPP should hold better in the long run than in the short run. When economic *news* is received, both exchange rates and prices may change. For instance suppose the Federal Reserve announces today that it will promote a 100% increase in the US money supply over the next 12 months. Such a change would cause greater inflation because more money in circulation leads to higher prices. The dollar would also fall in value relative to other currencies because the supply of dollars rises relative to the demand.

Following the Fed's announcement, would you expect goods prices in the United States to rise before the dollar depreciates on the foreign exchange market? While there are some important issues in exchange rate determination that must wait until later chapters, we generally can say here that the dollar would depreciate immediately following the announcement. If traders believe that the dollar will be worth less in the future, they will attempt to sell dollars now, and this selling activity drives down the dollar's value today. There should be some similar forces at work in the goods market as traders expecting higher prices in the future buy more goods today. But for most goods, the immediate short-run result will be a depletion of inventories at constant prices. Only over time will most goods prices rise.

Fig. 7.2 illustrates how the exchange rate will shift with news. The figure illustrates the quantity of dollars bought and sold on the horizontal axis and the yen price of the dollar on the vertical axis. Initially the foreign exchange market equilibrium occurs where the demand curve, D_0, intersects the supply curve, S_0, at an exchange rate of 120 yen/dollar with quantity Q_0 of dollars being bought and sold. Suppose the Federal Reserve now issues a statement causing people to expect the US money supply to grow more rapidly in the future. This causes foreign exchange traders to expect the dollar to depreciate in the future. As a result, they attempt to sell more dollars

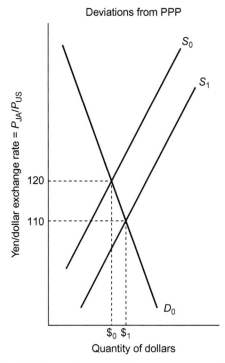

Figure 7.2 Shifts in the foreign exchange market and deviations from PPP.

now, shifting the supply curve out to S_1 in Fig. 7.2. This shift in supply, with constant demand, causes the dollar to depreciate down to 110 yen/dollar. At this new exchange rate, a quantity Q_1 is traded.

Suppose initially PPP holds, so that $E = 120 = P_{JA}/P_{US}$. The announced change in monetary policy has an immediate effect on the exchange rate because currencies are traded continuously throughout the day. Prices of goods and services will change much more slowly. In the short run the ratio of the price level in Japan to the price level in the United States may remain unchanged at 120. So while E falls today to 110 in Fig. 7.2, the ratio of the national price levels is still equal to the initial exchange rate of 120, and there is an apparent deviation from PPP.

Therefore periods with important economic news will be periods when PPP deviations are large—the exchange rate adjusts while prices lag behind. In addition to the differential speed of adjustment between exchange rates and prices, periods dominated by news are likely to be periods involving much relative price change, so that PPP deviations would tend to appear even without exchange rates and prices changing at different speeds.

Deviations from PPP are also likely because international trade involves lags between order and delivery. Prices are often set by contract today for goods that are to be delivered several months later. If we compare goods prices and exchange rates today to evaluate PPP, we are using the exchange rate applicable to goods delivered today with prices that were set some time in the past. Ideally we should compare contract prices in each country at the time contracts are signed with the exchange rate that is expected to prevail in the future period when goods are actually delivered and payment is made. If the exchange rate actually realized in the future period is the same as that expected when the goods prices were agreed upon, then there would be no problem in using today's exchange rate and today's delivered goods prices. The problem is that, realistically, exchange rates are very difficult to forecast, so that seldom would today's realized exchange rate be equal to the trader's forecast at some past period.

Let us consider a simple example. Suppose that on September 1, Mr. U.S. agrees to buy books from Ms. U.K. for £1 per book. At the time the contract is signed, books in the United States sell for $2, and the current exchange rate of $E_{\$/£} = 2$ ensures that the law of one price holds—a £1 book from the United Kingdom is selling for the dollar equivalent of $2 (the pound book price of 1 times the dollar price of the pound of $2). If the contract calls for delivery and payment on December 1 of £1 per book and Mr. U.S. expects the exchange rate and prices to be unchanged until December 1, he *expects* PPP to hold at the time the payment is due. Suppose that on December 1, the actual exchange rate is £1 = $1.50. An economist researching the law of one price for books would compare book prices of £1 and $2 with the exchange rate of $E_{\$/£} = 1.50$, and examine if $E_{\$/£} = P_{US}/P_{UK}$. Since $1.50 < 2/1$, he would conclude that there are important deviations from PPP. Yet these deviations are *spurious*. At the time the prices were set, PPP was expected to hold. We generate the appearance of PPP deviations by comparing exchange rates today with prices that were set in the past.

The possible explanations for deviations from PPP include factors that would suggest permanent deviations (shipping costs and tariffs), factors that would produce temporary deviations (differential speed of adjustment between financial asset markets and goods markets, or real relative price changes), and factors that cause the appearance of deviations where none may actually exist (comparing current exchange rates with prices set in the past or using national price indexes when countries consume different baskets of goods). Since PPP measurements convey information regarding the relative purchasing power of currencies, such measurements have served as a basis for economic policy discussions. The next section will provide an example of policy-related information contained in PPP measurement.

OVERVALUED AND UNDERVALUED CURRENCIES

If we observe E, P, and P^F over time, we find that the absolute PPP relationship does not hold very well for any pair of countries. If, over time, P^F rises faster than P, then we would expect E, the domestic currency price of the foreign currency, to fall. If E does not fall by the amount suggested by the lower P/P^F, then we could say that the domestic currency is undervalued or (the same thing) that the foreign currency is overvalued.

In the early 1980s there was much talk of an *overvalued* dollar. The foreign exchange value of the dollar appeared to be too high relative to the inflation differentials between the United States and the other developed countries. The term overvalued suggests that the exchange rate is not where it should be yet. However, if the free-market supply and demand factors are determining the exchange rate, then the overvalued exchange rate is actually the free-market equilibrium rate. This means that the term overvalued might suggest that this equilibrium is merely a temporary deviation from PPP, and over time the exchange rate will fall in line with the inflation differential.

In the early 1980s the foreign exchange price of the dollar grew at a faster rate than the inflation differential between the other industrial nations and the United States. It appears, then, that for more than 4 years, a dollar overvaluation developed. Not until 1985 did the exchange rate begin to return to a level consistent with PPP. Fig. 7.3 illustrates the actual level of the yen/dollar exchange rate and the implied PPP exchange rate of the yen/dollar. The implied PPP exchange rate is measured by the inflation rate differential between Japan and the United States. The line labeled "PPP exchange rate" measures the values the exchange rate would take if the percentage change in the exchange rate equaled the inflation differential between Japan and the United States.

Fig. 7.3 shows that the dollar appears to be overvalued in the early 1980s, in that the actual exchange rate is above that implied by PPP as measured by inflation differentials. By 1985 the dollar begins to depreciate

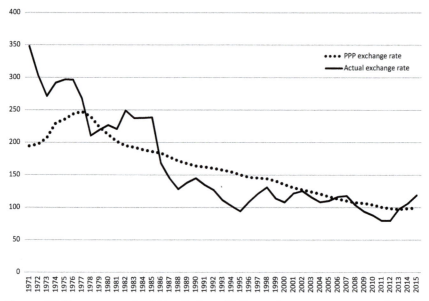

Figure 7.3 The computed PPP-implied yen/dollar exchange rate compared to the actual rate, 1971–2015. *FRED database, authors' calculations.*

against the yen and move toward the PPP value of the exchange rate. In the 1990s the dollar becomes substantially undervalued, bottoming out in around the mid-1990s. However, by the end of 1990s the dollar value again returns to the PPP level. During the second half of the 2000s the yen/dollar exchange rate starts to dip below the implied PPP values, with the low point reached in early 2012. Then the dollar strengthens considerably and becomes overvalued in 2015.

Since we know that PPP does not hold well for any pair of countries with moderate inflation in the short run, we must always have currencies that appear overvalued or undervalued in a PPP sense. The issue becomes important when the apparent over- or undervaluation persists for some time and has significant macroeconomic consequences. In the early 1980s the United States political issue at the forefront of this apparent dilemma was that the overvalued dollar was hurting export-oriented industries. The US goods were rising in price to foreign buyers as the dollar appreciated. The problem was made visible by a large balance of trade deficit that became a major political issue. In 1985 intervention in the foreign exchange market by major central banks contributed to a dollar depreciation that reduced the PPP-implied dollar overvaluation.

FAQ: What Is the PPP-adjusted GDP?

To measure how an economy is performing, economists use GDP per capita as the most common indicator. This measures how much is produced in a country divided by the population. To compare how different countries are performing becomes more difficult if the exchange rate is not at the "correct" level. In this chapter we have shown that the exchange rate can be temporarily overvalued or undervalued. Therefore if we use the current exchange rate we would over or undervalue a country's GDP. To provide a way for economists to compare GDP per capita across countries, a group of economists at the University of Pennsylvania have set up *The Penn World Tables*. These tables adjust GDP per capita, by using the PPP values instead of the current exchange rate. As can be seen in the accompanying table, the ranking of countries can change depending on whether the current exchange rate is used or the implied exchange rate from the PPP relationship. For example, Sweden has a higher current dollar GDP per capita relative to the United States, but falls seven spots below the United States when purchasing power is used to compute GDP. The opposite can also occur. Brunei Darussalam is only 20th in current dollar GDP per capita, but moves to 4th using the implied exchange rate from PPP. The Penn World Tables are available online for free at: pwt. econ.upenn.edu/.

Rank	Current dollar GDP per capita		PPP-adjusted GDP per capita	
1	Qatar	$97,519	Qatar	$146,178
2	Norway	$97,363	Macao SAR, China	$139,767
3	Macao SAR, China	$96,038	Singapore	$82,763
4	Australia	$61,887	Brunei Darussalam	$76,754
5	Denmark	$60,634	United Arab Emirates	$66,009
6	Sweden	$58,887	Norway	$64,893
7	Singapore	$56,287	Hong Kong SAR, China	$55,084
8	United States	$54,629	United States	$54,629
9	Ireland	$53,314	Saudi Arabia	$51,924
10	Iceland	$52,111	Ireland	$47,804
11	Netherlands	$51,590	Netherlands	$47,131
12	Austria	$51,127	Austria	$46,165
13	Canada	$50,271	Germany	$45,616
14	Finland	$49,541	Bahrain	$45,479
15	Germany	$47,627	Sweden	$45,144
16	Belgium	$47,517	Denmark	$44,863
17	United Kingdom	$45,603	Canada	$44,089
18	United Arab Emirates	$44,204	Australia	$43,902
19	France	$42,733	Iceland	$43,393
20	Brunei Darussalam	$41,344	Belgium	$42,725

Source: World Bank Data, 2015 for year 2014.

Besides the dollar overvaluation relative to the other developed countries' currencies, from time to time many developing countries have complained that their currencies are overvalued against the developed countries' currencies, and thus their balance of trade sustains a larger deficit than would otherwise occur. If PPP applied only to internationally traded goods, then we could show how lower labor productivity in developing countries could contribute to apparently overvalued currencies. For nontraded goods we assume that production methods are similar worldwide. It may make more sense to think of the nontraded goods sector as being largely services. In this case more productive countries tend to have higher wages and thus higher prices in the service sector than less-productive, low-wage countries. We now have a situation in which the price indexes used to calculate PPP vary with productivity and hence with wages in each country.

If we assume that exchange rates are determined only by traded goods prices (the idea being that if a good does not enter into international trade, there is no reason for its price to be equalized internationally and thus no reason for changes in its price to affect the exchange rate), then we can find how price indexes vary with service prices while exchange rates are unaffected. For instance the price of a haircut in Paris should not be affected by an increase in haircut prices in Los Angeles. So if the price of haircuts should rise in Los Angeles, other things being equal, the average price level in the United States increases. But this US price increase should not have any impact on the dollar per euro exchange rate. If, instead, the price of an automobile rises in the United States relative to French auto prices, we would expect the dollar to depreciate relative to the euro because demand for French autos (and thus euros) increases while demand for US autos (and thus dollars) decreases.

If the world operates in the way just described, then we would expect that the greater are the traded goods productivity differentials between countries, the greater will be the wage differentials reflected in service prices, and thus the greater will be the deviations from absolute PPP over time. Suppose that developing countries, starting from lower absolute levels of productivity, have higher productivity growth rates. If per capita income differences between countries give a reasonable measure of the productivity differences, then we would anticipate that as developing country per capita income increases relative to developed country per capita income, the developing country price index will grow faster than that of the developed country. But at the same time, the depreciation of the developing country's currency lags behind the inflation differentials, as measured by the average price levels in each country that include traded and nontraded goods prices. Thus, over time, the currency of the developing country will tend to appear overvalued (the foreign exchange value of the developing country's money has not depreciated as much as called for by the movements in the average price levels), whereas the developed country's currency will appear undervalued (the exchange value of the developed country's money has not appreciated as much as the price level changes would indicate).

Does the preceding discussion describe the real world? Do you believe that labor-intensive services (domestic servants, haircuts, etc.) are cheaper in poorer countries than in wealthy countries? Researchers have provided evidence suggesting that the deviations from PPP as previously mentioned do indeed occur systematically with changes in per capita income.

What is the bottom line of the foregoing consideration? National price indexes are not particularly good indicators of the need for exchange rate adjustments. In this respect it is not surprising to find that many studies have shown that absolute PPP does not hold. The idea that currencies are undervalued or overvalued can be misleading if exchange rates are free to change with changing market conditions. Only if central bank or government intervention interrupts the free adjustment of the exchange rate to market clearing levels can we really talk about a currency as being overvalued or undervalued (and in many such instances black markets develop where the currency is traded at free-market prices). The fact that changes in PPP over time present the appearance of an undervalued currency in terms of the price indexes of two countries is perhaps more an indicator of the limitations of price indexes than of any real market phenomena.

REAL EXCHANGE RATES

All discussions of exchange rates so far have been with respect to the *nominal exchange rate*. This is the exchange rate that is actually observed in the foreign exchange market. However, economists sometimes utilize the concept of the *real exchange rate* to represent changes in the competitiveness of a currency. The real exchange rate is an alternative way to think about currencies being over- and undervalued. The real exchange rate is measured as

$$E_{\text{real}} = E/(P/P^F) \tag{7.4}$$

or the nominal exchange rate adjusted for the ratio of the home price level relative to the price level abroad. In Fig. 7.3 one sees that the dollar appeared to be significantly overvalued against the yen in the early 1980s and then significantly undervalued in the mid-1990s. In terms of real exchange rate changes, this would mean that the real exchange rate in terms of yen per dollar would have risen in the early 1980s as the nominal exchange rate (yen per dollar) rose relative to the ratio of Japanese prices to US prices. Then, in the 1990s, the real yen/dollar exchange rate fell as the nominal exchange rate decreased relative to the ratio of Japanese prices to US prices.

If absolute PPP always held, the real exchange rate would equal 1. In such a world nominal exchange rates would always change to mirror the change in the ratio of home prices to foreign prices. Since the real world has deviations from PPP, we also observe real exchange rates rising and falling. When the real exchange rate rises beyond some point, concern is expressed about an exchange rate overvaluation. When the real exchange rate falls beyond some point, concern is expressed about exchange rate undervaluation. As stated in the preceding section, terms like *overvaluation* and *undervaluation* must be used carefully. Such terms may sometimes reflect shortcomings of price indexes as inputs into measures of currency values.

SUMMARY

1. PPP explains the relationship between product price levels and exchange rates.
2. If the exchange rate between two currencies is equal to the ratio of average price levels between two countries, then the absolute PPP holds.
3. If the percentage change in the exchange rate is equal to the inflation rate differential between two countries, then relative PPP holds.
4. PPP holds better for high-inflation countries due to the movement of price levels overwhelms any relative price changes.
5. From empirical evidence, exchange rates seem to deviate from PPP in the short run, but PPP tends to hold in the long run.
6. Deviations from PPP may arise from the presence of nontraded good prices in price indexes, differentiated goods, transactions costs, government restrictions, different consumption bundles in price indexes across countries, and adjustment lags between exchange rates and product prices.

7. A currency is overvalued (undervalued) if it has appreciated more (less) than the inflation rate differential between two countries as implied by PPP.

EXERCISES

1. Assume that the cost of a particular basket of goods is equal to $108 in the United States and ¥14,000 in Japan.
    a. What should the ¥/$ exchange rate be according to absolute PPP?
    b. If the actual exchange rate were equal to 120, would the dollar be considered undervalued or overvalued?
2. Suppose that the inflation rate in India is 100% and the inflation rate in the United States is 5%. According to relative PPP, what would happen to the value of dollar/rupee exchange rate?
3. If nontradable goods prices rise faster in country A than in country B, and tradable goods prices remain unchanged, determine whether currency A will appear to be overvalued or undervalued.
4. Explain why relative PPP may hold when absolute PPP does not?
5. List four reasons why deviations from PPP might occur; then carefully explain how each causes such deviations?
6. What is the "real exchange rate"? What does the real exchange rate equal if absolute PPP holds?

FURTHER READING

Lothian, J.R., Taylor, M.P., 1996. Real exchange rate behavior: the recent float from the perspective of the past two centuries. J. Polit. Econ. 104 (3), 488–509.

Officer, L.H., 1982. Purchasing Power Parity and Exchange Rates: Theory, Evidence, and Relevance. JAI Press, Greenwich.

Ravn, M.O., Schmitt-Grohe, S., Uribe, M., 2007. Pricing to habits and the law of one price. Am. Econ. Rev. 97 (2), 232–238. May.

Taylor, A.M., Taylor, M.P., 2004. The purchasing power parity debate. J. Econ. Perspect. 18 (4), 135–158.

The Economist online, 2016. The Big Mac Index, Patty Purchasing Parity. July 23.

APPENDIX A   THE EFFECT ON PPP BY RELATIVE PRICE CHANGES

Arbitrage in goods markets makes it easy to understand why price level changes affect exchange rates, but the effect of relative price changes is more subtle. The following example will illustrate how exchange rates can change because of relative price change even though there is no change in the overall price level (no inflation). Table 7.A summarizes the argument. Let us suppose there are two countries, France and Japan, and each consumes wine and sake. Initially, in period 0, wine and sake each sell for 1 euro in France and 1 yen in Japan. In a simple world of no transport costs or other barriers to the law of one price, the exchange rate, $E = €/¥$, must equal 1. Note that initially the relative price of one bottle of wine is equal to one bottle of sake (since sake and wine sell for the same price in each country). To determine the inflation rate in each country, we must calculate price indexes that indicate the value of the items consumed in each country for each period. Suppose that initially France consumes 9 units of wine and 1 unit of sake, whereas Japan consumes 1 wine and 9 sake. At the domestic prices of 1 unit of domestic currency per unit of wine or sake, we can see that the total value of the basket of goods consumed in France is 10 euros, whereas the total value of the goods consumed in Japan is 10 yen.

Now let us suppose that there is a bad grape harvest, so that in the next period wine is more expensive. In terms of relative prices, we know that the bad harvest will make wine rise in price relative to sake. Suppose now that instead of the original relative price of 1 sake = 1 wine, we now have 1.5 sake = 1 wine. Consumers will recognize this change in relative prices and tend to decrease their consumption of wine and increase consumption of sake. Suppose in period 1 the French consume 8 wine and 1.5 sake, whereas the Japanese consume 0.333 wine and 9.5 sake. Let us further assume that the central banks of Japan and France follow a policy of zero inflation, where inflation is measured by the change in the cost of current consumption. With no inflation, the value of the consumption basket will be unchanged from period 0 and will equal 10 in each country. Thus although average prices have not changed, we know that individual prices must change because of the rising price of wine relative to sake.

The determination of the individual prices is a simple exercise in algebra, but is not needed to understand the central message of the example; therefore, students could skip this paragraph and still retain the benefit of the lesson. Since we know that France consumes 8 wine and 1.5 sake with a total value of 10 francs and that the relative price is 1.5 sake = 1 wine, we can solve for the individual prices by letting $1.5P_s = P_w$, and we can then substitute this into our total spending equation ($8P_w + 1.5P_s = 10$) to determine the prices. In other words we have a system with two equations and two unknowns that is solvable:

$$8P_w + 1.5P_s = 10 \qquad (7.A1)$$

Table 7.A The effect of a relative price change on the exchange rate

France

	Period 0		Period 1	
	Price (in Euros)	Quantity consumed	Price (in Euros)	Quantity consumed
Wine	1	9	1.111	8
Sake	1	1	0.741	1.5
Value of consumption	10		10	

Japan

	Period 0		Period 1	
	Price (in Yen)	Quantity consumed	Price (in Yen)	Quantity consumed
Wine	1	1	1.5	0.333
Sake	1	9	1	9.5
Value of consumption	10		10	

Source: Adapted from Solnik, B., 1978. International parity conditions and exchange risk. J. Banking Financ. 289.
Note: Exchange rate, €/¥, in period 0 = 1; exchange rate, €/¥, in period 1 = 0.741.

$$1.5P_s = P_w \qquad (7.A2)$$

Substituting Eq. (7.A2) into the previous equation, we obtain

$$8P_w + 1P_w = 10 \qquad (7.A3)$$
$$=> P_w = 10/9 = 1.111$$

Since $P_w = 1.111$, we can use this to determine Ps:

$$1.5P_s = 1.111 => P_s = 1.111/1.5 = 0.741 \qquad (7.A4)$$

Thus we have our prices in France in period 1. For Japan it is even easier:

$$0.333P_w + 9.5P_s = 10 \qquad (7.A5)$$

$$1.5P_s = P_w \qquad (7.A6)$$

Substituting Eq. (7.A6) into the preceding equation, we obtain

$$0.333P_w + 6.333P_w = 10 => P_w = 1.5 \qquad (7.A7)$$

Thus

$$1.5P_s = 1.5 => P_s = 1 \tag{7.A8}$$

Given the new prices in period 1, we can now determine the exchange rate implied by the law of one price. Since sake sells for 0.741 euros in France and 1 yen in Japan, the euro price of yen must be €/¥ = 0.741.

In summary this example has shown how exchange rates can change because of real economic events, even when average price levels are constant. Since PPP is usually discussed in terms of price indexes, we find that real events, such as the relative price changes brought about by a poor harvest, will cause deviations from absolute PPP as the exchange rate changes, even though the price indexes are constant. Note also that the relative price effect leads to an appreciation of the currency in the country where consumption of the good that is increasing in price is heaviest. In our example the euro appreciates as a result of the increased relative price of wine.

PART III

Risk and International Capital Flows

CHAPTER 8

Foreign Exchange Risk and Forecasting

Contents

International business involves foreign exchange risk since the value of transactions in different currencies will be sensitive to exchange rate changes. Although it is possible to manage a firm's foreign-currency-denominated assets and liabilities to avoid exposure to exchange rate changes, the benefit involved is not always worth the effort.

The appropriate strategy for the corporate treasurer and the individual speculator will be at least partly determined by expectations of the future path of the exchange rate. As a result exchange rate forecasts are an important part of the decision-making process of international investors.

In this chapter we first consider the issue of foreign exchange risk, which is the presence of risk that arises from uncertainty regarding the future exchange rate; this uncertainty makes forecasting necessary. If future exchange rates were known with certainty, there would be no foreign exchange risk.

TYPES OF FOREIGN EXCHANGE RISK

One problem we encounter when trying to evaluate the effect of exchange rate changes on a business firm arises in determining the appropriate concept of exposure to foreign exchange risk.

We can identify three principal concepts of *exchange risk* exposure:

1. *Translation exposure*: This is also known as accounting exposure. It is the difference between foreign-currency-denominated assets and foreign-currency-denominated liabilities.

2. *Transaction exposure*: This is an exposure resulting from the uncertain domestic currency value of a foreign-currency-denominated transaction to be completed at some future date.

3. *Economic exposure*: This is an exposure of the firm's value to changes in exchange rates. If the value of the firm is measured as the present value of future after-tax cash flows, then economic exposure is concerned with the sensitivity of the real domestic currency value of long-term cash flows to exchange rate changes.

Economic exposure is the most important to the firm. Rather than worry about how accountants will report the value of our international operations (translation exposure), it is far more important to the firm (and to rational investors) to focus on the purchasing power of long-run cash flows insofar as these determine the real value of the firm.

Let us consider an example of a hypothetical firm's situation to illustrate the differences among the alternative exposure concepts. Suppose we have the balance sheet of XYZ-France, a foreign subsidiary of the parent US firm XYZ, Inc. The balance sheet in Table 8.1 initially shows the

Table 8.1 Balance sheet of XYZ-France, May 31

Cash	€1,000,000	Debt	€5,000,000
Accounts receivable	3,000,000	Equity	6,000,000
Plant and equipment	5,000,000		
Inventory	2,000,000		
	€11,000,000		**€11,000,000**

Dollar translation on May 31 $1 = €1

Cash	$1,000,000	Debt	$5,000,000
Accounts receivable	3,000,000	Equity	6,000,000
Plant and equipment	5,000,000		
Inventory	2,000,000		
	$11,000,000		**$11,000,000**

Dollar translation on June 1 $0.90 = €1

Cash	$900,000	Debt	$4,500,000
Accounts receivable	2,700,000	Equity	5,400,000
Plant and equipment	4,500,000		
Inventory	1,800,000		
	$9,900,000		**$9,900,000**

position of XYZ-France in terms of euros. A balance sheet is simply a recording of the firm's assets (listed on the left side) and liabilities (listed on the right side). A balance sheet must balance. In other words the value of assets must equal the value of liabilities so that the sums of the two columns are equal. Equity is the owners' claims on the firm and is a sort of residual value in that equity will change to keep liabilities equal to assets.

Although the balance sheet at the top of Table 8.1 is stated in terms of euros, the parent company, XYZ Inc., consolidates the financial statements of all foreign subsidiaries into its own statements. Thus the euro-denominated balance sheet items must be translated into dollars to be included in the parent company's balance sheet. *Translation* is the process of expressing financial statements measured in one unit of currency in terms of another unit of currency.

Assume that initially the exchange rate equals €1 = $1. The balance sheet in the middle of Table 8.1 uses this exchange rate to translate the balance sheet items into dollars. Current US accounting standards, introduced in 1981, require all foreign-denominated assets and liabilities to be translated at current exchange rates. In the United States, accounting standards are set by the Financial Accounting Standards Board (FASB). On December 7, 1981, the FASB issued Financial Accounting Standard No. 52, commonly referred to as FAS 52. FAS 52 essentially requires that balance sheet accounts be translated at the exchange rate prevailing at the date of the balance sheet. The issue in translation exposure is the sensitivity of the equity account of the balance sheet to exchange rate changes. The equity account equals assets minus liabilities and measures the accounting or book value of the firm. As the domestic currency value of the foreign-currency-denominated assets and liabilities of the foreign subsidiary changes, the domestic currency book value of the subsidiary will also change.

The top two balance sheets in Table 8.1 give us the euro and dollar position of the firm on May 31. However, suppose there is a devaluation of the euro on June 1 from $1 = €1 to $0.90 = €1. The balance sheet in terms of dollars will change as illustrated by the new translation at the bottom of the table. Now the owners' claim on the firm in terms of dollars, or in terms of the book value measured by equity, has fallen from $6 to $5.4 million. Given the current method of translating exchange rate changes, when the currency used to denominate the foreign subsidiaries' statements is depreciating relative to the dollar, then the owners' equity will fall. We must realize that this drop in equity does not necessarily represent any real loss to the firm or real drop in the value of the firm.

The euro position of the firm is unchanged; only the dollar value to the US parent is altered by the exchange rate change.

Since the balance sheet translation of foreign assets and liabilities does not by itself indicate anything about the real economic exposure of the firm, we must look beyond the balance sheet and the translation exposure. Transaction exposure can be viewed as a kind of economic exposure, since the profitability of future transactions is susceptible to exchange rate change, and these changes can have a big effect on future cash flows—as well as on the value of the firm. Suppose XYZ-France has contracted to deliver goods to a Japanese firm and allows 30 days' credit before payment is received. Furthermore suppose that at the time the contract was made, the exchange rate was 100 yen/euro (¥100 = €1). Suppose also that the contract called for payment in yen of exactly ¥100,000 in 30 days. At the current exchange rate the value of ¥100,000 is €1,000. But if the exchange rate changes in the next 30 days, the value of ¥100,000 would also change. Should the yen depreciate unexpectedly, then in 30 days XYZ-France will receive ¥100,000; however, this will be worthless than €1,000, so that the transaction is not as profitable as originally planned. This is transaction exposure. XYZ has committed itself to this future transaction, thereby exposing itself to exchange risk. Had the contract been written to specify payment in euros, then the transaction exposure to XYZ-France would have been eliminated; the Japanese importer would now have the transaction exposure. Firms can, of course, hedge against future exchange rate uncertainty in the forward-looking markets discussed in Chapter 4, Forward-Looking Market Instruments. The Japanese firm could buy yen in the forward market to be delivered in 30 days and thus eliminate the transaction exposure.

The example of transaction exposure, just analyzed, illustrates how exchange rate uncertainty can affect the future profitability of the firm. The possibility that exchange rate changes can affect future profitability, and therefore the current value of the firm, is indicative of economic exposure. Managing foreign exchange risks involves the sorts of operations considered in Chapter 4, Forward-Looking Market Instruments. There we covered the use of forward markets, swaps, options, futures, and borrowing and lending in international currencies, and so will not review that information here. Note, however, that firms should manage cash flows carefully, with an eye toward expected exchange rate changes, and should not always try to avoid all risks since risk taking can be profitable. Firms practice risk minimization subject to cost constraints and eliminate foreign exchange risk only when the expected benefits from it exceed the costs.

Although forward exchange contracts may be an important part of any corporate hedging strategy, there exist other alternatives that are frequently used. For example, suppose a firm has assets and liabilities denominated both in a weak currency X, which is expected to depreciate, and in a strong currency Y, which is expected to appreciate. The firm's treasurer would try to minimize the value of accounts receivable denominated in X, which could mean tougher credit terms for customers paying in currency X. The firm may also delay the payment of any accounts payable denominated in X, because it expects to be able to buy X for repayment at a cheaper rate in the future. Insofar as is possible, the firm will try to reinforce these practices on payables and receivables by invoicing its sales in currency Y and its purchases in X. Although institutional constraints may exist on the ability of the firm to specify the invoicing currency, it would certainly be desirable to implement such policies.

We see, then, that corporate hedging strategies involve more than simply minimizing holdings of currency X and currency-X-denominated bank deposits. Managing cash flows, receivables, and payables will be the daily activity of the financial officers of a multinational firm. In instances when it is not possible for the firm successfully to hedge a foreign currency position internally, there is always the forward or futures market. If the firm has a currency-Y-denominated debt and it wishes to avoid the foreign exchange risk associated with the debt, it can always buy Y currency in the forward market and thereby eliminate the risk.

In summary foreign exchange risk may be hedged or eliminated by the following strategies:

1. Trading in forward, futures, or options markets
2. Invoicing in the domestic currency
3. Speeding (slowing) payments of currencies expected to appreciate (depreciate)
4. Speeding (slowing) collection of currencies expected to depreciate (appreciate).

THE FOREIGN EXCHANGE RISK PREMIUM

Let us now consider the effects of foreign exchange risk on the determination of forward exchange rates. As mentioned previously the forward exchange rate may serve as a predictor of future spot exchange rates. We may question whether the forward rate should be equal to the expected future spot rate, or whether there is a *risk premium* incorporated in the forward rate that serves as an insurance premium inducing others to take the risk, in which case the forward rate would differ from the expected future spot rate by this premium. The empirical work in this area has dealt with the issue of whether the forward rate is an unbiased predictor of future spot rates. An *unbiased* predictor is one that is correct on average, so that over the long run the forward rate is just as likely to overpredict the future spot rate as it is to underpredict. The property of unbiasedness does not imply that the forward rate is a good predictor. For example, there is the story of an old lawyer who says, "When I was a young man I lost many cases that I should have won; when I was older I won many that I should have lost. Therefore, on average, justice was done." Is it comforting to know that on average the correct verdict is reached when we are concerned with the verdict in a particular case? Likewise the forward rate could be unbiased and "on average" correctly predict the spot rate without ever actually predicting the future realized spot rate. All we need for unbiasedness is that the forward rate is just as likely to guess too high as it is to guess too low.

The effective return differential between two countries' assets should be dependent on the perceived risk of each asset and the risk aversion of the investors. Now let us clarify what we mean by *risk* and *risk aversion*. The risk associated with an asset is the contribution of that particular asset to the overall portfolio. Modern financial theory has commonly associated the riskiness of a portfolio with the variability of the returns from that portfolio. This is reasonable in that investors are concerned with the future value of any investment, and the more variable the return from an investment is, the less certain we can be about its value at any particular future date. Thus we are concerned with the variability of any individual asset insofar as it contributes to the variability of our portfolio return (our portfolio return is simply the total return from all our investments).

Risk aversion implies that an investor who is faced with two assets with equal return will prefer the asset with the lowest risk. In terms of investments two individuals may agree on the degree of risk associated with two assets, but the more risk-averse individual would require a higher interest rate on the riskier asset to induce him or her to hold it than would the less risk-averse individual. Risk aversion implies that people must be paid to take risk. Individuals with bad credit must pay a higher interest rate than those with good credit, otherwise lenders would only lend to the good credit individuals.

FAQ: Are Entrepreneurs Risk Lovers?

It is a common perception that entrepreneurs love to take risks, and are a "special breed" of business people. That seems to contradict the idea in economics that people are risk averse. In an article in *The New Yorker*, Malcolm Gladwell discusses this by examining the behavior of some famous successful entrepreneurs.[1] After studying the behavior of entrepreneurs such as Ted Turner and John Paulson, he concludes that entrepreneurs are in fact very risk averse. They spend a lot of time to make sure that their risk is minimal in their investments, or spend large amounts on research to make sure that the expected return is sufficient. John Paulson, e.g., did a lot of research on the housing market in the United States in the mid-2000s, deciding that the housing bubble must burst. By buying *Credit Default Swaps* that gave him a short position, he benefited a great deal from the downturn. In fact in 2007 alone he had profits of $15 billion. So entrepreneurs are just like other people, trying to minimize their risk exposure and only investing where the expected payoff is large enough to cover the risk of the investment.

It was already stated that the effective return differential between assets of two countries is a function of risk and risk aversion. The effective return differential between a US security and a security in the United Kingdom is

$$i_{US} - (E^\star_{t+1} - E_t)/E_t - i_{UK} = f(\text{risk aversion}, \text{risk}) \qquad (8.1)$$

The left-hand side of the equation is the effective return differential measured as the difference between the domestic US return, i_{US}, and the foreign asset return, $(E^\star_{t+1} - E_t)/E_t - i_{UK}$. We must remember that the effective return on the foreign asset is equal to the interest rate in terms of foreign currency plus the expected change in the exchange rate, where $E^\star_{t+1}$ is the expected dollar price of pounds next period. The right-hand side of Eq. (8.1) indicates that changes in risk and risk aversion will cause changes in the return differential.

We can view the effective return differential shown in Eq. (8.1) as a risk premium. Let us begin with the approximate interest parity relation:

$$i_{US} - i_{UK} = (F - E_t)/E_t \qquad (8.2)$$

---

[1] Gladwell, Malcolm, "The Sure Thing." *The New Yorker*, January 18, 2010, p. 24.

To convert the left-hand side to an effective return differential, we must subtract the expected change in the exchange rate (but since this is an equation, whatever is done to the left-hand side must also be done to the right-hand side):

$$i_{US} - (E_{t+1}^* - E_t)/E_t - i_{UK} = (F - E_t)/E_t - (E_{t+1}^* - E_t)/E_t \qquad (8.3)$$

or

$$i_{US} - (E_{t+1}^* - E_t)/E_t - i_{UK} = (F - E_{t+1}^*)/E_t$$

Thus we find that the effective return differential is equal to the percentage difference between the forward and expected future spot exchange rate. The right-hand side of Eq. (8.3) may be considered a measure of the risk premium in the forward exchange market. Therefore if the effective return differential is zero, then there would appear to be no risk premium. If the effective return differential is positive, then there is a positive risk premium on the domestic currency (the currency in the numerator of E_t, in this case the dollar) since the expected future spot price of dollars is higher than the prevailing forward rate. In other words, traders offering to buy dollars for pounds in the future will receive a premium using the forward market, in that dollars are expected to appreciate (relative to pounds) by an amount greater than the current forward rate. Thus the trader can buy cheaper dollars using the forward market. Conversely, traders wishing to sell dollars for delivery next period will pay a premium to be able to use the forward market to ensure a set future price.

For example, suppose $E_t = \$2.10$, $E_{t+1}^* = \$2.00$, and $F = \$2.05$. The foreign exchange risk premium is

$$(F - E_{t+1}^*)/E_t = (\$2.05 - \$2.00)/\$2.10 = 0.024$$

and the expected change in the exchange rate is equal to

$$(E_{t+1}^* - E_t)/E_t = (\$2.00 - \$2.10)/\$2.10 = -0.048$$

The forward discount on the pound is

$$(F - E_t)/E_t = (\$2.05 - \$2.10)/\$2.10 = -0.024$$

Thus the dollar is expected to appreciate against the pound by approximately 4.8%, but the forward premium indicates an appreciation of only 2.4% if we use the forward rate as a predictor of the future spot rate. The discrepancy results from the presence of a risk premium that makes the forward rate a biased predictor of the future spot rate. Specifically the forward rate overpredicts the future dollar price of pounds in order to allow the risk premium.

Given the positive risk premium on the dollar, the expected effective return from holding a UK bond will be less than the domestic return to US residents holding US bonds. To continue with the previous example, let us suppose that the UK interest rate is 0.124, whereas the US rate is 0.100. Then the interest rate differential is

$$i_{US} - i_{UK} = -0.024$$

The expected return from holding a UK bond is

$$i_{UK} + (E^*_{t+1} - E_t)/E_t = 0.124 - 0.048 = 0.076$$

The return from the US bond is 0.10, which exceeds the expected effective return on the foreign bond; yet this can be an equilibrium solution given the risk premium. Investors are willing to hold UK investments yielding a lower expected return than comparable US investments because there is a positive risk premium on the dollar. Thus the higher dollar return is necessary to induce investors to hold the riskier dollar-denominated investments.

MARKET EFFICIENCY

Although the previous example had a nonzero effective return differential, it might still be an *efficient market*. A market is said to be *efficient* if prices reflect all available information. In the foreign exchange market, this means that spot and forward exchange rates will quickly adjust to any new information. For instance, an unexpected change in US economic policy that informed observers feel will be inflationary (like an unexpected increase in money supply growth) will lead to an immediate depreciation of the dollar. If markets were inefficient, then prices would not adjust quickly to the new information, and it would be possible for a well-informed investor to make profits consistently from foreign exchange trading that would otherwise be excessive relative to the risk undertaken.

With efficient markets, the forward rate would differ from the expected future spot rate only by a risk premium. If this were not the case, and the forward rate exceeded the expected future spot rate plus a risk premium, an investor could realize certain profits by selling forward currency now, because she or he would be able to buy the currency at a lower price in the future than the forward rate at which the currency will be sold. Although profits can most certainly be earned from foreign exchange speculation in the real world, it is also true that there are no sure profits. The real world is characterized by uncertainty regarding the future spot rate, since the future cannot be foreseen. Yet forward exchange rates adjust to the changing economic picture according to revisions of what the future spot rate is likely to be (as well as to changes in the risk attached to the currencies involved). It is this ongoing process of price adjustments in response to new information in the efficient market that rules out any certain profits from speculation. Of course, the fact that the future will bring unexpected events ensures that profits and losses will result from foreign exchange speculation. If an astute investor possessed an ability to forecast exchange rates better than the rest of the market, the profits resulting would be enormous. Foreign exchange forecasting will be discussed in the next section.

Many studies have tested the efficiency of the foreign exchange market. The fact that they have often reached different conclusions regarding the efficiency of the market emphasizes the difficulty involved in using statistics in the social sciences. Such studies have usually investigated whether the forward rate contains all the relevant information regarding the expected future spot rate. They test whether the forward rate alone predicts the future spot rate well or whether additional data will aid in the prediction. If further information adds nothing beyond that already embodied in the forward rate, the market is said to be efficient. On the other hand, if some data are found that would permit a speculator consistently to predict the future spot rate better than can be done using the forward rate (including a risk premium), then this speculator would earn a consistent profit from foreign exchange speculation, and one could conclude that the market is not efficient.

It must be recognized that such tests have their weaknesses. Although a statistical analysis must make use of past data, speculators must actually predict the future. The fact that a researcher could find a forecasting rule that would beat the forward rate in predicting past spot rates is not particularly useful for current speculation and does not rule out market efficiency. The key point is that such a rule was not known during the time the data were actually being generated. So if a researcher in 2017 claims to have found a way to predict the spot rates observed in 2015 better than the 2015 forward rates, this does not mean that the foreign exchange market in 2015 was necessarily inefficient. Speculators in 2015 did not have the forecasting rule developed in 2017, and thus could not have used such information to outguess the 2015 forward rates consistently.

FOREIGN EXCHANGE FORECASTING

Since future exchange rates are uncertain, participants in international financial markets can never know for sure what the spot rate will be 1 month or 1 year ahead. As a result forecasts must be made. If we could forecast more accurately than the rest of the market, the potential profits would be enormous. An immediate question is: What makes a good forecast? In other words how should we judge a forecast of the future spot rate?

We can certainly raise objections to rating forecasts on the basis of simple forecast errors. Even though, other things being equal, we should prefer a smaller forecast error to a larger one, in practice other things are not equal. To be successful, a forecast should be on the "correct side" of the forward rate. The "correct side" means that the forecast makes the market participant choose correctly whether to use the forward market or not. For instance consider the following example:

Current spot rate: ¥120 = $1
Current 12-month forward rate: ¥115 = $1
Mr. A forecasts: ¥106 = $1
Ms. B forecasts: ¥116 = $1
Future spot rate realized in 12 months: ¥113 = $1

A Japanese firm has a $1 million receipt due in 12 months and uses the forecasts to help decide whether to cover the dollar receivable with a forward contract or wait and sell the dollars in the spot market in 12 months. In terms of forecast errors, Mr. A's prediction of ¥106 = $1 yields an error of −6.2% ((106 − 113)/113) against a realized future spot rate of ¥113. Ms. B's prediction of ¥116 = $1 is much closer to the realized spot rate, with an error of only 2.6% ((116 − 113)/113). While Ms. B's forecast is closer to the rate eventually realized, this is not the important feature of a good forecast, in this case. Ms. B forecasts a future spot rate in excess of the forward rate, so if it followed her prediction, the Japanese firm would wait and sell the dollars in the spot market in 12 months (or would take a *long position* in dollars). Unfortunately since the future spot rate ¥113 = $1 is less than the current forward rate at which the dollars could be sold

(¥115 = $1), the firm would receive ¥113 million rather than ¥115 million for the $1 million.

Following Mr. A's forecast of a future spot rate below the forward rate, the Japanese firm would sell dollars in the forward market (or take a *short position* in dollars). The firm would then sell dollars at the current forward rate of ¥115 per dollar rather than wait and receive only ¥113 per dollar in the spot market in the future. The forward contract yields ¥2 million more than the uncovered position. The important lesson is that a forecast should be on the correct side of the forward rate; otherwise, a small forecasting error is not useful. Corporate treasurers or individual speculators want a forecast that will give them the direction the future spot rate will take relative to the forward rate.

If the foreign exchange market is efficient so that prices reflect all available information, then we may wonder why anyone would pay for forecasts. There is some evidence that advisory services have been able to "beat the forward rate" at certain times. If such services could consistently offer forecasts that are better than the forward rate, what can we conclude about market efficiency? Evidence that some advisory services can consistently beat the forward rate is not necessarily evidence of a lack of market efficiency. If the difference between the forward rate and the forecast represents transaction costs, then there is no abnormal return from using the forecast. Moreover, if the difference is the result of a risk premium, then any returns earned from the forecasts would be a normal compensation for risk bearing. Finally we must realize that the services are rarely free. Although the economics departments of larger banks sometimes provide free forecasts to corporate customers, professional advisory services charge anywhere from several hundred to many thousands of dollars per year for advice. If the potential profits from speculation are reflected in the price of the service, then once again we cannot earn abnormal profits from the forecasts.

FUNDAMENTAL VERSUS TECHNICAL TRADING MODELS

Exchange rate forecasters typically use two types of models: technical or fundamental. A *fundamental model* forecasts exchange rates based on variables that are believed to be important determinants of exchange rates. As we shall learn later in the text, fundamentals-based models of exchange rates view as important things like government monetary and fiscal policy, international trade flows, and political uncertainty. An expected change in some fundamental variable leads to a current change in the forecast. A *technical trading model* uses the past history of exchange rates to predict future movements. Technical traders are sometimes called *chartists* because they use charts or diagrams depicting the time path of an exchange rate to infer changing trends. Finance scholars typically have taken a dim view of technical analysis, since the ability to predict future price movements by looking only at the past would bring the concept of efficient markets into question. However, recent research has led to a more supportive view of technical analysis by some scholars and the method is widely popular among foreign exchange market participants. Surveys indicate that nearly 90% of foreign exchange dealers use some sort of technical analysis to form their expectations of exchange rates. However, the same surveys suggest that technical models are seen as particularly useful for short-term forecasting, while fundamentals are seen as more important for predicting long-run changes.

Although the returns to a superior forecaster would be considerable, there is no evidence to suggest that abnormally large profits have been produced by following the advice of professional advisory services. But then if you ever developed a method that consistently outperformed other speculators, would you tell anyone else?

SUMMARY

1. Foreign exchange risk includes translation exposure, transaction exposure, and economic exposure.
2. Foreign exchange risk could be minimized by trading in forward-looking market instruments, invoicing prices in domestic currency, speeding payments of currencies expected to appreciate, and speeding collections of currencies expected to depreciate.
3. The foreign exchange risk premium is the difference between the forward exchange rate and the expected future spot exchange rate.
4. A risk-averse investor will prefer an investment with a lower risk when he/she faces two investments of similar expected returns.
5. The difference between the return on a domestic asset and the effective return on a foreign asset depends on the risk of the assets and the degree of risk aversion.
6. The effective return differential is equal to the risk premium in the forward exchange market.

7. If the effective return differential is zero, then there would be no risk premium. If the effective return differential is positive, then there would be a positive risk premium on the domestic currency.

8. If a positive risk premium on the domestic currency exists, investors would be willing to hold foreign investments even if the foreign investments yield lower effective returns than the domestic investments.

9. In an efficient market, prices reflect all available information. If the foreign exchange market is efficient, the forward exchange rate would differ from the expected future spot exchange rate only by a risk premium.

10. For multinational firms, a good forecast is not necessarily minimizing forecasting errors, but it should be on the correct side of the forward exchange rate.

EXERCISES

1. Distinguish among translation exposure, transaction exposure, and economic exposure. Define each concept and then indicate how they may be interrelated.

2. The 6-month interest rate in the United States is 10%; in Mexico it is 12%. The current spot rate (dollars per peso) is $0.40.
   a. What do you expect the 6-month forward rate to be?
   b. Is the peso selling at a premium or discount?
   c. If the expected spot rate in 6 months is $0.38, what is the risk premium?

3. We discussed risk aversion as being descriptive of investor behavior. Can you think of any real-world behavior that you might consider to be evidence of the existence of risk preferrers?

4. Does an efficient market rule out all opportunities for speculative profits? If so, why? If not, why not?

5. You are the treasurer of a US firm that has a €1 million commitment due to a German firm in 90 days. The current spot rate is $1.00 per euro, and the 90-day forward rate is $1.11. Ali forecasts that the spot rate in 90 days will be $1.01. Jahangir forecasts that the spot rate will be $1.12 in 90 days. The actual spot rate in 90 days turns out to be $1.10. Who had the best forecast and why?

6. It was reported in the *Financial Times* that "Toyota suffers a ¥20 billion drop in operating profits for every ¥1 rise (in the exchange rate, yen per dollar) against the dollar." Does this statement have implications for transaction, translation, or economic exposure primarily?

FURTHER READING

Bacchetta, P., van Wincoop, E., 2009. Infrequent portfolio decisions: a solution to the forward discount puzzle. Am. Econ. Rev. 100, 870–904.

Bams, D., Walkowiak, K., Wolff, C.C.P., 2004. More evidence on the dollar risk premium in the foreign exchange market. J. Int. Money Financ 23 (2), 271–282.

Bekaert, G., Hodrick, R.J., 1993. On biases in the measurement of foreign exchange risk premiums. J. Int. Money Financ April 12, 115–138.

Boothe, P., Longworth, D., 1986. Foreign exchange market efficiency tests: implications of recent empirical findings. J. Int. Money Financ June 5, 135–152.

Elliott, G., Ito, T., 1999. Heterogeneous expectations and tests of efficiency in the Yen/Dollar forward exchange market. J. Monet. Econ., 435–456.

Engel, C., 1996. The forward discount anomaly and the risk premium: a survey of recent evidence. J. Empir. Financ. September 3, 123–192.

Lui, Y., Mole, D., 1998. The use of fundamental and technical analysis by foreign exchange dealers: Hong Kong evidence. J. Int. Money Financ. June 17, 535–545.

Wang, P., Jones, T., 2002. Testing for efficiency and rationality in foreign exchange markets. J. Int. Money Financ. April 21, 223–239.

CHAPTER 9

Financial Management of the Multinational Firm

Contents

Since multinational firms are involved in payables and receivables denominated in different currencies, product shipments across national borders, and subsidiaries operating in different political jurisdictions, they face a different set of problems than firms with a purely domestic operation. The corporate treasurer and other financial decision makers of the multinational firms operate in a cosmopolitan setting that offers profit and loss opportunities never considered by the executives of purely domestic firms. This chapter looks at the unique attributes of financial management in the multinational firm. The basic issues—control, cash management, trade credit, intrafirm transfers, and capital budgeting—face all firms. The problems particular to the internationally oriented firm are the ones addressed.

FINANCIAL CONTROL

Any business firm must evaluate its operations periodically to better allocate resources and increase income. The financial management of a multinational firm involves exercising control over foreign operations. The responsible individuals at the parent office or headquarters review financial reports from foreign subsidiaries with a view toward modifying operations and assessing the performance of foreign managers.

173

Typical control systems are based on setting standards with regard to sales, profits, inventory, or other specific variables and then examining financial statements and reports to evaluate the achievement of such goals. There is no "correct" system of control. Methods vary across industries and even across firms in a single industry. All methods have the common goal of providing management with a means of monitoring the performance of the firm's operations, new strategies, and goals as conditions change. However, establishing a useful control system is more difficult for a multinational firm than for a purely domestic firm. For instance, should foreign subsidiary profits be measured and evaluated in foreign currency or in the domestic currency of the parent firm? The answer to this question depends on whether foreign managers are to be held responsible for currency translation gains or losses.

If top management wants foreign managers to be involved in currency management and international financing issues, then the domestic currency of the parent would be a reasonable choice. On the other hand, if top management wants foreign managers to concern themselves with production operations and behave as other managers in companies in the foreign country would, then the foreign currency would be the appropriate currency for evaluation.

Some multinational firms prefer a decentralized management structure in which each subsidiary has a great deal of autonomy and makes most financing and production decisions subject only to general parent company guidelines. In this management setting, the foreign manager may be expected to operate and think as the stockholders of the parent firm would want, so the foreign manager makes decisions aimed at increasing the parent's domestic currency value of the subsidiary. The control mechanism in such firms is to evaluate foreign managers based on their ability to increase that value.

Other firms prefer more centralized management in which financial managers at the parent make most of the decisions. They choose to move funds among divisions based on a system-wide view rather than what is best for a single subsidiary. A highly centralized system would have foreign managers evaluated on their ability to meet goals established by the parent for key variables like sales or labor costs. The parent-firm managers assume responsibility for maximizing the value of the firm, with foreign managers basically responding to directives from the top. We then see that the appropriate control system is largely determined by the management style of the parent.

Considering the discussion to this point, it is clear that managers at foreign subsidiaries should be evaluated only on the basis of things they control. Foreign managers often may be asked by the parent to follow policies and relations with other subsidiaries of the firm that the managers would never follow if they sought solely to maximize their subsidiary's profit. Actions of the parent that lower a subsidiary's profit should not result in a negative view of the foreign manager. In addition, other actions beyond the foreign manager's control—changing tax laws, foreign exchange controls, or inflation rates—could result in reducing foreign profits through no fault of the foreign manager. The message to parent company managers is to place blame fairly where the blame lies. In a dynamic world, corporate fortunes may rise and fall because of events entirely beyond any manager's control.

CASH MANAGEMENT

Cash management involves using the firm's cash as efficiently as possible. Given the daily uncertainties of business, firms must maintain some liquid resources. *Liquid assets* are those that are readily spent. Cash is the most liquid asset. But since cash (and the traditional checking account) earns no interest, the firm has a strong incentive to minimize its holdings of cash. There are highly liquid short-term securities that serve as good substitutes for actual cash balances and yet pay interest. The corporate treasurer is concerned with maintaining the correct level of liquidity at the minimum possible cost.

The multinational treasurer faces the challenge of managing liquid assets denominated in different currencies. The challenge is compounded by the fact that subsidiaries operate in foreign countries where financial market regulations and institutions differ.

When a subsidiary receives a payment and the funds are not needed immediately by this subsidiary, the managers at the parent headquarters must decide what to do with the funds. For instance, suppose a US multinational's Mexican subsidiary receives 500 million pesos. Should the pesos be converted to dollars and invested in the United States, or placed in Mexican peso investments, or converted into any other currency in the world? The answer depends on the current needs of the firm as well as the current regulations in Mexico. If Mexico has strict foreign exchange controls in place, the 500 million pesos will have to be kept in Mexico and invested there until a future time when the Mexican subsidiary will need them to make a payment.

Even without legal restrictions on foreign exchange movements, we might invest the pesos in Mexico for 30 days if the subsidiary faces a large payment in 30 days. This assumes that there is no need for the funds in another area of the firm, and that the return on the Mexican investment is comparable to what we could earn in another country on a similar investment (which interest rate parity would suggest). By leaving the funds in pesos, we do not incur any transaction costs for converting pesos to another currency now and then going back to pesos in 30 days. In any case, we would never let the funds sit idly in the bank for 30 days.

There are times when the political or economic situation in a country is so unstable that we keep only the minimum possible level of assets in that country. Even when we will need pesos in 30 days for the Mexican subsidiary's payable, if there exists a significant threat that the government could confiscate or freeze bank deposits or other financial assets, we would incur the transaction costs of currency conversion to avoid the political risk associated with leaving the money in Mexico.

Multinational cash management involves centralized management. Subsidiaries and liquid assets may be spread around the world, but they are managed from the home office of the parent firm. Through such centralized coordination, the overall cash needs of the firm are lower. This occurs because all subsidiaries do not have the same pattern of cash flows. For instance, one subsidiary may receive a dollar payment and finds itself with surplus cash, while another subsidiary faces a dollar payment and must obtain dollars. If each subsidiary operated independently, there would be more cash held in the family of multinational foreign units than if the parent headquarters directed the surplus funds of one subsidiary to the subsidiary facing the payable.

Centralization of cash management allows the parent to offset subsidiary payables and receivables in a process called *netting*. Netting involves the consolidation of payables and receivables for one currency so that only the difference between them must be bought or sold. For example, suppose Oklahoma Instruments in the United States sells C$2 million worth of car phones to its Canadian sales subsidiary and buys C$3 million worth of computer frames from its Canadian manufacturing subsidiary. If the payable and receivable both are due on the same day, then the C$2 million receivable can be used to fund the C$3 million payable, and only C$1 million must be bought in the foreign exchange market. Rather than buy C$3 million to settle the payable and sell the C$2 million to convert the receivable into dollars, incurring transaction costs twice on the full C$5 million, the firm has one foreign exchange transaction for C$1 million.

Table 9.1 Intrafirm payments for netting million-dollar values (week of January 15)
Payments

Receipts	Canada	United Kingdom	Germany	Mexico	Total
Canada	–	1.2	2.0	0.0	3.2
United Kingdom	0.0	–	1.1	0.1	1.2
Germany	0.5	0.0	–	0.0	0.5
Mexico	0.2	0.1	0.0	–	0.3
Total	0.7	1.3	3.1	0.1	5.2

Had the two Canadian operations not been subsidiaries, the financial managers would still practice netting but on a corporate-wide basis, buying or selling only the net amount of any currency required after aggregating the receivables and payables of all subsidiaries overall currencies. Effective netting requires accurate and timely reporting of transactions by all divisions of the firm.

As an example of intrafirm netting, let us consider a US parent firm with subsidiaries in Canada, the United Kingdom, Germany, and Mexico. Table 9.1 sets up the report for the week of January 15. We assume that netting occurs weekly. Each division's scheduled payments and receipts are converted to dollars so that aggregation across all units can occur. Table 9.1 indicates that the Canadian subsidiary will pay $0.7 million (total of column 2) and receive $3.2 million (total of row 1), so it will have a cash surplus of $2.5 million. The UK subsidiary will pay $1.3 million and receive $1.2 million, so it will have a cash shortage of $0.1 million. The German subsidiary will pay $3.1 million and receive $0.5 million, so it has a shortage of $2.6 million, and, finally, the Mexican subsidiary will pay $0.1 million and receive $0.3 million, so it has a surplus of $0.2 million. The parent financial managers determine the net payer or receiver position of each subsidiary for the weekly netting. Only these net amounts are transferred within the firm. The firm does not have to change $0.7 million worth of Canadian dollars into the currencies of Germany and Mexico to settle the payable of the Canadian subsidiary and then convert $3.2 million worth of pounds, euros, and pesos into Canadian dollars. Only the net cash surplus flowing to the Canadian subsidiary of $2.5 million must be converted into Canadian dollars.

So far we have considered netting when the currency flows occur at the same time. What if the payments and receipts are not for the same date? Suppose in our Oklahoma Instruments example that the C$3 million payable is due on October 1, and the C$2 million receivable is due September 1. Netting could still occur by *leading* or *lagging* currency flows. The sales subsidiary could lag its C$2 million payment by 1 month, or the C$3 million could lead 1 month and be paid on September 1. Leads and lags increase the flexibility of parent financial managers, but require excellent information flows between all divisions and headquarters.

LETTERS OF CREDIT

Once a company decides to export a good, they want to make sure that a payment will be made by the importer of the good. Because it is difficult to enforce contracts across countries, an intermediary is often necessary to enforce the contract. A *letter of credit* (LOC) is a written instrument issued by a bank at the request of an importer that obligates the bank to pay a specific amount of money to an exporter. The time at which payment is due is specified, along with conditions regarding necessary documents to be presented by the exporter prior to payment. The LOC may stipulate that a *bill of lading* be presented that evidences no damaged goods. A *bill of lading* is a detailed list of the content that is shipped, and can be used to identify missing or damaged items. Perhaps some minimal level of damage (like 2% of the boxes or crates) is stipulated. In any case such conditions in an LOC allow the importer to retain some quality control prior to payment.

Fig. 9.1 illustrates a simple LOC. Note that this is an *irrevocable* LOC. This means that the agreement cannot be modified without the express permission of all parties. Most LOCs are of this type. A *revocable* LOC may be altered by the account party—the importer buying the goods. Since the importer is free to alter the LOC, we might wonder why any exporter would ever accept a revocable LOC. The exporter may interpret the issuance of the LOC as a favorable credit report on the buyer. The exporter will call the issuing bank prior to shipment to make sure that the LOC has not been altered or revoked, and then present the necessary documents and collect payment as soon as possible. The revocable LOC is still safer than shipping goods based only on the importer's promise to pay, with no bank credit backing up the transaction. Still revocable LOCs primarily are used only when there is no question of revocation. This form of LOC may save bank fees, which are higher with irrevocable LOCs; so if there is no chance of revocation, it may pay to use the revocable LOC.

The sales contract stipulates the method of payment. The use of LOCs is widespread, so let us assume the contract calls for payment by LOC. The

*[Bank letterhead (Name & Address
of Importer's Bank)]*

LETTER OF CREDIT NO.   ACCOUNT PARTY
DATE: (Buyer's Name & Address)

                                                             BENEFICIARY
                                                      (Seller's Name & Address)

TO: *(Seller's Bank & Address)*

WE HAVE OPENED AN IRREVOCABLE LETTER OF CREDIT IN FAVOR OF: *(Seller's Name)*
FOR THE AMOUNT OF: $ _____
                                 (Dollar amount is written in words here)

AVAILABLE WITH US AGAINST THE FOLLOWING DOCUMENTS:
                        (Required documents are listed here)

TRANSSHIPMENTS: *(Permitted or not)*

PARTIAL SHIPMENTS: *(Permitted or not)*

THIS CREDIT IS VALID UNTIL *(Date)* FOR PRESENTATION OF DOCUMENTS TO US.
DOCUMENTS ARE TO BE PRESENTED WITHIN *(Number)* DAYS AFTER DATE OF
ISSUANCE OF BILLS OF LADING.
PLEASE ADVISE THE BENEFICIARY OF YOUR CONFIRMATION.

THIS CREDIT IS SUBJECT TO THE UNIFORM CUSTOMS AND PRACTICE FOR
DOCUMENTARY CREDITS. INTERNATIONAL CHAMBER OF COMMERCE
PUBLICATION NO. 500.
THIS CREDIT IS IRREVOCABLE AND WE HEREBY ENGAGE WITH THE DRAWERS THAT
DRAWINGS IN ACCORD WITH THE TERMS OF THIS CREDIT WILL BE DULY HONORED BY US.

                                                             Yours truly,

                                                             (Signature)

                                                      International Department

Figure 9.1 Letter of credit (LOC).

importer must then apply for an LOC from a bank. The importer requests
that the LOC stipulate no payment until appropriate documents are presented by the exporter to the bank. These document stipulations cannot
violate the sales contract since the bank is at risk to ensure that the documents are in order at the time of payment.

If the bank considers the importer an acceptable credit risk, the LOC is issued and sent to the exporter. The exporter then examines the LOC to ensure that it conforms to the sales contract. If it does not, then modifications must be made before the goods are shipped. Once the exporter fulfills all obligations in delivering the goods, the documentary proof is presented to the bank for examination. If the documents conform to the LOC, payment is made, with the bank collecting from the importer and then paying the exporter.

If the importer does not pay the bank, the bank is still obligated to pay the exporter. The exporter is then satisfied, and any problems must be settled between the importer and the bank. Banks may or may not require that the underlying goods serve as collateral for the LOC. If the bank does require an interest in the goods, then the bill of lading is consigned to the bank. With an unsecured LOC, the bank assumes the credit risk of a buyer default. With a secured LOC, the bank assumes the risk of changes in the value of the goods and the cost of disposal. Even if the importer is a sound credit risk, the bank assumes the risk that it misses a document discrepancy and that the importer refuses to pay as a result.

What are the risks for the buyer and seller? The exporter faces the risk of shipping goods without being able to meet all terms listed in the LOC. If the goods are shipped and a document discrepancy exists, then the seller will not be paid. The buyer risks fraud from the seller. The goods may not meet the specifications ordered, but the seller fraudulently prepares documents stating otherwise. The bank is not responsible for such fraudulent documents, so the risk is the buyer's.

Banks charge a flat fee for issuing and amending LOCs. A percentage of the amount paid is also charged at the time payment is made. These charges generally apply to the importer, unless the parties agree otherwise.

AN EXAMPLE OF TRADE FINANCING

Let us consider an example that applies some of the issues covered so far. Suppose a US firm, New York Wine Importers, wants to import wine from a French firm, Paris Wine Exporters. Fig. 9.2 illustrates the steps involved in the transaction. First, the importer and exporter must agree on the basics of the transaction. The sales contract will stipulate the amount and kind of wine, price, shipping date, and payment method.

Following the sales contract, the importer requests a LOC from its bank, New York First Bank. The bank issues an LOC that authorizes

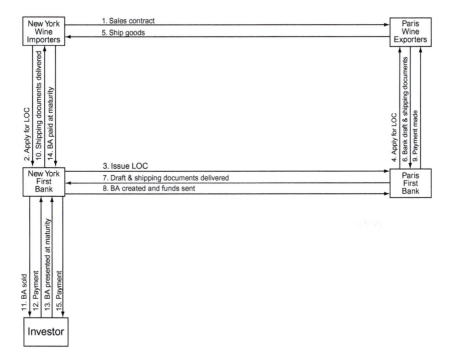

Figure 9.2 Steps involved in a US import transaction.

Paris Wine Exporters to draw a bank draft on New York First Bank for payment. The bank draft is like a check, except that it is dated for maturity at some time in the future when payment will be made. Paris Wine Exporters ships the wine and gives its bank, Paris First Bank, the bank draft along with the necessary shipping documents for the wine. Paris First Bank then sends the bank draft, shipping documents, and LOC to New York First Bank.

When New York First Bank accepts the bank draft, a *bankers' acceptance* (BA) is created. A *banker's acceptance* is a contractual obligation of a bank for a future payment. At this point, Paris Wine Exporters may receive payment of a discounted value of the BA, as the BA does not mature until sometime in the future. New York First Bank discounts the BA and sends the funds to Paris First Bank for the account of Paris Wine Exporters. New York First Bank delivers the shipping documents to New York Wine Importers, and the importer takes possession of the wine.

New York First Bank is now holding the BA after paying a discounted value to Paris First Bank. Instead of holding the BA until maturity, New

York First Bank sells it to an investor. Upon maturity, the investor will receive the face value of the BA from New York First Bank, and New York First Bank will receive the face value from New York Wine Importers.

INTRAFIRM TRANSFERS

Since the multinational firm is made up of subsidiaries located in different political jurisdictions, transferring funds among divisions of the firm often depends on what governments will allow. Beyond the transfer of cash, as covered in the preceding section, the firm will have goods and services moving between subsidiaries. The price that one subsidiary charges another subsidiary for internal goods transfers is called a *transfer price*. The setting of transfer prices can be a sensitive internal corporate issue because it helps to determine how total firm profits are allocated across divisions. Governments are also interested in transfer pricing since the prices at which goods are transferred will determine tariff and tax revenues.

The parent firm always has an incentive to minimize taxes by pricing transfers in order to keep profits low in high-tax countries and by shifting profits to subsidiaries in low-tax countries. This is done by having intrafirm purchases by the high-tax subsidiary made at artificially high prices, while intrafirm sales by the high-tax subsidiary are made at artificially low prices.

Governments often restrict the ability of multinationals to use transfer pricing to minimize taxes. The US Internal Revenue Code requires *arm's-length pricing* between subsidiaries—charging prices that an unrelated buyer and seller would willingly pay. When tariffs are collected on the value of trade, the multinational has the incentive to assign artificially low prices to goods moving between subsidiaries. Customs officials may determine that a shipment is being "underinvoiced" and may assign a value that more truly reflects the market value of the goods.

Transfer pricing may also be used for "window-dressing"—i.e., to improve the apparent profitability of a subsidiary. This may be done to allow the subsidiary to borrow at more favorable terms, since its credit rating will be upgraded as a result of the increased profitability. The higher profits can be created by paying the subsidiary artificially high prices for its products in intrafirm transactions. The firm that uses transfer pricing to shift profits from one subsidiary to another introduces an additional problem for financial control. It is important that the firm be able to evaluate each subsidiary on the basis of its contribution to corporate income. Any

Table 9.2 Transfer pricing example
Waikiki Shirt Co. makes T-shirts in low-tax country L (with a 20% tax rate) and ships them to a distribution center in high-tax country H (with a 40% tax rate)

	Manufacturing country L	Distribution country H
Arm's-length pricing		
Sales price	$5	$20
Cost	$1	$5
Pretax profit	$4	$15
Tax	$0.80 (0.2 × $4)	$6 (0.4 × $15)
After-tax profit	$3.20	$9
Global profit = $12.20		
Distorted prices		
Sales price	$10	$20
Cost	$1	$10
Pretax profit	$9	$10
Tax	$1.80 (0.2 × $9)	$4 (0.4 × $10)
After-tax profit	$7.20	$6
Global profit = $13.20		

artificial distortion of profits should be accounted for so that corporate resources are efficiently allocated.

Table 9.2 provides an example of transfer pricing for the Waikiki Shirt Co. Waikiki Shirt Co. manufactures shirts in a low-tax country, country L, and then ships the shirts to a distribution center in a high-tax country, country H. The tax rate in L is 20% and the tax rate in H is 40%. Given these differential tax rates, Waikiki Shirt Co. will increase its global profit if profits earned by the high-tax distribution operation in country H are transferred to country L, where they would be taxed at a lower rate. The top half of the table provides the outcome when the firm uses arm's-length pricing in transferring shirts from the manufacturing operation to the distribution operation. The manufactured shirts produced in country L are sold to the distribution operation in country H at a price of $5. Since shirts cost $1 to produce, the pretax profit in country L is $4 per shirt. With a tax rate of 20%, there is a tax of $0.80 per shirt so that the after-tax profit of the manufacturing operation is $3.20. The distribution center pays $5 per shirt and then sells the shirts for $20, earning a pretax profit of $15 per shirt. With a 40% tax rate in country H, the firm must pay $6 tax per shirt so that the after-tax profit is $9 per shirt. By summing the after-tax profit earned in countries L and H, the firm earns a global profit of $12.20 per shirt.

Now suppose the firm uses distorted transfer pricing to lower the global tax liability and increase the global profit. This involves having the manufacturing operation in the low-tax country L charge a price above the arm's-length (true market) value for the shirts it sells to the distribution operation in the high-tax country H. The bottom half of Table 9.2 illustrates how this might work. Now the manufacturing operation sells the shirts to the distribution operation for $10 per shirt. The cost of production is still the same $1 so the pretax profit is $9 per shirt. A 20% tax rate means that a tax of $1.80 per shirt must be paid, and the after-tax profit is $7.20 per shirt. The distribution operation now pays $10 for the shirt and still sells it for $20, so the pretax profit is $10. At 40%, the tax is $4 per shirt, and the after-tax profit is $6. Summing the after-tax profit of the operations in country L and country H, we find that the global profit is $13.20 per shirt.

The firm is able to increase the profit per shirt by $1 through the transfer pricing distortion of the value of the shirt transferred from country L to country H. In this manner, firms can increase profits by shifting profits from high-tax to low-tax countries. Of course, the tax authorities in country H would not permit such an overstatement of the transfer value of the shirt (and consequent underpayment of taxes in country H), if they could determine the true arm's-length shirt value. For this reason, tax authorities frequently ask multinational firms to justify the prices they use for internal transfers.

CAPITAL BUDGETING

Capital budgeting refers to the evaluation of prospective investment alternatives and the commitment of funds to preferred projects. Long-term commitments of funds expected to provide cash flows extending beyond 1 year are called *capital expenditures*. Capital expenditures are made to acquire *capital assets*, like machines or factories or whole companies. Since such long-term commitments often involve large sums of money, careful planning is required to determine which capital assets to acquire. Plans for capital expenditures are usually summarized in a capital budget.

Multinational firms considering foreign investment opportunities face a more complex problem than do firms considering only domestic investments. Foreign projects involve foreign exchange risk, political risk, and foreign tax regulations. Comparing projects in different countries requires a consideration of how all factors will change over countries.

There are several alternative approaches to capital budgeting. A useful approach for multinational firms is the adjusted present value approach. We work with *present value* because the value of a dollar to be received today is worth more than a dollar to be received in the future, say 1 year from now. As a result we must discount future cash flows to reflect the fact that the value today will fall depending on how long it takes before the cash flows are realized. The Appendix A to this chapter reviews present value calculations for readers unfamiliar with the concept.

For multinational firms, the adjusted present value approach is presented here as an appropriate tool for capital budgeting decisions. The *adjusted present value (APV)* measures total present value as the sum of the present values of the basic cash flows estimated to result from the investment (operations flows) plus all financial effects related to the investment, or

$$APV = -I + \sum_{t=1}^{T} \frac{CF_t}{(1+d)^t} + \sum_{t=1}^{T} \frac{FIN_t}{(1+df)^t} \qquad (9.1)$$

where $-I$ is the initial investment or cash outlay, Σ is the summation operator, t indicates time or year when cash flows are realized (t extends from year 1 to year T, where T is the final year), CF_t represents estimated basic cash flows in year t resulting from project operations, d is the discount rate on those cash flows, FIN_t is any additional financial effect on cash flows in year t (these will be discussed shortly), and df is the discount rate applied to the financial effects.

CF_t should be estimated on an after-tax basis. Problems of estimation include deciding whether cash flows should be those directed to the subsidiary housing the project, or only to those flows remitted to the parent company. The appropriate combination of cash flows can reduce the taxes of the parent and subsidiary.

Several possible financing effects should be included in FIN_t. These may include depreciation charges arising from the capital expenditure, financial subsidies, or concessionary credit terms extended to the subsidiary by a government or official agency, deferred or reduced taxes given as incentive to undertake the expenditure, or a new ability to circumvent exchange controls on remittances.

Each of the flows in Eq. (9.1) is discounted to the present. The appropriate discount rate should reflect the uncertainty associated with the flow. CF_t is not known with certainty and could fluctuate over the life of the project. Furthermore the nominal cash flows from operations will change over time as inflation changes. The discount rate, d, could be equal to the risk-free rate plus a risk premium that reflects the systematic risk of the project. The financial terms in FIN_t are likely to be fixed in nominal terms over time. In this case current market interest rates may be acceptable as discount rates, df.

Consider this example to illustrate the APV approach to capital budgeting decisions. Suppose Midas Gold Extractors has an opportunity to enter a small, developing country and apply its new gold recovery technique to some old mines that no longer yield profitable amounts of ore under conventional mining. Midas estimates that the cost of establishing the foreign operation will be $10 million. The project is expected to last for 2 years, during which period the operating cash flows from the new gold extracted will be $7.5 million/year. In addition, the new operating unit will allow Midas to repatriate an additional $1 million/year in funds that have been tied up in the developing country by capital controls. If Midas applies a discount rate of 10% to operating cash flows and 6% to the funds that will be freed from controls, then the APV is:

$$APV = -10 + \frac{7.5}{1.10} + \frac{7.5}{1.10^2} + \frac{1}{1.06} + \frac{1}{1.06^2}$$
$$= -10 + 14.85 = 4.85$$

So the adjusted present value of the gold recovery project equals $4.85 million. The firm can compare this value to the APV of other projects it is considering in order to budget its capital expenditures in the optimum manner.

Capital budgeting is an imprecise science, and forecasting future cash flows is sometimes viewed as more art than science. The typical firm experiments with several alternative scenarios to test the sensitivity of the budgeting decision to different assumptions. One of the key assumptions in projects considered for unstable countries is the level of political risk that must be accounted for. Cash flows should be adjusted for the threat of loss resulting from government expropriation or regulation.

SUMMARY

1. Financial control is necessary in order to monitor the multinational firm's operations.
2. The firm's management style determines whether to decentralize or centralize its financial management between the parent and the foreign subsidiaries.
3. Multinational cash management involves managing the firm's liquid assets (in domestic and foreign currencies) as efficiently as possible.
4. Cash management is centralized management, which allows the parent firm to offset subsidiary payables and receivables such that the overall cash needs for the firm are low.
5. Netting is the consolidation of payables and receivables in a currency so that only the difference between them must be bought or sold.
6. A LOC is a contract written by a bank to guarantee that the bank will pay the exporter the amount of money owed by the importer.
7. The LOC stipulates that payment will be made only upon presentation of required documents by the exporter to the bank. Once the exporter fulfills all obligations, the payment will be made with the bank collecting from the importer to pay the exporter. Failure to pay by the importer will not affect the exporter's receivable.
8. A bill of lading is a record of the shipper's receipt and the shipment of goods.
9. A bankers' acceptance is a draft drawn on a firm and accepted by banks as payable at maturity.
10. A transfer price is the price that one subsidiary charges another subsidiary of internal good transfers.
11. Transfer prices may be used by the multinational firms to minimize taxes on profits from subsidiaries in high-tax countries and shift profits to subsidiaries in low-tax countries.
12. Capital budgeting is a process by which the firm decides which long-term investments to make. It involves the calculation of each project's future cash flow by period, the present value of the cash flows after considering the time value of money, the number of years it takes for a project's cash flow to pay back the initial cash investment, an assessment of risk, and other factors.

13. The adjusted present value is the sum of the project's initial investment cost, the present values of cash flows, and all financial effects related to the investment.

EXERCISES

1. Suppose that the Japanese firm Sanpo will receive $1.5 million from its US sales subsidiary on June 3. Moreover, on June 3 a US bank is due $2.3 million from Sanpo as repayment of a loan. Explain how netting by Sanpo would apply to this example, and what the advantages are?

2. What could be done if Question 1 is modified so that Sanpo owes the $2.3 million on June 13, but the $1.5 million receivable is still scheduled for June 3?

3. Give an example of how transfer pricing can be used to
   a. shift profits to a low-tax subsidiary in Ireland?
   b. reduce the tariff on a shipment of computer parts from a subsidiary in Taiwan to a subsidiary in Brazil?
   c. increase profits in a French subsidiary that will soon be applying for a loan?

4. What is arm's-length pricing?

5. Suppose a US multinational firm estimates that a $150 million capital expenditure in a new plant in an unstable developing country will have a life of 2 years before it is confiscated by the foreign government. During this 2-year period, the operating cash flows will be $100 million each year. In addition, the firm will be able to use the new facility to repatriate $10 million each year in funds that have been held in the country involuntarily. If the discount rate for the operations cash flows is 10% and the discount rate for the exchange control avoidance is 8%, what is the adjusted present value of the project?

6. What is a LOC? What risks do the parties to a LOC take?

FURTHER READING

Ahn, J., Amiti, M., Weinstein, D., 2011. Trade finance and the great trade collapse. Am. Econ. Rev. 101 (3), 298–302.

Assef, S., Mitra, S., 1999. Making the most of transfer pricing. Insur. Exec, 2–4.

Dembeck, J.L., Stout, D.E., 1996. Transfer pricing in a global economy. Small. Bus. Contr. 9 (1), 38–46.

Gudmundsson, A.K., 2009. Lost in transfer pricing: the pitfalls of EU transfer pricing documentation. Int. Transf. Pricing J 16 (1), 2–28.

Holland, J., 1990. Capital budgeting for international business: a framework for analysis. Manage. Finance. 16 (2), 1–6.

Lessard, D.R., 1985. Evaluating foreign projects: an adjusted present value approach. In: Lessard, D.R. (Ed.), International Financial Management, Wiley, New York.

Mitchell, P., 1997. Alternative financing techniques in trade with Sub-Saharan Africa. Bus. Am. 118 (2), 29.

Venedikian, H.M., Warfield, G.A., 1996. Export-Import Finance. Wiley, New York.

APPENDIX A PRESENT VALUE

What would you pay today to receive $1000 in 1 year? The answer will vary from individual to individual, but we would all want to pay less than $1000 today. How much less depends on the *discount rate*—a measure, like an interest rate or rate of return, that we would use to discount to the present the $1000 to be received in 1 year.

Suppose that I require a 10`% return on all my investments. Then one way of viewing present value is as the principal amount today that when invested at 10% simple interest would be worth $1000 when the principal and interest are summed after 1 year. To find the required principal amount, we divide the future value (FV) of $1000 by 1 plus the discount rate (d) of 10%, or the present value (PV) formula, which is

$$PV = \frac{FV}{1 + d} = \frac{\$1,000}{1.10} = \$909.09 \qquad (9A.1)$$

I would pay $909.09 for the right to receive $1000 in 1 year. Another way of stating this is to say that the present value of $1000 to be received in 1 year is $909.09.

For amounts to be received at some year n in the future, the formula is modified to

$$PV = \frac{FV}{(1 + d)^n} \qquad (9A.2)$$

In the example just used, the $1000 is received in 1 year, so n equals 1. What if the $1000 is to be received in 2 years? Then the formula gives us

$$PV = \frac{\$1,000}{(1 + 0.10)^2} = \frac{\$1,000}{(1.10)(1.10)}$$
$$= \frac{\$1,000}{1.21} = \$826.45 \qquad (9A.3)$$

The present value of $1000 to be received in 2 years is $826.45. The farther into the future we go, the lower the present value of any future value. Furthermore the higher the discount rate, the lower the present value of any future value to be received.

If a capital outlay will generate a stream of earnings to be received over many years, we simply sum the present value of each individual year to obtain the present value of the future cash flows associated with the expenditure. Then we subtract the initial investment or cash outflow to find the present value of the project. If Σ is the summation operator and t denotes time (like years), then the present value of an investment of I dollars today yielding cash flows of CF_t over each year t in the future for T years is

$$PV = -I + \sum_{t=1}^{T} \frac{CF_t}{(1+d)^t} \qquad (9A.4)$$

If we can estimate the after-tax cash flows (CF_t) associated with a capital expenditure (I) today, and we can choose an appropriate discount rate (d), then the present value of the project is indicated by Eq. (9A.4).

CHAPTER 10

International Investment

Contents

In the early 1960s, international investment was viewed as being motivated by interest differentials among countries. If the interest rate in one country exceeded that of another, then financial capital was expected to flow between the countries until the rates were equal. Modern capital market theory provided a new basis for analysis. There were obvious problems with the old theory, since interest differentials can explain one-way flows of capital, from the low- to the high-interest-rate country; yet, realistically, capital flows both ways between most pairs of countries.

In this chapter, we apply some basic ideas of modern finance to understand and analyze the incentives for international portfolio investment, foreign direct investment, and capital flight.

PORTFOLIO DIVERSIFICATION

No doubt the differences in the returns on various countries' assets provide an incentive for capital flows. However, we would not expect interest rates to be equalized throughout the world, since risk differs from one asset to another. Furthermore, we would anticipate a certain random component in international capital flows, because money flows to new investment opportunities as they open up in various countries. Given the short time needed to shift funds around the world, the expected profit (adjusted for risk differences) from investing in different assets should be equal. If this were not the case, then money would flow internationally until it was true.

Yet even with constant interest rates internationally, there would still be an incentive for international capital flows. This additional incentive is provided by the desire to hold diversified portfolios. It is this diversification motive that leads to the two-way flows of capital between countries. Besides the return on an investment, investors are concerned with the risk attached to the investment. It is very unlikely that an individual who has $100,000 to invest will invest the entire amount in one asset. By choosing several investment alternatives and holding a *diversified portfolio*, the investor can reduce the risk associated with his or her investments. Modern financial literature has emphasized the concept of variability of return as a measure of risk. This is reasonable in that investors are interested in the future value of their portfolios, and the more variable the value of the portfolios, the less certain they can be of the future value.

By diversifying and selecting different assets (including assets of different countries) for a portfolio, we can reduce the variability of the portfolio returns. To see the effects of diversification, let us consider a simple example of an investor facing a world with two investment opportunities: asset A and asset B. The investor will hold a portfolio of A and B, with the share of the portfolio devoted to A denoted by a and the share devoted to B denoted by b. The shares, a and b, are fractions of the portfolio between 0 and 1, where $a + b = 1$. Thus, if the investor holds only A, then $a = 1$ and $b = 0$. If only B is held, then $a = 0$ and $b = 1$. Most likely the investor will choose some amount of diversification by holding both A and B.

The return on the portfolio (R_p) can be written as a weighted average of the returns on the individual assets $(R_A$ and $R_B)$:

$$R_p = aR_A + bR_B \tag{10.1}$$

The expected future return on the portfolio will then be determined by the expected future return in the individual assets:

$$R_p^\star = aR_A^\star + bR_B^\star \tag{10.2}$$

where $R_p^\star, R_A^\star,$ and $R_B^\star$ are the expected values of the portfolio and individual asset returns, respectively. We said earlier that the idea of portfolio risk was associated with the variability of the return on the portfolio.

The measure of the degree to which a variable deviates from its mean or average value is known as the *variance*. The variance of the portfolio will depend on the share of the portfolio held by each asset and the variance of the individual assets, as well as their covariance. Specifically,

$$\text{var}(R_p) = a^2 \, \text{var}(R_A) + b^2 \, \text{var}(R_B) + 2ab \, \text{cov}(R_A, R_B) \quad (10.3)$$

where *var* stands for variance and *cov* stands for covariance. The *covariance* is a measure of the degree to which the two assets move together. If, when one return is higher than average, the return on the other asset is lower than average, the covariance is negative. Looking at Eq. (10.3), we see that a negative covariance could contribute greatly to reducing the overall portfolio variance and, therefore, risk.

To see the effects of diversification more clearly, let us use a simple example. Table 10.1 shows a set of hypothetical investment opportunities. This table is a hypothetical assessment of the investment opportunity that is available. If we hold only asset A, our expected return is 10%, with a variance of 0.00605. If we hold only asset B, our expected return is 8% with a variance of 0.00545. Thus, asset A yields a higher expected return than asset B, but the variability of the returns is also higher with asset A than B. By holding 50% of our portfolio in A and 50% in B, our expected return is $R_p = 0.5(10\%) + 0.5(8\%) = 9\%$ with a variance (using Eq. (10.3)) of

$$\text{var}(R_p) = .25(0.00605) + .25(0.00545) + 2 \times .25(-0.0048252)$$
$$= 0.0004625$$

We need not be concerned with the statistical theory underlying the example. The important result for our use is the large reduction in variability of return achieved by diversification. By investing half of our wealth in A and half in B, we expect to receive a return on our portfolio that is halfway between what we would expect from just holding A or B alone.

Table 10.1 Hypothetical returns for two assets

Probability	R_A (%)	R_B (%)
0.25	−2	16
0.25	9	9
0.25	19	−4
0.25	14	11

Note: $R_A^* = 10\%$; $R_B^* = 8\%$; $\text{var}(R_A) = 0.00605$; $\text{var}(R_B) = 0.00545$; $\text{cov}(R_A, R_B) = -0.004825$.

However, the variance of our return is much less than half the variance of either R_A or R_B. The substantially lower risk achieved by diversification will lead investors to hold many different assets, including assets from different countries.

As the size of the investor's portfolio grows, the investor will want to buy more assets in the proportions that are already held in order to maintain the desired degree of diversification. This means that as wealth increases, we could anticipate international capital flows between countries, as investors maintain these optimal portfolios. Thus, even with constant international interest rates, we should expect to observe two-way flows of capital as international wealth increases.

We should recognize that diversification will not eliminate all risk to the investor, since there will still exist *systematic risk*—the risk present in all investment opportunities. For instance, in the domestic context, we know that different industries have different time patterns of performance. While one industry is enjoying increasing sales and profits, another industry might be languishing in the doldrums. Then, at some later period, the reverse might be true, and the once-thriving industry is now the stagnant one. This is similar to the example of opportunities A and B previously presented. The negative covariance between them indicates that when one is enjoying better-than-average times, the other is suffering, and vice versa. Yet there is still a positive portfolio variance, even when we diversify and hold both assets. The variance that can be eliminated through diversification is called *nonsystematic risk*; this is the risk that is unique to a particular firm or industry. Systematic risk is common to all firms and remains even in diversified portfolios. Systematic risk results from events that are experienced jointly by all firms, like the overall business cycle of recurrent periods of prosperity and recession that occur at the national level.

By extending our investment alternatives internationally, we can gain by international diversification. There appears to be nonsystematic risk at the national level that can be reduced with international portfolio diversification. Moreover, business cycles do not happen uniformly across countries, so when one country is experiencing rapid growth, another may be in a recession. By investing across countries, we eliminate part of the cyclical fluctuation in our portfolio that would arise from the domestic business cycle. Therefore, some of what would be considered systematic risk, in terms of strictly domestic investment opportunities, becomes nonsystematic risk when we broaden our opportunities to include foreign as well as domestic investment. Thus, we can say that not only will investors tend to diversify their portfolio holdings across industries, but they can also realize additional gains by diversifying across countries.

One might wonder whether the gains from international diversification could be realized by investing in domestic multinational firms. If we consider a multinational firm—a firm doing business in many countries—to be affected significantly by foreign factors, then we may view multinational stock as similar to an international portfolio. Since multinational firms have operations in many countries, we may hypothesize that multinational stock prices behave more like an internationally diversified portfolio than like just another domestic stock. The evidence indicates that domestic multinational firms are poor substitutes for international diversification. While the variability of returns from a portfolio of US multinational stock tends to be somewhat lower than the variability of a portfolio of purely domestic-oriented stocks, a portfolio invested across different national stock markets can reduce portfolio return variance by substantially more.

REASONS FOR INCOMPLETE PORTFOLIO DIVERSIFICATION

Many studies have demonstrated the gain from international diversification. However, recent research has indicated that investors seem to greatly favor domestic assets and invest much less in foreign assets than one would expect given the expected gains from diversification. Tesar and Werner (1995) examined the foreign investment positions of major industrial countries for the 1970–90 period and found that international investment as a fraction of the total domestic market for stocks and bonds equaled about 3% for the United States, 4% for Canada, 10% for Germany, 11% for Japan, and 32% for the United Kingdom. Calculations of an "optimal" investment portfolio would have much higher fractions devoted to international assets.

Recent studies have shown an increase in the international investment positions, but nowhere near the levels of an "optimal" investment portfolio. For example, Ferreira and Miguel (2011) show that the foreign bond position for the 1997–2009 period was slightly above 4% for the United States, 5% for Canada, 25% for Germany, 21% for Japan, and 47% for the United Kingdom. In general, EMU countries had a high international investment position, with Ireland leading the sample of countries with a 91% international investment. However, the international investment for the European Monetary Union (EMU) countries was only 12%, implying that many of the "foreign" purchases of EMU countries were with other EMU countries.

Why do investors seem to have this bias in favor of domestic securities? There are several possible reasons: taxes, transaction costs, or something else that is missing from the standard model of international investment. Let us consider the alternatives in turn:

1. *Taxes.* If home bias is due to taxes, then the tax on foreign securities would have to be high enough to offset the higher return (or lower risk) expected from these securities. However, taxes paid to foreign governments can usually be credited against domestic taxes. Even if there is some net increase in the tax paid on foreign investment, it is unlikely that this increase could be high enough to discourage foreign investment to the extent observed.

2. *Transaction costs.* The cost associated with buying and selling foreign securities includes explicit monetary costs, like fees, commissions, and bid-ask spreads, and implicit costs such as differences in regulations protecting investors, language differences, and costs of obtaining information about foreign investment opportunities. Familiarity with domestic assets and lower explicit costs of trading at home may lead to home bias.

3. *What else?* One possibility is that the gains from international diversification have been overstated. If countries tend to specialize in the production of certain goods and services and trade with the rest of the world for other goods and services, it is possible to imagine a situation where incomes fluctuate less than one might think based on fluctuations in domestic production. As output fluctuates for certain industries, relative prices change and this relative price change helps to smooth out income fluctuations. For instance, if the Philippines specializes in pineapple production and bad weather reduces the harvest, pineapple prices rise due to the reduction in supply. This price increase helps to cushion the fall in income related to the poor harvest. In this manner, relative price changes may serve as a natural hedge against output fluctuations, so that there is less income variability to be reduced through diversification.

The puzzle of home bias has not been answered adequately. It may be that there is no answer that can be related easily to financial models of investment. The surprisingly low level of international securities in investment portfolios may reflect investors' decisions to hold undiversified portfolios, both internationally as well as domestically. Further research is needed to understand these issues better.

Although the investor risk considered so far has focused on the variability of portfolio return, it should be realized that in international investment there is always the potential for political risk, which may involve the confiscation of foreigners' assets. The next chapter will consider the analysis of such risk and includes a recent ranking of countries in terms of the perceived political risk attached to investments made in that country.

INTERNATIONAL INVESTMENT OPPORTUNITIES

As with domestic markets, there are international investment opportunities in stocks, bonds, and mutual funds. The United States is the largest market. Ferreira and Miguel (2011) show that the United States has a share of 41.3% of the world's bond market, with Japan a distant second with 14.2%, followed by Germany with 6.7%. The differences in size of the various national markets can (and does at times) prove problematic for investors seeking to trade quickly in the smaller markets.

A good example of the problems that can arise in turbulent times is provided by the stock market collapse of October 1987. In mid-October, prices collapsed dramatically in all stock markets around the world. The price fall brought huge orders to sell stocks as investors liquidated their positions and mutual funds raised cash to pay off customers' redemption requests. Stock exchanges in the United States are relatively *deep*— meaning that there are enough potential buyers and sellers and a large number of securities traded so that the market permits trading at all times. Other markets are relatively *thin*—with a much smaller number of potential buyers and sellers and a smaller volume of securities traded.

During the stock market collapse in 1987, the New York Stock Exchange was able to trade 600 million shares, while markets in Hong Kong, Singapore, Italy, Spain, France, and Germany were not as liquid. In fact, at the peak of the trading frenzy, the Hong Kong market closed for a week. Can you imagine the frustration of a US portfolio manager wanting to sell shares in Hong Kong while trading has stopped?

THE GLOBALIZATION OF EQUITY MARKETS

If we go back to just a couple of decades ago, many countries had equity (stock) markets that were segmented. A *segmented market* is one in which foreign investors are not allowed to buy domestic stocks and domestic investors are not allowed to buy foreign stocks. Part of the process of the globalization of world economies is the liberalization of stock market

Table 10.2 Date of first stock market liberalization

Argentina	November 1989
Brazil	March 1988
Chile	May 1987
Colombia	December 1991
Greece	December 1987
India	June 1986
Indonesia	September 1989
Jordan	December 1995
South Korea	June 1987
Malaysia	May 1987
Mexico	May 1989
Nigeria	August 1995
Pakistan	February 1991
Philippines	May 1986
Portugal	July 1986
Taiwan	May 1986
Thailand	January 1988
Turkey	August 1989
Venezuela	January 1990
Zimbabwe	June 1993

Source: From Henry, P. B., 2000. Stock market liberalization, economic reform, and emerging market equity prices. J. Financ. 55, 529–564; Beckaert, G., Harvey, C. R., 2000. Foreign speculators and emerging equity markets. J. Financ. 55, 565–614.

restrictions to open markets to the world. Table 10.2 provides dates of first stock market liberalizations for several countries.

What happens when a country moves from a segmented market, cut off from foreign investors and foreign markets, to a globalized market in which the domestic restrictions are lifted, the domestic stock market is now freely open to the world, and domestic investors can hold stocks of both domestic and foreign firms?

To answer this question, we shall assume that risk is represented by the variance of the return on a portfolio of assets as discussed earlier in the chapter. Now, we can think about a risk premium that must be paid to compensate investors for taking risk. Let us denote the return on the risk-free asset (like a US government security) as Rf. Then we can consider the risk premium on small country C's assets as being equal to the return on C's assets minus the risk-free rate of return, or: Risk Premium = $R_C - Rf$. The size of this risk premium should depend upon the variance of the return on the market portfolio and the price of risk.

In a segmented market, the variance of returns is just the variance of the domestic market return, so the risk premium before globalization is:

$$\text{Risk Premium in segmented market} = P \, \text{var}[R_C] \qquad (10.4)$$

where P is the price of risk. So, the risk premium required on domestic stocks in segmented financial market C will just depend upon the variance of stock prices in country C multiplied by the price of risk P. P is determined by the degree of risk aversion of investors. If all investors are the same everywhere, then P is a constant across countries. In a world of segmented markets, a country with a variance of returns twice as high as another country would have twice the risk premium on its stocks. This risk premium is what investors require in order to willingly hold shares of the stocks.

In the globalized equity market we can think of the portfolio return volatility for the residents of small country C as the variance of a portfolio comprised of the stocks of country C and the stocks of the rest of the world. Using the formula for portfolio variance introduced earlier in the chapter, this would be:

$$\text{Var}[R_p] = w^2 \, \text{var}[R_w] + c^2 \, \text{var}[R_C] + 2wc \, \text{cov}[R_w, R_C] \quad (10.5)$$

where w and c are the fraction of the portfolio devoted to stocks from the rest of the world and the small country, respectively; R_W and R_C are the returns on the stocks of the rest of the world and small country C, respectively. Eq. (10.5) shows that the variance of the portfolio is determined by the amount invested in each area, the variance of returns on the stocks of the two areas, and the covariance between the returns on the two kinds of stocks.

If country C is a segmented market, then the portfolio return variance would just be equal to the variance of the return on country C stocks as in Eq. (10.4), as w would equal zero and c would equal one. Now, think what would happen if the government of country C would liberalize its financial markets to become more globalized. The risk premium on C's stock should depend upon the contribution of C's stock to the variance of the world portfolio, which is given by the covariance of the return on stock in country C with the returns in the rest of the world, or

$$\text{Risk Premium in globalized market} = P \, \text{cov}[R_W, R_C] \qquad (10.6)$$

Should we expect the risk premium on country C stock to rise or fall with globalization? To answer that question, compare Eqs. (10.4) and (10.6). For globalization to reduce the risk premium on country C, we need $\text{var}(R_C) >$ $\text{cov}(R_W, R_C)$. Note that the square root of the variance is known as the *standard deviation* (SD). So $\text{SD}(R_C)$ is equal to the sqrt(var(R_C)). The SD is just another measure of how a variable deviates from its mean or average value. What is useful for our purposes is that the covariance is equal to the correlation coefficient between two variables multiplied by the product of their SDs, or $\text{cov}(R_W, R_C) = \rho\text{SD}(R_W)\text{SD}(R_C)$ where ρ is the correlation coefficient. The correlation coefficient is a number between 1 and -1 that indicates how these two variables change together. If $\rho = 1$, then the two variables are perfectly correlated and move together about their respective means. If $\rho = -1$, then the two variables are perfectly negatively correlated and move exactly opposite to each other, so that when one is above its mean value, the other is below its mean value. If $\rho = 0$, then the two variables are independent and have no relationship.

Now we can find the conditions under which globalizing a financial market will reduce the risk premium on a country's stock. Comparing Eqs. (10.4) and (10.6) again, we need $\text{var}(R_C) > \text{cov}(R_W, R_C)$, which may be written as:

$$\text{var}(R_C) > \rho\text{SD}(R_W)\text{SD}(R_C) \tag{10.7}$$

If we divide both sides of this inequality by $\text{SD}(R_W)\text{SD}(R_C)$, we have:[1]

$$\text{SD}(R_C)/\text{SD}(R_W) > \rho \tag{10.8}$$

So the risk premium on country C stock will fall with globalization, if the ratio of the SD of the stock returns in C to the stock returns in the rest of the world is greater than the correlation coefficient between the two. Since SDs are always positive, if the correlation coefficient is negative, then this must always be true. In this case, country C stock prices would tend to rise when the rest-of-the-world stock prices tend to fall, and the risk premium on C's stock will always fall with globalization. In general, we need a relatively small ρ and a large $\text{SD}(R_C)$ relative to $\text{SD}(R_W)$. This is, in fact, what one usually observes in the world. Small countries with segmented stock markets typically have relatively small correlations of their stock prices with the rest of the world. In addition, the volatility of their stock prices tends to be high relative to rest-of-the-world volatility. So, in general, we expect that when a government liberalizes its financial markets to become globalized, or integrated with the rest of the world, the risk premium on its stock falls.

---

[1] Note that $\text{var}(R_C) = (\text{SD}(R_C))^2$ so that $\text{var}(R_C)/(\text{SD}(R_W)\text{SD}(R_C)) = \text{SD}(R_C)/\text{SD}(R_W)$.

This, then, points out a major benefit of globalized financial markets: A lower risk premium on domestic financial assets allows domestic firms to lower their *cost of capital*. The cost of capital is what firms have to pay investors to raise new funds. If a domestic firm sells new shares of stock, then the lower the risk premium, the smaller dividends or cash flows the firm must pay stockholders. This allows firms to raise money more cheaply and will allow greater investment spending and expansion than otherwise.

FOREIGN DIRECT INVESTMENT

The previous sections have dealt with international portfolio investment. A particular type of portfolio investment is labeled Foreign Direct Investment (FDI). *FDI* is the spending by a domestic firm to establish foreign operating units. In the US balance of payments, direct investment is distinguished from portfolio investment solely on the basis of percentage of ownership. Capital flows are designated as FDI when a foreign entity owns 10% or more of a firm, regardless of whether the capital flows are used to purchase a new plant and equipment or to buy an ownership position in an existing firm. The growth of FDI spending corresponds to the growth of the multinational firm. Although FDI is properly emphasized in international trade discussions of the international movement of factors of production, students should be able to distinguish portfolio investment from direct investment.

The motives for portfolio investment are easily seen in terms of the risk and return concepts already examined. In a general sense, the concern with a firm's return, subject to risk considerations, may be thought of as motivating all firm decisions, including those of direct investment. However, a literature has developed to offer more specific motives for desiring domestic ownership of foreign production facilities. Theories of FDI typically explain the incentive for such investment in terms of some imperfection in free-market conditions. If markets were perfectly competitive, the domestic firm could just as well buy foreign securities to transfer capital abroad rather than actually establishing a foreign operating unit. One line of theorizing on foreign investment is that individual firms may not attempt to maximize profits, which would be in the interest of the firm's stockholders; instead, they would attempt to maximize growth in terms of firm size. This is a concept that relies on an oligopolistic form of industry that would allow a firm to survive without maximizing profits. In this case, FDI is preferred since domestic firms cannot depend on foreign-managed firms to operate in the domestic firm's best interests.

Other theories of FDI are based on the domestic firm possessing superior skills, knowledge, or information as compared to foreign firms. Such advantages would allow the foreign subsidiary of the domestic firm to earn a higher return than is possible by a foreign-managed firm.

FDI has become an increasingly important source of finance for both developing and developed countries. Fig. 10.1 illustrates how inflows of FDI to developed and developing countries have changed in recent times. Developing and transition economies have seen a fairly steady upward trend on FDI inflows during the 1990–2015 period, except following the US recessions of 2000 and 2008. Fig. 10.1 also shows an upward trend in FDI in the developed countries. In addition to the trend, there are two periods of higher than usual investment. From the mid-1990s to the end of the 1990s, Europe and the United States saw a sharp increase in the investment flow. This has been called the "the great IT investment boom." A similar boom occurred about 2003–07 and was associated with increased housing speculative activity. Also here Europe and the United States were the favorite targets for the investment flows. By 2009 the investment boom had disappeared and FDI appears to be back at its normal trend. Recently FDI has increased, especially in 2015. However, this increase is not due to an increase in new FDI (greenfield investment projects). Instead it is mainly due to mergers and acquisitions and restructuring of companies.

FDI occurs in both developing and developed countries. Fig. 10.1 shows that in most years the FDI is slightly larger in the developing and transition countries as opposed to developed economies. However, in 2015 developing economies experienced a substantially higher FDI at $936 billion compared to $764 billion for the developing and transition nations. The dominance of FDI in developed countries is mainly due to mergers and acquisitions, and due to a slowdown in investment in the BRIC countries (Brazil, Russia, India, and China).

FDI is often politically unpopular in developing countries, and increasingly so also in developed countries, because it is associated with an element of foreign control over domestic resources. Nationalist sentiment, combined with a fear of exploitation, has often resulted in laws restricting direct investment. Although FDI is feared, it may be very beneficial for countries. FDI may contribute more to economic development than do bank loans, since more of the funds go to actual investment in productive resources. In contrast, bank loans to sovereign governments were (and are) often used for consumption spending rather than investment. If foreign

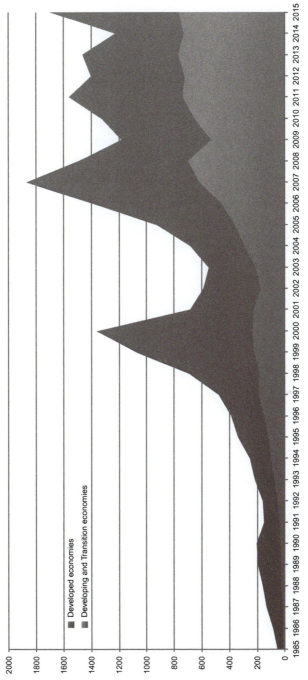

Figure 10.1 Foreign direct investment. *From UNCTAD statistics, billions of USD in current prices and exchange rates.*

firms make a bad decision regarding an FDI, the loss is sustained by the foreign firm, and no repayment would be necessary. In contrast, if the domestic government uses bank loans inefficiently, the country still faces a repayment obligation to the foreign banks. In addition, FDI may involve an adoption of new technologies and productive expertise not available in the domestic economy. Empirical work has shown benefits of FDI for developing nations, but some argue that the primary benefit may be the greatest contribution of FDI. For example, Wang and Wang (2015) found that Chinese companies benefitted more from the access to global financial markets rather than the adoption of new technologies.

CAPITAL FLIGHT

In the discussion of portfolio investment, we emphasized expected risk and return as determinants of foreign investment. When the risk of doing business in a country rises sharply or the expected return falls, we sometimes observe large outflows of investment funds so that the country experiences massive capital account deficits. Such net outflows of funds are often descriptively referred to as *capital flight*. The change in the risk–return relationship that gives rise to capital flight may be the result of political or financial crisis, tightening capital controls, tax increases, or fear of a domestic currency devaluation.

One of the issues arising from the developing-country debt crisis of the 1980s was an assertion by bankers that some of the borrowed money was not put to use in the debtor nations but, instead, was misappropriated by individuals and deposited back in the developed countries. In addition to allegedly misappropriated funds, wealthy individuals and business firms often shipped capital out of the debtor nations at the same time that these nations were pleading for additional funds from developed-country banks.

It is estimated that over the period from 1977 to 1987, $20 billion of flight capital left Argentina. This $20 billion is almost half of the debt, totaling $46 billion, that was incurred through 1984. The data suggest a crude interpretation that for every $1 borrowed by Argentina, about 50 cents came out of the country as flight capital. Similar statements might be made for other countries. An important aspect of the capital outflows is that fewer resources are available at home to service the debt, and more borrowing is required. In addition, capital flight may be associated with a loss of international reserves and greater pressure for devaluation of the domestic currency.

The discussion of capital flight highlights the importance of economic and political stability for encouraging domestic investment. Business firms and individuals respond to lower risk and higher return. The stable and growing developing country faces little, if any, capital flight and attracts foreign capital to aid in expanding the productive capacity of the economy.

CAPITAL INFLOW ISSUES

The early 1990s were characterized by a surge of capital inflows to developing countries. Interest in countries with emerging financial markets stimulated both direct and portfolio investment in these countries. The inflows were welcome in that they helped poor countries finance domestic infrastructure to aid in development, and they provided additional opportunities for international diversification for investors. However, some countries that experienced particularly large capital inflows exhibited problems that could reduce the positive effects of the capital flows.

A large capital inflow in a short period of time can lead to an appreciation of the recipient country's currency. This appreciation may reduce the competitiveness of the nation's export industries and cause a fall in output and rise in unemployment in these industries. We learned in Chapter 3, The Balance of Payments that a large rise in the capital account surplus will be accompanied by a large rise in the current account deficit. The capital inflow may also be associated with a rapid increase in the country's money supply, which would create inflationary conditions. As a result of potential problems associated with capital inflows, some countries have imposed policies aimed at limiting the effects of these inflows.

Fiscal restraint is a policy of cutting government expenditures, or raising taxes, so that the expansionary effect of the capital flows is partially offset by the contractionary fiscal policy. Chile, Malaysia, and Thailand followed such policies. Many countries have used some sort of exchange rate policy measures. Generally, these involved an appreciation of the currency in countries where the exchange rate has maintained little flexibility. Allowing the currency to appreciate may hurt export industries, but it allows the money supply to be insulated from the capital flow so that inflationary monetary policy does not occur. Some countries also permitted greater exchange rate flexibility as a way to insulate the domestic money supply from the capital flows. Some countries imposed capital controls to limit the inflow of capital. Such measures include taxes and quantity quotas on capital flows, increased reserve requirements on bank borrowing in foreign currency, or limits on foreign exchange transactions.

Overall, the experience of the 1990s has created an awareness that capital inflows can be both a blessing and a curse. The attempts to manage the risks associated with such inflows have met with varied degrees of success, and further studies of the experiences of countries that followed different policies will yield suggestions for appropriate government policy measures.

SUMMARY

1. Portfolio diversification explains the two-way flow of capital between countries, even when interest rates are equalized among countries.

2. The variability of returns on a portfolio is measured by variance, which is the degree of deviations from the average value. The smaller the variance, the more certain the returns on the portfolio.

3. By including various assets in the portfolio, investors can reduce the variability of the portfolio's returns.

4. Portfolio diversification eliminates the nonsystematic risk that is unique to an individual asset. The systematic risk, which is commonly shared by all assets, still remains.

5. The home-bias puzzle of portfolio diversification indicates that investors prefer to hold a large proportion of domestic assets in their portfolios, even though by holding some international assets they could reduce the variability of the portfolio's returns.

6. Some possible explanations for the home-bias portfolio puzzle are: (1) different taxes between home and foreign assets, (2) higher transactions (information) costs of foreign assets, and (3) overestimated benefits of international diversification.

7. Before financial liberalization in the 1980s, stock markets in many countries were segmented markets, which did not allow foreign investors to buy/sell domestic stocks and domestic investors to buy/sell foreign stocks.

8. After liberalization, many financial markets become globalized. The globalized financial market will reduce the risk premium of a home country's assets, if the ratio of SDs of the asset returns in the home country to the rest-of-the-world asset returns is greater than the correlation coefficient between home and international assets.

9. FDI is the capital flow of investment to acquire 10% or more of voting stocks of a firm abroad.

10. The motives for ownership of foreign operations can be explained by imperfect competitive market conditions and superior expertise of the domestic firm.

11. There have been two episodes of sharp increases in FDI in Europe and the United States during the late 1990s and 2003–07. The first investment surge was the "Great IT Investment Boom" and the second one was due to the housing market boom.

12. Capital flight is the sudden outflow of funds. It is usually an outcome of political instability, financial crisis, or a fear of currency devaluation.

13. A rapid increase in capital inflow could harm an economy. It could cause an appreciation of the recipient country's currency and reduce competitiveness of exporting industries.

EXERCISES

1. Explain how investment flows can be motivated by interest rate differentials and still allow two-way capital flows between countries.
2. What is the difference between systematic and nonsystematic risk? Give examples of both risks.
3. Explain how portfolio diversification can reduce risk.
4. Explain why US portfolios do not have a large enough international diversification.
5. Assume that you have a choice of two assets, A and B, and a portfolio of an equal share of the two assets. Assume also that the assets have the following statistics:

	Return	Variance	Covariance
Asset A	20%	0.10	−0.01
Asset B	16%	0.02	

   a. What does the negative covariance between the assets A and B mean?
   b. As a risk-averse investor, would you choose the asset A, B, or the portfolio? Explain your reason.

FURTHER READING

Carrieri, F., Errunza, V., Hogan, K., 2007. Characterizing world market integration through time. J. Financ. Quant. Anal. 42, 915–940.

Didier, T., Rigobon, R., Schmukler, S.L., 2013. Unexploited gains from international diversification: patterns of portfolio holdings around the world. Rev. Econ. Stat.

Ferreira, M.A., Miguel, A.F., 2011. The determinants of domestic and foreign bond bias. J. of Multinational Financ. Management. 21 (5).

Foerster, S.R., Karolyi, G.A., 1999. The effects of market segmentation and investor recognition on asset prices: evidence from foreign stocks listing in the United States. J. Financ. June.

Hasan, I., Simaan, Y., 2000. A rational explanation for home country bias. J. Int. Money Financ. June.

International Monetary Fund, 1997. Developing countries get more private investment, less aid. Financ. Dev.

Kasa, K., 1994. Measuring the gains from international portfolio diversification. FRBSF Wkly. Lett.

Kho, B., Stulz, R.M., Warnock, F., 2009. Financial globalization, governance, and the evolution of the home bias. J. Account. Res. 47 (2), 597–635.

Kim, Y., 2000. Causes of capital flows in developing countries. J. Int. Money Financ. April

Stulz, R.M., 1999. Globalization, corporate finance, and the cost of capital. J. Appl. Corp. Financ. 12 (3), 8–25.

Tesar, L.L., Werner, I.M., 1995. Home bias and high turnover. J. Int. Money Financ.

Wang, J., Wang, X., 2015. Benefits of foreign ownership: evidence from foreign direct investment in China. J. Int. Econ. 97 (2).

APPENDIX A AMERICAN DEPOSITARY RECEIPTS

It is not always necessary to transfer funds abroad to buy foreign securities. Many foreign stocks are traded in the United States in the form of *American depositary receipts* (*ADRs*). ADRs are negotiable instruments certifying that shares of a foreign stock are being held by a foreign custodian. ADRs are popular because they offer an easy way for US investors to diversify internationally and allow non-US firms access to raising money in the United States. Even though these stocks are bought and sold on the US market, they are still subject to foreign exchange risk because the dollar price of the ADR shares reflects the dollar value of the foreign currency price of the stock in the foreign country of origin. Furthermore, foreign government policy will have an impact on the value of ADRs. For instance, in April 1987, the British government imposed a 5% tax on conversion of British stocks into ADRs. Trading in these ADRs dropped dramatically until the British government reduced the tax.

Firms that list their stocks as ADRs have some choice as to what type of listing they desire. The available types of ADR programs include the following:
- *Level I ADR*
  - No requirement to file financial statements that conform to US accounting standards.
  - Traded in the so-called over-the-counter (OTC) market and are not traded on an exchange like NASDAQ or the New York Stock Exchange.

- Created from existing shares in foreign market; no new capital can be raised.
- *Level II ADR*
  - Must file financial statements conforming to US accounting standards.
  - Traded on organized exchanges like NASDAQ or the New York Stock Exchange.
  - Created from existing shares in foreign market; no new capital can be raised.
- *Level III ADR*
  - Must file financial statements conforming to US accounting standards.
  - Trade on organized exchanges like NASDAQ or the New York Stock Exchange.
  - New issues of stock in order to raise new capital for firm.
- *Rule 144A ADR*
  - No requirement to file financial statements conforming to US accounting standards.
  - Not traded on OTC or exchanges; strictly for private trades among qualified institutional buyers.
  - New issues of stock in order to raise new capital for firm.

In addition to ADRs, there are also *global depositary receipts* (GDRs), which are traded in more than one market location. For instance, a firm may have a GDR that is traded in the United States, London, and Tokyo.

Why do non-US firms list their shares in the United States? The US listing provides the following benefits: an enlarged investor base, the ability to raise new capital in the world's largest financial market, and lower transaction costs than in the home market. In addition, a firm generally finds that the price of its home market shares rises with a US listing. This is likely due to the greater liquidity of trade in the firm's stock, meaning that there are more counterparties with which to trade and the ease of buying or selling at a good price is enhanced. In addition, a firm that is located in a country with weak accounting standards sends a signal to investors of its quality when it lists in the United States and files financial statements conforming to US accounting standards. In addition, non-US firms may list on a US exchange to use the ADR as a means to take over a US firm. For instance, when Daimler Benz bought Chrysler Corporation, Daimler exchanged ADRs for shares of Chrysler stock.

CHAPTER 11

International Lending and Crises

Contents

In many ways, international lending is similar to domestic lending. Lenders care about the risk of default and the expected return from making loans whether they are lending across town or across international borders. In this chapter, we will continue our discussion of capital flows, by looking at international lending. In addition, the chapter will examine the problems that borrowing countries may experience.

INTERNATIONAL LENDING

International lending has had recurrent horror stories where regional financial crises have imposed large losses on lenders. In the 1980s, there was a Latin American debt crisis in which many countries were unable to service the international debts they had accumulated. Table 11.1 illustrates the commitment of US banks to lending in each of the crisis areas. The table indicates that the situation from the perspective of US banks was much more dire in the 1982 Latin American crisis than in the more recent cases. The 1980 debtor nations owed so much money to international banks that a default would have wiped out the biggest banks in the world. As a result, debts were *rescheduled* rather than allowed to default. A debt rescheduling postpones the repayment of interest and principal so that banks can claim the loan as being owed in the future rather than in default

Table 11.1 US bank loans in financial crisis countries as a percentage of US bank capital
Latin America in 1982

Argentina	12%
Brazil	26%
Chile	9%
Mexico	37%
Mexico in 1994	11%

Asia in 1997

Indonesia	2%
Korea	3%
Thailand	1%

Source: From Kamin, S., 1998. The Asian financial crisis in historical perspective: a review of selected statistics. Working Paper, Board of Governors of the Federal Reserve System.

now. This way, banks do not have to write off the debt as a loss—which would have threatened the existence of many large banks due to the large size of the loans relative to the capitalization of the bank. For instance, the Mexican debt to US banks in 1982 was equal to 37% of US bank capital. Banks simply could not afford to write off bad debt of this magnitude as loss. By rescheduling the debt, banks would avoid this alternative.

In contrast to the heavy exposure of international banks to Latin American borrowers in 1982, the Asian financial crisis of 1997 involved a much more manageable debt position for US banks. Many international investors lost money in the Asian crisis, but the crisis did not threaten the stability of the world banking system to the extent the 1980s crisis did. However, the debtor countries required international assistance to recover from the crisis in all recent crisis situations. This recovery involves new loans from governments, banks, and the International Monetary Fund (IMF). Later in this chapter, we consider the role of the IMF in more detail. First, it is useful to think about what causes financial crises.

CAUSES OF FINANCIAL CRISES

The causes of the recent Asian financial crisis are still being debated. Yet, it is safe to say that certain elements are essential in any explanation, including external shocks, domestic macroeconomic policy, and domestic financial system flaws. Let us consider each of these in turn.

1. *External shocks.* Following years of rapid growth, the East Asian economies faced a series of external shocks in the mid-1990s that may have
   contributed to the crisis. The Chinese renminbi and the Japanese
   yen were both devalued, making other Asian economies with fixed
   exchange rates less competitive relative to China and Japan. Because
   electronics manufacturing is an important export industry in East Asia,
   another factor contributing to a drop in exports and national income
   was the sharp drop in semiconductor prices. As exports and incomes
   fell, loan repayment became more difficult and property values started
   to fall. Since real property is used as collateral in many bank loans, the
   drop in property values made many loans of questionable value so that
   the banking systems were facing many defaults.

2. *Domestic macroeconomic policy.* The most obvious element of macroeconomic policy in most crisis countries was the use of fixed exchange
   rates. Fixed exchange rates encouraged international capital flows into
   the countries, and many debts incurred in foreign currencies were
   not hedged because of the lack of exchange rate volatility. Once pressures for devaluation began, countries defended the pegged exchange
   rate by central bank intervention—buying domestic currency with
   dollars. Because each country has a finite supply of dollars, countries
   also raised interest rates to increase the attractiveness of investments
   denominated in domestic currency. Finally, some countries resorted
   to capital controls, restricting foreigners access to domestic currency
   to restrict speculation against the domestic currency. For instance, if
   investors wanted to speculate against the Thai baht, they could borrow baht and exchange them for dollars, betting that the baht would
   fall in value against the dollar. This increased selling pressure on the
   baht could be reduced by capital controls limiting foreigners' ability to
   borrow baht. However, ultimately the pressure to devalue is too great,
   as even domestic residents are speculating against the domestic currency and the fixed exchange rate is abandoned. This occurs with great
   cost to the domestic financial market. Because international debts were
   denominated in foreign currency and most were unhedged because of
   the prior fixed exchange rate, the domestic currency burden of the
   debt was increased in proportion to the size of the devaluation. To aid
   in the repayment of the debt, countries turn to other governments and
   the IMF for aid.

3. *Domestic financial system flaws.* The countries experiencing the Asian
   crisis were characterized by banking systems in which loans were not

always made on the basis of prudent business decisions. Political and social connections were often more important than expected return and collateral when applying for a loan. As a result, many bad loans were extended. During the boom times of the early to mid-1990s, the rapid growth of the economy covered such losses. However, once the growth started to falter, the bad loans started to adversely affect the financial health of the banking system. A related issue is that banks and other lenders expected the government to bail them out if they ran into serious financial difficulties. This situation of implicit government loan guarantees created a *moral hazard* situation. A moral hazard exists when one does not have to bear the full cost of bad decisions. If institutions or individuals taking the risk are assured of not being held liable for losses, then it creates excessive risk taking. So if banks believe that the government will cover any significant losses from loans to political cronies that are not repaid, they will be more likely to extend such loans.

Considerable resources have been devoted to understanding the nature and causes of financial crises in hopes of avoiding future crises and forecasting those crises that do occur. Forecasting is always difficult in economics, and it is safe to say that there will always be surprises that no economic forecaster foresees. Yet there are certain variables that are so obviously related to past crises that they may serve as warning indicators of potential future crises. The list includes the following:

1. *Fixed exchange rates.* Countries involved in recent crises, including Mexico in 1993–94, the Southeast Asian countries in 1997, and Argentina in 2002, all utilized fixed exchange rates prior to the onset of the crisis. Generally, macroeconomic policies were inconsistent with the maintenance of the fixed exchange rate. When large devaluations ultimately occurred, domestic residents holding unhedged loans denominated in foreign currency suffered huge losses.

2. *Falling international reserves.* The maintenance of fixed exchange rates may be no problem. One way to detect whether the exchange rate is no longer an equilibrium rate is to monitor the international reserve holdings of the country (largely the foreign currency held by the central bank and treasury). If the stock of international reserves is falling steadily over time, that is a good indicator that the fixed exchange rate regime is under pressure and there is likely to be a devaluation.

3. *Lack of transparency.* Many crisis countries suffer from a lack of transparency in governmental activities and in public disclosures of business

conditions. Investors need to know the financial situation of firms in order to make informed investment decisions. If accounting rules allow firms to hide the financial impact of actions that would harm investors, then investors may not be able to adequately judge when the risk of investing in a firm rises. In such cases, a financial crisis may appear as a surprise to all but the "insiders" in a troubled firm. Similarly, if the government does not disclose its international reserve position in a timely and informative manner, investors may be caught by surprise when a devaluation occurs. The lack of good information on government and business activities serves as a warning sign of potential future problems.

This short list of warning signs provides an indication of the sorts of variables an international investor must consider when evaluating the risks of investing in a foreign country. Once a country finds itself with severe international debt repayment problems, it has to seek additional financing. Because international banks are not willing to commit new money where prospects for repayment are slim, the IMF becomes an important source of funding. Before we examine the role of the IMF, we will examine the recent financial crisis in the United States and the debt crisis in Greece.

INTERNATIONAL LENDING AND THE GREAT RECESSION

The recent financial crisis shares some similarities with past crises, but is also different in some ways. The recent crisis, starting in the end of 2007, has been called the *Great Recession*, because of its sharp effect on output across the world. Economists are still debating the causes of the crisis, but some general observations can be made. The Great Recession was caused by an overexpansion of credit and a lack of transparency into the riskiness of the investments. This is similar to the Asian financial crisis. However, the transmission effect of the crisis was a bit different for the Great Recession than the Asian financial crisis. The effects of the US housing crisis were transmitted throughout the international financial world from a highly interconnected global financial market. Specifically, the sharp increase in securitization during the beginning of the 2000s integrated financial markets across the world and led to an unexpected *systemic risk*. *Systemic risk* is the possibility that an event, such as a failure of a single firm, could have a serious effect on the entire economy.

The beginning of the crisis occurred in the housing sectors in five states in the United States, namely: Arizona, California, Florida, Nevada, and Virginia. The housing market crash in these five states caused financial markets across the world to momentarily break down. How could

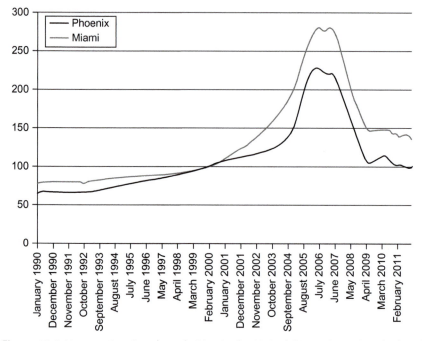

Figure 11.1 House prices in selected cities in the United States. *From Standard and Poors' Shiller-Case Home Price Index, authors' calculation, February 2012.*

the housing market in a few states cause such a big effect? The answer lies in the way mortgage lending has become an international market. Fig. 11.1 shows the home prices in two big US cities. These two cities are typical for the price behavior in the five states, experiencing the housing market crash. Fig. 11.1 shows how from 2001 to 2006 home prices rapidly increased, and then in 2007 the prices fell back down even faster. Note that, in particular, in 2004–06 the prices in both cities show a remarkable rise.

The sharp fall in home price in the United States appeared to have been a surprise for home speculators and also for some mortgage investors. The delinquency rates on mortgages rose to unprecedented levels, as seen in Fig. 11.2. The large increase in foreclosures and short sales, following the fall of home prices, resulted in mortgage losses to banks and other financial investors. However, such losses were not confined only to the domestic US financial markets. Instead, financial markets across the world were affected by the US mortgage problems.

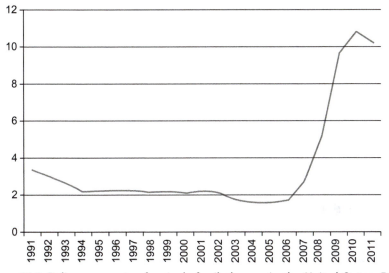

Figure 11.2 Delinquency rates for single-family homes in the United States. *From Mortgage Bankers Association, authors' calculations, January 2011.*

The reason for the spread of the losses across the world was the high degree of securitization of the US mortgages. The process of home ownership in the United States involves a loan originator, using money from an original lender for the mortgage. The original lender rarely holds the loan, instead bundling mortgages into a *Mortgage Backed Security* (MBS). This practice enables the loan originator to continue lending, thereby increasing the availability of mortgage funds. The loan originator charges a fee, but does not end up with the risk of the loan not being repaid. The fact that the loan originator did not end up holding the mortgage resulted in less careful screening of individuals applying for home loans.

Once the original lender has a sufficient number of mortgages, the lender will bundle the mortgages into an MBS. An MBS is a number of different mortgages that are bundled together and sold in such a way that different MBS products have different risk levels. In this way, investors can choose how high a risk they are willing to accept. To reduce the risk, one can also buy a hedge for default risk, such as a *Credit Default Swap* (CDS) that we discussed in Chapter 4, Forward–Looking Market Instruments.

The MBS makes it easy for investors across the world to invest in the US housing market. It is almost impossible for a foreign bank to offer a mortgage to an individual in the United States, because of the monitoring costs of the loan. However, an MBS is a bundle of mortgages with a specific risk. Thus international investors do not need to worry about what the MBS contains. This made international investment in MBSs particularly attractive. In addition, the MBS could be hedged using the CDS market, which made the international investors feel protected. Therefore, loans to individuals that are seen as risky (subprime or nonprime loans) increased with the introduction of the MBS market. According to DiMartino and Duca (2007) nonprime loans increased from 9% of new mortgages in 2001 to 40% in 2006.

The MBS and CDS markets grew sharply in 2004–07. The CDS market was $6.4 trillion in 2004 and grew to $57.9 trillion in 2007. However, the protection had one flaw: There still was a *counterparty risk*. A counterparty risk is the risk that a firm that is part of the hedge defaults. Thus, one can set up a perfect hedge against default risk of the MBS, but if one firm that sold you the CDS defaults then your investment is suddenly unhedged. Once your portfolio is unhedged, your chance of default increases. Thus, one firm defaulting can have a spreading effect across financial institutions and individuals across the globe. In general, this systemic risk seems to have been unanticipated by the financial market.

In March 2008, the first major problem appeared with Bear Stearns, an investment bank in the United States, nearing bankruptcy. Bear Stearns was highly interconnected with both domestic and international financial markets through MBSs and CDSs. To forestall the systemic risk possibility, the Federal Reserve and Treasury decided to intervene. However, when Lehman Brothers ran into the same type of problem in October 2008, it was allowed to go into bankruptcy. At the time of its bankruptcy, Lehman had close to a million CDS contracts, with hundreds of firms all over the world. Therefore the ripple effects from Lehman Brothers default were felt throughout the world with the cost of risk hedges increasing sharply and many banks and financial firms edging closer to bankruptcy. In the United States, Countrywide (the largest US mortgage lender) failed and Fannie Mae and Freddie Mac (the largest backers of mortgages in the United States) were taken over by the government. In addition, the world's largest insurance company, AIG, became virtually bankrupt in October 2008, primarily due to CDS problems. In the rest of the world, major financial companies defaulted or were taken over by the government. For example, in the United Kingdom Northern Rock and Bradford & Bingley were taken over by the UK government, while in Iceland the whole banking system defaulted pushing the entire country into default in October 2008.

The reason for the multitude of bankruptcies across the world was the high levels of *leverage* for many financial institutions. Financial institutions need to have equity to back up the loans they make. The more equity they have, the lower the leverage level. Let us assume that you have $1, and lend it to Sam for 10% interest. You now will receive an interest payment of 10 cents when the loan matures. In this example the leverage level is one, because your equity (the cash you invested in the company) is equal to your assets (the loan you made). Now assume that you want to lend $10 more to Joe. You are out of cash to lend Joe so you borrow money from Roger (at 5%) to lend to Joe (at 10%). You now have $1 in equity plus $10 in liabilities (to Roger) and assets of $11. Your leverage level is now 11 to 1. Note that the higher the leverage level, the higher your profit will be, unless someone defaults. If Joe defaults on his loan then you do not have any equity to pay back your loan, and consequently have to go bankrupt. The higher the leverage level is, the higher the risk that you will become bankrupt from a bad loan.

Traditional banks have to hold liquid capital to back up their asset portfolios. The riskier the assets are, the higher the capital that is required to hold. To prevent bank insolvency, the *Bank for International Settlements*, located in Switzerland, sets the international rules for capitalization of banks. The most recent framework is called the Basel III rules. In addition to the Basel III regulation, the Federal Reserve sets additional rules for US banks. In contrast, investment banks and hedge funds have fewer rules. Thus, they may have higher leverage levels than traditional banks. At the start of the Great Recession, many investment banks had leverage ratios of 30 to 1, meaning that 30 dollars of assets had only 1 dollar of equity. Even a small reduction in the value of the assets wiped out the equity, making the financial institution insolvent.

INTERNATIONAL LENDING AND THE GREEK DEBT CRISIS

The Greek debt crisis of 2010 followed the Great Recession and was related to the response of the financial industries to the financial crisis. Greece has struggled with fiscal deficits for a long time and succeeded in reducing the fiscal deficit far enough to join the Eurozone in 2001. Fig. 11.3 shows the fiscal deficit shrinking from more than 10% of GDP in 1995 to slightly less than 4% in 2001. However, the fiscal deficits grew worse again in the 2000s. Gradually the fiscal deficit returned to the 10% mark in 2008 and bottomed out at 16% in 2009! In addition to the fiscal deficit, Fig. 11.3 also shows the current account deficit. In the 2000s the fiscal deficit and the current account

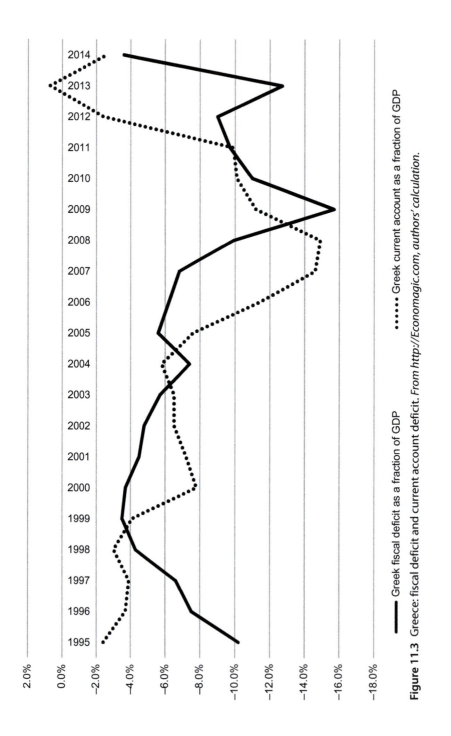

Figure 11.3 Greece: fiscal deficit and current account deficit. *From http://Economagic.com, authors' calculation.*

— Greek fiscal deficit as a fraction of GDP

•••••• Greek current account as a fraction of GDP

deficits both increase rapidly. This implies that the cause of the current account deficit was foreign capital flows financing the fiscal deficit. In Chapter 3, The Balance of Payments, we discussed such a situation as a case of "twin deficits." Government borrowing pressured up interest rates and attracted financial investment from Germany and other countries. The use of foreign funds to finance the government borrowing made it easier for Greek people to continue consuming, because they did not have to buy government debt themselves. In addition, the foreign financial flows meant that the Greek government was not pressured to reduce government spending or raise taxes to eliminate the fiscal deficit.

The convenient position of using foreign financial flows to pay for the fiscal deficit came to an end after the Great Recession. When the US financial crisis spread through the world in 2008, financial firms became cautious about taking on risk, following the default of several major financial firms. The lack of risk appetite led to a sharp increase in the cost of hedging risk. This affected firms, municipalities, states, and countries that had high indebtedness. Among the countries affected was Greece, which saw its cost of funds increasing sharply. Fig. 11.4 illustrates the added cost of borrowing for selected countries in comparison to the cost of borrowing for Germany. The figure illustrates that the cost of borrowing for Greece was at par with Germany in 2007 and only slightly more in 2008–09. However, in the 2010–12 period the cost of borrowing

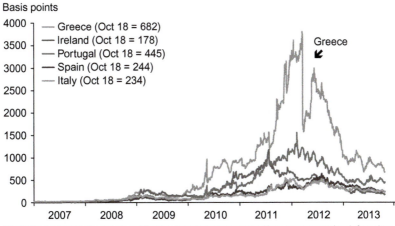

NOTE: The chart shows the spread, or difference, in interest rates between 10-year government bonds for various countries and German 10-year government bonds.

Figure 11.4 Borrowing rates for selected European countries. *From Globalization & Monetary Policy Institute, Federal Reserve of Dallas.*

skyrocketed for Greece. At one point Greece had to pay over 3500 basis points (35 percentage points) more than Germany! The tremendously high borrowing costs meant that the Greek government had to increase its borrowing just to finance the cost of borrowing. Clearly this was not a sustainable position. In May 2010 Greece had no choice but to ask the IMF for assistance. In the next section, we look at how the role of the IMF has changed from supervising the Bretton Woods system to a lender of last resort.

IMF CONDITIONALITY

The IMF has been an important source of loans for debtor nations experiencing repayment problems. The importance of an IMF loan is more than simply having the IMF "bail out" commercial bank and government creditors. The IMF requires borrowers to adjust their economic policies to reduce balance of payments deficits and improve the chance for debt repayment. Such IMF-required adjustment programs are known as *IMF conditionality.*

Part of the process of developing a loan package includes a visit to the borrowing country by an IMF mission. The mission comprises economists who review the causes of the country's economic problems and recommend solutions. Through negotiation with the borrower, a program of conditions attached to the loan is agreed upon. The conditions usually involve targets for macroeconomic variables, such as money supply growth or the government deficit. The loan is disbursed at intervals, with a possible cutoff of new disbursements if the conditions have not been met.

The importance of IMF conditionality to creditors can now be understood. Loans to sovereign governments involve risk management from the lenders' point of view just as loans to private entities do. Although countries cannot go out of business, they can have revolutions or political upheavals leading to a repudiation of the debts incurred by the previous regime. Even without such drastic political change, countries may not be able or willing to service their debt due to adverse economic conditions. International lending adds a new dimension to risk since there is neither an international court of law to enforce contracts nor any loan collateral aside from assets that the borrowing country may have in the lending country. The IMF serves as an overseer that can offer debtors new loans if they agree to conditions. Sovereign governments may be offended if a foreign creditor government or commercial bank suggests changes in the debtor's domestic policy, but the IMF is a multinational organization of over 180 countries. The members of the IMF mission to the debtor nation will be of many different nationalities, and their advice will be nonpolitical. However, the IMF is still criticized at times as being dominated by the interests of the advanced industrial countries. In terms of voting power, this is true.

Votes in the IMF determine policy, and voting power is determined by a country's quota. The quota is the financial contribution of a country to the IMF and it entitles membership. Each country receives 250 votes, plus one additional vote for each SDR100,000 of its quota. (At least 75% of the quota may be contributed in domestic currency, with less than 25% paid in reserve currencies or SDRs.) Table 11.2 shows that the United States has by far the most votes, at 16.6% of the total votes. Japan and China follow with slightly more than 6% of the votes. Although the BRIC countries (Brazil, Russia, India, and China) are becoming more powerful in terms of votes, the United States, Japan, Germany, France, and the United Kingdom together have almost 40% of the votes in the IMF. With such a large share of the votes, these five developed countries can dominate voting, especially with the help of other smaller European countries.

The IMF has been criticized for imposing conditions that restrict economic growth and lower living standards in borrowing countries. The typical conditionality involves reducing government spending, raising taxes, and restricting money growth. For example, in May 2010, Greece signed

Table 11.2 Top 10 countries with most votes in the IMF 2016

Country	Votes (in %)
United States	16.6
Japan	6.2
China	6.1
Germany	5.3
France	4.1
United Kingdom	4.1
Italy	3
India	2.6
Russia	2.6
Brazil	2.2

Source: From http://IMF.org

a €30 billion loan agreement with the IMF. In addition, the European Union agreed to provide funds making the total financing package reach €110 billion. At the heart of the agreement Greece would impose fiscal discipline that would reduce the budget deficit from its 15.4% level in 2009, to well below 3% of GDP by 2014. To accomplish this the Greek authorities committed to reduce government spending and increase taxes. Note that in this case monetary growth was not an issue as Greece belonged to the Eurozone and cannot adjust monetary growth.

In the original statement by the IMF and Greek authorities, it is recognized that the austerity package could lead to short-run output contraction. However, the view was that the structural reforms and fiscal discipline would improve the competitiveness and long-run recovery of the economy. Such policies may be interpreted as austerity imposed by the IMF, but the austerity is intended for the borrowing government in order to permit the productive private sector to play a larger role in the economy.

The view of the IMF is that adjustment programs are unavoidable in debtor countries facing repayment difficulties. However, the short-run contraction can be quite burdensome. In Greece, for example, the unemployment rate increased substantially. Fig. 11.5 shows the Greek unemployment rate. From a usual unemployment at or below 10% the unemployment skyrocketed to over 25% in a 5-year period. With one in four unemployed it leaves citizens with much time to be upset about the current conditions.

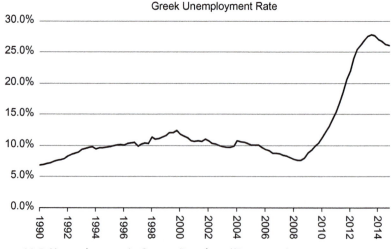

Figure 11.5 Unemployment in Greece. *From http://Economagic.com*

Consequently it is no surprise that Greece has had more than a half dozen changes in government since 2009. The IMF maintains that adjustments required are those that promote long-run growth. While there may indeed be short-run costs of adjusting to a smaller role for government and fewer and smaller government subsidies, in the long run the required adjustments should stimulate growth to allow debt repayment.

THE ROLE OF CORRUPTION

Corrupt practices by government officials have long reduced economic growth. Payment of money or gifts in order to receive a government service or benefit is quite widespread in many countries. Research shows that there is a definite negative relationship between the level of corruption in a country and both investment and growth.

Research shows that corruption thrives in countries where government regulations create distortions between the economic outcomes that would exist with free markets and the actual outcomes. For instance, a country where government permission is required to buy or sell foreign currency will have a thriving black market in foreign exchange where the black market exchange rate of a US dollar costs much more domestic currency than the "official rate" offered by the government. This distortion allows government officials an opportunity for personal gain by providing access to the official rate.

Generally speaking, the more competitive a country's markets are, the fewer the opportunities for corruption. So policies aimed at reducing corruption typically involve reducing the discretion that public officials have in granting benefits or imposing costs on others. This may include greater transparency of government practices and the introduction of merit-based competitions for government employment. Due to the sensitive political nature of the issue of corruption in a country, the IMF has only recently begun to include this issue in its advisory and lending functions. When loans from the IMF or World Bank are siphoned off by corrupt politicians, the industrial countries providing the major support for such lending are naturally concerned and pressure the international organizations to include anticorruption measures in loan conditions. In the late 1990s, both the IMF and World Bank began explicitly including anticorruption policies as part of the lending process to countries when severe corruption is ingrained in the local economy.

COUNTRY RISK ANALYSIS

International financial activity involves risks that are missing in domestic transactions. There are no international courts to enforce contracts and a bank cannot repossess a nation's collateral, because typically no collateral is pledged. Problem loans to sovereign governments have received most of the publicity, but it is important to realize that loans to private firms can also become nonperforming because of capital controls or exchange rate policies. In this regard, even operating subsidiary units in foreign countries may not be able to transfer funds to the parent multinational firm, if foreign exchange controls block the transfer of funds.

It is important for commercial banks and multinational firms to be able to assess the risks involved in international deals. *Country risk analysis* has become an important part of international business. *Country risk analysis* refers to the evaluation of the overall political and financial situation in a country and the extent to which these conditions may affect the country's ability to repay its debts. In determining the degree of risk associated with a particular country, we should consider both qualitative and quantitative factors. The qualitative factors include the political stability of the country. Certain key features may indicate political uncertainty:

1. Splits between different language, ethnic, and religious groups that threaten to undermine stability.
2. Extreme nationalism and aversion to foreigners that may lead to preferential treatment of local interests and nationalization of foreign holdings.
3. Unfavorable social conditions, including extremes of wealth.
4. Conflicts in society evidenced by frequency of demonstrations, violence, and guerrilla war.
5. The strength and organization of radical groups.

Besides the qualitative or political factors, we also want to consider the financial factors that allow an evaluation of a country's ability to repay its debts. Country risk analysts examine factors such as these:

1. *External debt.* Specifically, this is the debt owed to foreigners as a fraction of GDP or foreign exchange earnings. If a country's debts appear to be relatively large, then the country may have future repayment problems.
2. *International reserve holdings.* These reserves indicate the ability of a country to meet its short-term international trade needs should its export earnings fall. The ratio of international reserves to imports is used to rank countries according to their liquidity.

3. *Exports.* Exports are looked at in terms of the foreign exchange earned as well as the diversity of the products exported. Countries that depend largely on one or two products to earn foreign exchange may be more susceptible to wide swings in export earnings than countries with a diversified group of export products.

4. *Economic growth.* Measured by the growth of real GDP or real per capita GDP, economic growth may serve as an indicator of general economic conditions within a country.

Although no method of assessing country risk is foolproof, by evaluating and comparing countries on the basis of some structured approach, international lenders have a base on which they can build subjective evaluations of whether to extend credit to a particular country.

Recognizing the desire of investors to have reliable information about country risk, *BlackRock Investment Institute* launched a new ranking of country risk in 2011. This ranking ranks countries according to the likelihood of debt default, devaluation of the currency or above-trend deflation. Foreign investors would not only be concerned about a country defaulting on the debt, but would also be concerned about a sharp loss of the foreign currency value by a high inflation or devaluation of the currency.

There are four components to BlackRock's country risk analysis:

1. *Fiscal Space*, with a 40% weight, examines several macroeconomic factors that could lead to a debt path that is unsustainable.

2. *External Finance Position*, with a 20% weight, examines the vulnerability of a country to external shocks.

3. *Financial Sector Health*, with a 10% weight, measures the risk exposure that the private sector banks impose on the country's financial health.

4. *Willingness to Pay*, with a 30% weight, measures how a country's institutions can handle debt payment.

The first three components deal with a country's ability to pay, whereas the last one deals with the willingness to pay. Fig. 11.6 shows the results of the July 2015 ranking of country risk.

The Scandinavian countries are ranked very high in the index. Norway leads the index, with Sweden, Finland, and Denmark also in the top 10. Norway has extremely low levels of debt and has strong institutions backing the country. On the other extreme are countries with large levels of debt or high political instability. The Euro debt crisis still remains a problem resulting in Greece, Portugal, Croatia, Slovenia, and Italy ranking among the lowest 10 countries. Others among the bottom 10 countries are having political instability, such as Ukraine, Venezuela, and Egypt.

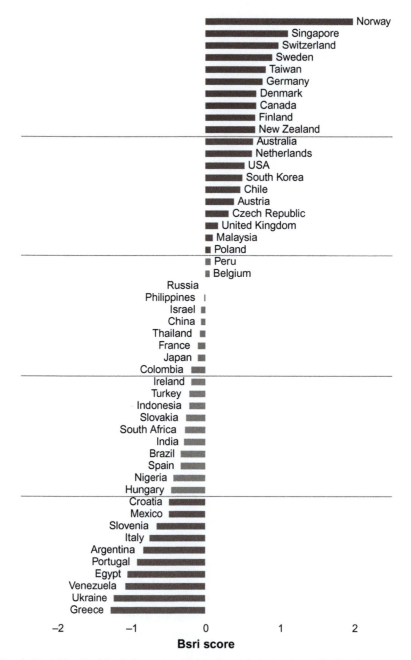

Figure 11.6 The BlackRock Sovereign Risk Index, July 2015. *From BlackRock Investment Institute. 2011. Introducing the BlackRock Sovereign Risk Index: a more comprehensive view of credit quality.*

The United States ranks 13th, close to the top among the second tier of countries in the risk index. Note also that the differences are small between the score that United States has and the scores of the five countries ahead, implying that from the view of riskiness, the top 20 countries in the ranking have a relatively low riskiness.

SUMMARY

1. The Latin American debt crisis in the 1980s had threatened the solvency of large banks and creditors, so debts were rescheduled to postpone the repayments rather than allowed for default.
2. The causes of the Asian financial crisis of 1997 were external shocks, weak macroeconomic fundamentals, and domestic financial system flaws.
3. A fixed exchange rate system, a decline in foreign reserves, and a lack of transparency in governmental activities could serve as warning indicators of potential financial crisis.
4. The Great Recession of 2008–09 in the United States spread to global financial markets because foreign investors had invested in MBSs backed by US mortgages.
5. Since the risk of MBS could be hedged by using CDS market, many investors felt protected and highly leveraged their investments. This practice led to bankruptcies of several giant investment banks.
6. When a country seeks financial assistance from IMF to overcome its problem, the government is subject to a set of agreed macroeconomic policy changes and structural reforms, known as the IMF conditionality, to ensure ability to repay the loan.
7. The IMF has included a clause of anticorruption into its lending process.
8. Country risk analysis is the evaluation of a country's overall political and financial situations that may influence the country's ability to repay its loans.
9. Country risk analysis is based on structural modeling of variables such as the amount of external debt to GDP, international reserve holdings, the volume of exports, and the pace of economic growth.

EXERCISES

1. Why would a debtor nation prefer to borrow from a bank rather than the IMF, other things being equal? Can "other things" ever be equal between commercial bank and IMF loans?

2. Pick three developing countries and create a country risk index for them. Rank them ordinally in terms of factors that you can observe (like exports, GDP growth, reserves, etc.) by looking at *International Financial Statistics* published by the IMF. Based on your evaluation, which country appears to be the best credit risk? How does your ranking compare to that found in the most recent *BlackRock Investment* survey?

3. How did each of the following contribute to the Asian financial crisis of the late 1990s: external shocks, domestic macroeconomic policy, and domestic financial system flaws?

4. Explain how the fixed exchange rate arrangement could lead to a financial crisis.

5. Imagine yourself in a job interview for a position with a large international bank. The interviewer mentions that, recently, the bank has experienced some problem loans to foreign governments. The interviewer asks you what factors you think the bank should consider when evaluating a loan proposal involving a foreign governmental agency. How do you respond?

6. Explain what a highly leveraged investment practice is. How does it relate to financial crisis?

FURTHER READING

Bird, G., Hussain, M., Joyce, J.P., 2004. Many happy returns? Recidivism and the IMF. J. Int. Money Financ. 23 (1), 231–251.

BlackRock Investment Institute, 2011. Introducing the BlackRock Sovereign Risk Index: A more Comprehensive View of Credit Quality. BlackRock Investment Institute, New York.

Brealey, R.A., Kaplanis, E., 2004. The impact of IMF programs on asset values. J. Int. Money Financ. 23 (2), 143–304.

Bullard, J., Neely, C.J., Wheelock, D.C., 2009. Systemic risk and the financial crisis: a primer. Fed. Reserve Bank St. Louis Rev 91, 403–417.

DiMartino, D., Duca, J.V., 2007. The rise and fall of subprime mortgages. Fed. Reserve Bank of Dallas Econ. Lett. 2 (11), 1–8.

Schadler, S., Bennett, A., Carkovic, M., Dicks-Mireaux, L., Mecagni, M., Morsink, J.H.J., Savastano, M.A., 1995. IMF Conditionality: Experience under Stand-By and Extended Arrangements. World Bank, Washigton, DC, International Monetary Fund Occasional Paper, No. 128.

Somerville, R.A., Taffler, R.J., 1995. Banker judgment versus formal forecasting models: the case of country risk assessment. J. Bank. Financ. 19 (2), 281–297.

Stulz, R.M., 2010. Credit default swaps and the credit crisis. J. Econ. Perspect. 24 (1), 73–92.

PART IV

Modeling the Exchange Rate and Balance of Payments

CHAPTER 12

Determinants of the Balance of Trade

Contents

Earlier chapters are full of discussions involving foreign exchange rates and the balance of payments. We now know the definitions and uses of these two important international finance terms, but have yet to consider what determines their values at any particular point in time. Why do some countries run a balance of trade surplus while others run deficits? It is worth noting that financial institutions, central banks, and governments invest many resources in trying to predict exchange rates and international trade and payments. The kinds of theories to be introduced in this chapter have shaped the way economists, investors, and politicians approach such problems. Exchange rate determination will be discussed in the next chapters.

ELASTICITIES APPROACH TO THE BALANCE OF TRADE

Economic behavior involves satisfying unlimited wants with limited resources. One implication of this fact of budget constraints is that consumers and business firms will substitute among goods as prices change to stretch their budgets as far as possible. For instance, if Italian-made shoes and US-made shoes are good substitutes, then as the price of US shoes rises relative to Italian shoes, buyers will substitute the lower-priced Italian shoes for the higher-priced US shoes. The crucial concept for determining consumption patterns is relative price—the price of one good relative to another. Relative prices change as relative demand and supply for individual goods change. Such changes may result from changes in tastes, or production technology, or government taxes or subsidies, or many other possible sources. If the changes involve prices of goods at home changing relative to foreign goods, then international trade patterns may be altered. The elasticities approach to the balance of trade is concerned with how changing relative prices of domestic and foreign goods will change the balance of trade.

A change in the exchange rate will change the domestic currency price of foreign goods. Suppose initially that a pair of shoes sells for $50 in the United States and €50 in Italy. At an exchange rate of €1 = $1, the shoes sell for the same price in each country when expressed in a common currency. If the euro is devalued to €1.2 = $1, and shoe prices remain constant in the domestic currency of the producer, then shoes selling for €50 in Italy will now cost the US buyer $41.67. After the devaluation, €1 = $0.8333, so €50 = $41.67, and the price of Italian shoes has fallen for US buyers. Conversely, the price of $50 US shoes to Italian buyers has risen from €50 to €60. The relative price effect of the euro devaluation should increase US demand for Italian goods and decrease Italian demand for US goods. How much quantity demanded changes in response to the relative price change is determined by the elasticity of demand.

In the beginning of economics courses, students learn that *elasticity* measures the responsiveness of quantity to changes in price. The *elasticities approach to the balance of trade* provides an analysis of how devaluations will affect the balance of trade depending on the elasticities of supply and demand for foreign exchange and foreign goods.

When demand or supply is elastic, it means that quantity demanded or supplied will be relatively responsive to the change in price. An inelastic demand or supply indicates that quantity is relatively unresponsive to price changes. We can make things more precise by using coefficients of elasticity. For instance, letting ε_d represent the coefficient of elasticity of demand, we can write ε_d as

$$\varepsilon_d = \%\Delta Q / \%\Delta P \qquad (12.1)$$

This implies that the coefficient of elasticity of demand is equal to the percentage change in the quantity demanded, divided by the percentage change in price. If the price increases by 5% and the quantity demanded falls by more than 5%, then ε_d exceeds 1 (in absolute value), and we say that demand is elastic. If the price increases by 5%, but quantity demanded falls by less than 5%, we would say that demand is inelastic and ε_d would be less than 1.

Just as we can compute a coefficient of elasticity of demand ε_d, so too can we compute a coefficient of elasticity of supply, ε_s, as the percentage change in the quantity supplied, divided by the percentage change in price. If ε_s exceeds 1, the quantity supplied is relatively responsive to price, and we say that supply is elastic. For ε_s less than 1, the quantity supplied is relatively unresponsive to price, so that the supply is inelastic.

Elasticity will determine what happens to total revenue (sales price times quantities sold) following a price change. For example, an elastic demand is when quantity changes exceed that of the price change. In such a case, the total revenue will move in the opposite direction from the price change. Suppose the demand for black velvet paintings from Mexico is elastic. If the peso price rises 10%, the quantity demanded falls by more than 10%, so that the revenue received from sales will fall as a result of the price change. In contrast, if the demand for Colombian coffee is inelastic, then a 10% increase in price will result in a fall in the quantity demanded of less than 10%. The high coffee price increase more than makes up for the lost sales. Thus, coffee sales revenues rise following the price change. Obviously, the elasticity of demand is very important in determining export and import revenues when international prices change.

Now let us consider an example of supply and demand in the foreign exchange market. Fig. 12.1 provides an example of the supply and demand for UK pounds. The demand curve labeled D is the demand for pounds, arising from the demand for British exports. The familiar downward slope indicates that the higher the price of pounds, the fewer the number of pounds demanded. The supply curve labeled S is the supply of pounds to the foreign exchange market. The upward slope indicates the positive relationship between the foreign exchange price of pounds and the quantity of pounds supplied. The point where the supply and demand curves intersect is the equilibrium point where the quantity of pounds demanded just equals the quantity supplied. Suppose initially we have an equilibrium at E_0 and £$_0$; that is, £$_0$ is the quantity of pounds bought and sold at the exchange rate E_0 (the dollar price of a pound). Now suppose there is an increase in demand for pounds (say, because of an increase in demand for UK exports) that shifts the demand curve to D_1. There are several possible responses to this shift in demand:

1. With freely floating exchange rates, the pound will appreciate, so that the exchange rate rises to E_1, and £$_1$ are bought and sold.

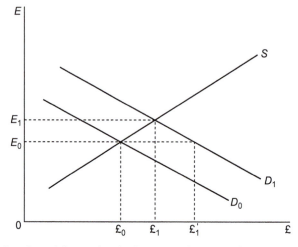

Figure 12.1 Supply and demand in the foreign exchange market.

2. Central banks can peg the exchange rate at the old rate E_0 by providing $£_1' - £_0$ from their reserves.
3. The supply and demand can be affected by imposing controls or quotas on the supply of, or demand for, pounds.
4. Quotas or tariffs could be imposed on foreign trade to maintain the old supply and demand for pounds.

The elasticities approach recognizes that the effect of an exchange rate change on the equilibrium quantity of currency being traded will depend on the elasticities of the supply and demand curves involved. It is important to remember that the elasticities approach is a theory of the balance of trade and can only be a theory of the balance of payments in a world without capital flows.

Suppose that in Fig. 12.1, the US central bank (the Federal Reserve) decides to fix the exchange rate at E_0. To do so the US central bank has to supply pounds to the market from US reserves in exchange for US dollars. Now the old exchange rate E_0 is maintained because of the central bank's addition of $£_1' - £_0$ to the market. If it becomes apparent that the increase in demand is a permanent change, then the Federal Reserve will have to devalue the dollar, driving up the dollar price of pounds. This, of course, means that UK goods will be more expensive to the United States, whereas US goods will be cheaper to the United Kingdom. Will this improve the US trade balance? It all depends on the elasticities of supply and demand. When the quantity demanded for the imports by American

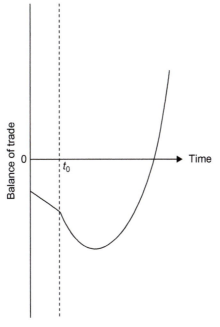

Figure 12.2 The J-curve.

consumers is not responsive to price changes, an increase in the price of imports could lead to an increase in total cost of imports. Likewise, with an inelastic demand for US exports in the United Kingdom, even though the price of imports from the United States falls, few more units are demanded. In this case, the US balance of trade deficit and the excess demand for pounds could actually increase following a devaluation. Such a response to a devaluation has been labeled a *J-curve*. The J-curve effect refers to the pattern of the balance of trade, following a devaluation. If the balance of trade is viewed over time, the initial decrease in the trade balance is followed by a growing trade balance, because of inelastic demand, and results in the time pattern of the trade balance shown in Fig. 12.2.

Note in the figure that the trade balance is initially negative, falling over time. The devaluation occurs at point t_0. Following the devaluation, the balance of trade continues to fall for a while before finally turning upward. The initial fall results from low elasticities in the short run. Over time, elasticities increase so that the balance of trade improves. This general pattern of the balance of trade falling before it increases traces a pattern that resembles the letter *J*.

ELASTICITIES AND THE J-CURVE

Devaluation is conventionally believed to be a tool for increasing a country's balance of trade. Yet the J-curve effect indicates that when devaluation increases the price of foreign goods to the home country and decreases the price of domestic goods to foreign buyers, there is a short-run period during which the balance of trade falls. We now consider the reasons for why there may be low elasticities in the short run, to see what the possible underlying reasons are for a J-curve. We can identify two different periods following a devaluation. Immediately following a devaluation the contracts that have already been negotiated become revalued. Such a period is called the *currency contract period*. Once the contracts have expired there may still be a limited response by traders. The short-run period following the expiration of contracts is called the *pass-through analysis*. During this period the traders have limited changes in the quantities in response to the new set of prices, but over time the response becomes complete. We will discuss each of these two short-run responses.

CURRENCY CONTRACT PERIOD

Immediately following a devaluation, contracts negotiated prior to the exchange rate change become due. This period is called the *currency contract period*. Fig. 12.3 illustrates the timing of events.

Contracts are signed at time t_1. After the contracts are established, there is a currency devaluation at time t_2. Then the payments specified in the contracts are due at a later period t_3. The effects of such existing contracts on the balance of trade depend on the currency in which the contract is denominated. For instance, let us suppose that the United States devalues the dollar. Before the devaluation the exchange rate is $1 per unit of foreign currency (to simplify matters, we will assume only one foreign currency); afterward the rate jumps to $1.25. If a US exporter has contracted to sell $1 worth of goods to a foreign firm payable in dollars, the exporter will still earn $1. However, if the export contract was written in terms of foreign currency (let FC stand for foreign currency), then the exporter

Contracts Signed	Currency Devaluation	Payments Due	
			Time
t_1	t_2	t_3	

Figure 12.3 The currency contract period.

expected to receive FC1, which would be equal to $1. Instead, the devaluation leads to FC1 = $1.25, so the US exporter receives an unexpected gain from the dollar devaluation. On the other hand, consider an import contract where a US importer contracts to buy from a foreign firm. If the contract calls for payment of $1, then the US importer is unaffected by the devaluation. If the contract had been written in terms of foreign currency so that the US importer owes FC1, then the importer would have to pay $1.25 to buy the FC1 that the exporter receives. In this case the importer faces a loss because of the devaluation.

In the simple world under consideration here, we would expect sellers to prefer a contract in the currency expected to appreciate, whereas buyers would prefer contracts written in terms of the currency expected to depreciate. Table 12.1 summarizes the possible trade balance effects during the currency contract period.

Table 12.1 divides the effects into four cells. Cell I represents the case in which US export contracts are written in terms of foreign currency, although import contracts are denominated in dollars. In this case the dollar value of exports will increase since the foreign buyer must pay in foreign currency, which is worth more after the devaluation. Because imports are paid for with dollars, the devaluation will have no effect on the dollar value of US imports. As a result, the balance of trade must increase.

Cell II indicates the trade balance effects when US exports and imports are paid for with foreign currency. Since the dollar devaluation increases the value of foreign currency, the dollar values of both exports

Table 12.1 US trade balance effects during currency contract period following a devaluation of the US dollar

US export contracts written in	US import contracts written in	
	Dollars	Foreign currency
Foreign currency	I. Exports increase Imports constant **Balance of trade increases**	II. Exports increase Imports increase **Initial surplus: balance of trade increases** **Initial deficit: balance of trade decreases**
Dollars	III. Exports constant Imports constant **Balance of trade unchanged**	IV. Exports constant Imports increase **Balance of trade decreases**

and imports will increase. The net effect on the US trade balance depends on the magnitude of US exports relative to imports. If exports exceed imports, so that there is an initial trade surplus, then the increase in export values will exceed the increase in imports and the balance of trade will increase. Conversely, if there is an initial trade deficit, so that imports exceed exports, then the increase in imports will exceed the increase in exports and the balance of trade will decrease.

If both exports and imports are payable in dollars, then the balance of trade is unaffected by a devaluation, as indicated in Cell III. But if exports are payable in dollars and imports require payment in foreign currency, the dollar value of exports will be unaffected by the devaluation and import values will increase; in this case the trade balance decreases as in Cell IV. Note that only in the case of Cell IV is there a decline in the trade balance during the currency contract period following a devaluation. A decline could also occur in Cell II, although only if there is an initial trade deficit. The key feature of Table 12.1 is that foreign-currency-denominated imports provide a necessary condition for the US trade balance to take the plunge observed in the J-curve phenomenon during the currency contract period.

PASS-THROUGH ANALYSIS

The currency contract period refers to the period following a devaluation when contracts negotiated prior to the devaluation come due. During this time it is assumed that goods prices do not adjust instantaneously to the change in currency values. Eventually, of course, as new trade contracts are negotiated, goods prices will tend toward the new equilibrium. *Pass-through* analysis considers the ability of prices to adjust in the short run. The kind of adjustment expected is an increase in the price of imported goods in the devaluing country and a decrease in the price of this country's exports to the rest of the world. If goods prices do not adjust in this manner, then spending patterns will not be altered, so that the desirable balance of trade effects of devaluation do not appear.

Devaluation is normally a response to a persistent and growing balance of trade deficit. As import prices rise in the devaluing country, fewer imports should be demanded. At the same time, the lower price of domestic exports to foreigners should increase the quantity demanded for exported goods. The combination of a higher demand for domestic exports and a lower domestic demand for imports should bring about

Table 12.2 US trade balance effects during pass-through period following a devaluation of the US dollar

US exports	US imports	
	Inelastic supply	Inelastic demand
Inelastic supply	I. Exports increase Imports constant **Balance of trade increases**	II. Exports increase Imports increase **Initial surplus: balance of trade increases** **Initial deficit: balance of trade decreases**
Inelastic demand	III. Exports constant Imports constant **Balance of trade constant**	IV. Exports constant Imports increase **Balance of trade decreases**

an improvement in the trade balance. In the short run, however, if the response to the new prices is so slow that the quantities traded do not change much, then the new prices could contribute to the J curve. For instance, if the demand for imports is inelastic, then buyers will be relatively unresponsive to the higher price of imports, and thus the total import bill could rise rather than fall after the devaluation. Such behavior is not unreasonable since it takes time to find good substitutes for the now higher-priced import goods. Eventually, such substitutions will occur. However, in the short-run buyers may continue to buy imports in large enough quantities so that the now higher price results in a greater rather than a smaller value of domestic imports after the devaluation. The same explanation could hold on the other side of the market if foreign demand for domestic exports is inelastic. In this case, foreign buyers will not buy much more in the short run, even though the price of domestic exports has fallen.

Table 12.2 summarizes the possible effects following a US devaluation during the brief pass-through period before quantities adjust. The worst case is presented in Cell IV. With an inelastic demand for US imports and an inelastic demand for US exports, there will be a full pass-through of prices.

The effects of a devaluation, summarized in Table 12.2, assume that the inelastic demand or supply holds the quantity fixed. To illustrate the pass-through effects we show the underlying supply and demand in Fig. 12.4. Fig. 12.4A illustrates the case of perfectly inelastic demand for US imports.

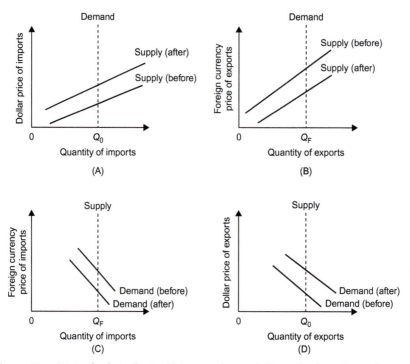

Figure 12.4 (A) Perfectly inelastic US import demand; (B) perfectly inelastic demand for US exports; (C) perfectly inelastic supply of US imports; (D) perfectly inelastic supply of US exports.

Who demands US imports? US buyers, so the relevant price in Fig. 12.4A is the dollar price of imports. Note that the US demand for imports is fixed at Q_0. This means that in the short run, US importers will buy Q_0 at any relevant price. After the devaluation, the supply curve shifts to the left, representing the fact that foreign exporters now want to charge a higher dollar price for their exports to the United States because the dollar is worth less. The vertical distance between the old and the new supply curves indicates how much more sellers wish to charge for any given quantity. Since the demand curve is a vertical line, fixed at Q_0, sellers will be able to pass through the full amount of the desired price increase to importers; thus importers will be buying Q_0 at a higher price than before, and the total dollar value of imports will increase. This is the situation in Cell IV of Table 12.2, where the US balance of trade decreases because of the full pass-through.

Fig. 12.4B shows why exports remain constant in Cell IV. In this case the foreigners' demand for US exports is perfectly inelastic. Because foreign buyers purchase US exports, the relevant price is the foreign currency price in Fig. 12.4B. Foreign buyers want to purchase Q_F amount of US exports regardless of the price in the short run. Note that now the relevant price to foreign buyers is the foreign currency price. After the devaluation, the supply curve shifts to the right to reflect the fact that US exporters are willing to sell goods for less foreign currency because foreign currency is now worth more. However, with the perfectly inelastic demand curve, there is a full pass-through, lowering the foreign currency price by the full amount of the devaluation. In other words, if the devaluation increased the value of foreign currency by 10%, the foreign currency price of US exports falls by 10% and the total dollar value of US exports remains constant.

Note that Cell III of Table 12.2 pairs the inelastic demand for US exports, as just discussed, with an inelastic supply of US imports. Fig. 12.4C illustrates the effect of the inelastic supply. Since imports into the United States are supplied by foreign sellers, the relevant price is the foreign currency price in Fig. 12.4C. In this case, foreign sellers will sell Q_F imports to the United States independent of price. After the devaluation, the US demand for imports in terms of foreign currency shifts to the left, indicating that buyers are willing to pay fewer units of foreign currency than before for a given quantity of imports. Because the supply curve is perfectly inelastic, the foreign currency price of imports falls by the amount of the devaluation, and thus there is no pass-through. In other words, the pass-through effect is completely offset by a fall in the foreign currency price of imports. After a dollar devaluation we expect imports to become more expensive to the United States; yet with a perfectly inelastic import supply curve, as in Fig. 12.4C, US dollar import prices are unchanged so that the dollar value of imports is also unchanged.

Cell II of Table 12.2 couples the inelastic US import demand, as previously discussed and illustrated in Fig. 12.4A, with an inelastic supply of US exports. Fig. 12.4D shows the supply effect. Because US exports are supplied by US sellers, the dollar price is the relevant price in Fig. 12.4D. After the devaluation, foreigners are willing to pay a higher dollar price for US exports because dollars are cheaper. With the perfectly inelastic supply curve, the dollar price of exports rises by the full amount of the devaluation. Thus, rather than having a devaluation pass-through lower US export prices to foreigners, the increase in dollar prices has foreign buyers paying the same price as before (because the foreign currency price is unchanged). But the higher dollar price results in an increase in the dollar value of US exports. Since the inelastic demand for US imports also causes the dollar value of imports to increase, the net result for the balance of trade depends on whether initially exports exceeded imports, in which case the increase in exports after the devaluation will be larger than the import increase. If imports initially exceeded exports, then the devaluation will lower the trade balance.

Finally, we have the case of Cell I, where the balance of trade clearly increases during the pass-through period when quantities are fixed. The inelastic supply of US exports leads to an increase in the dollar value of US exports, whereas the inelastic supply of imports results in the value of imports holding constant.

The portrayal of perfectly inelastic supply and demand curves is made for illustrative purposes. We cannot argue that in the real world there is absolutely no quantity response to changing prices in the short run. The important contribution of the pass-through analysis is to indicate how changing goods prices in the short run, when the quantity response is likely to be quite small, can affect the balance of trade. If it is more reasonable to expect producers to be less able to alter quantities supplied than buyers can alter quantity demanded, then Cell I of Table 12.2 is the most likely real-world case. In this instance, the supplies of US imports and exports are inelastic, so the US trade balance should improve during the pass-through period.

THE MARSHALL–LERNER CONDITION

Table 12.2 shows that the problematic case for the effect of a devaluation on the balance of trade is the case when the demand elasticity for imports is perfectly inelastic and the demand for exports is also perfectly inelastic (Cell IV). In this case the trade balance will not improve. As we just pointed out the zero elasticity case is an extreme case. What would then be the minimum elasticities of the demand for imports and demand for exports that is needed to improve the balance of trade? Alfred Marshall and Abba Lerner derived the necessary value, and this condition has become known as the *Marshall–Lerner condition*. The Marshall–Lerner condition states that the absolute value of the sum of the elasticities of the demand for imports and the demand for exports has to be greater than unity.

Rather than looking at the mathematical proof we can see the intuition using our cases in Fig. 12.4. Take the case in Fig. 12.4A, where the

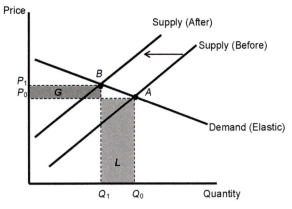

Figure 12.5 Elastic demand for imports.

demand for imports is perfectly inelastic. This case implies that domestic residents do not find any substitutes for the import and continue importing the same quantity no matter what the price is. With this assumption the import price goes up at the equivalent rate of the devaluation and the total value of imports always increases. However, if the demand for imports is elastic, then there will be a change in the quantity imported. Fig. 12.5 shows that the quantity demanded will decrease from Q_0 to Q_1, when the currency is devalued, if the demand for imports is not completely inelastic. In other words, domestic residents will find domestic substitutes and consume less of the imports when the import price goes up. Thus, the total imports have two areas. The rectangle G is an increase in the value of imports, whereas the area L is a decrease in the value of imports. The combination of these areas will determine the total change to the value of imports. Similarly, an elastic demand for exports will create a positive effect of the total value of exports.

Thus, the Marshall–Lerner condition explains the J-curve effect. If the sum of the short-run elasticities of demand for imports and the demand for exports is below unity, then the balance of trade will worsen. However, if in the longer run the elasticities increase so that the sum is now above unity, then the balance of trade will improve. It is very likely that long-run elasticities are higher than short-run ones, because consumers will find domestic substitutes in the long run. Thus, the combination of the short-run and long-run elasticities may cause a J-curve like shape for the response of the balance of trade to a devaluation.

THE EVIDENCE FROM DEVALUATIONS

The preceding discussion has shown the possible short-run effects of a devaluation on the trade balance through the currency contract and pass-through periods. What does the evidence of past devaluations have to offer regarding the *actual* effects? Unfortunately, the available evidence suggests that the effects of devaluation appear to differ across countries and time so that no strong generalizations are possible.

Some authors show that devaluation improves the trade account in the short run, while others disagree. The reasons for such disagreement come from the fact that different researchers use different sample periods and different statistical methodology. Several researchers have focused on the manner in which producers in different countries adjust the profit margins on exports to partially offset the effect of exchange rate changes. This appears to be an important factor in explaining differences in the pass-through effect across countries. For instance, if the Japanese yen appreciates against the US dollar, the yen appreciation would tend to be passed through to US importers as a higher dollar price of Japanese exports. Japanese exporters could limit this pass through of higher prices by reducing the profit margins on their products and lowering the yen price to counter the effect of the yen appreciation. This *pricing to market* behavior has been found to be especially prevalent among Japanese and German exporters but is much less common among US exporters. For example, Gagnon and Knetter (1995) analyzed automobile trade and estimated that a 10% depreciation of the dollar against the yen would result in Japanese auto firms reducing their prices so that the dollar price to US importers would rise by only 2.2%. There was no similar evidence of US auto firms reducing prices for exported autos in response to dollar appreciation. Klitgaard (1996) found that Japanese exporters tend to lower their profit margins on exports by 4% (relative to margins on domestic sales) for every 10% appreciation of the yen. He also showed that in addition to cutting profit margins, in the 1990s Japanese exporters responded to yen appreciation by shifting production to high-valued products that are less sensitive to price increases. The Japanese resistance to allowing pass-through effects is another reason why the Japanese balance of trade may be less responsive to exchange rate changes than the US trade balance.

There is some evidence that the impact of devaluations may differ over the short run and long run depending upon what happens to labor costs relative to the cost of capital. Forbes (2002) has found that in the short run following a devaluation, firm output and exports tend to rise as the cost of labor in the devaluing country falls and firms take advantage of this to expand production and increase their export sales. However, over time, capital becomes more expensive to firms in the devaluing country if the risk associated with that country rises or interest rates rise. So the net effect of devaluation depends upon the mix of capital and labor utilized in a nation's export industries. The evidence from a cross section of countries suggests that in countries where the ratio of capital to labor employed is low, devaluations are much more likely to result in export expansion and faster economic growth. But in countries where the capital/labor ratio is high, devaluations will tend to have little if any expansionary influence on exports and economic growth.

ABSORPTION APPROACH TO THE BALANCE OF TRADE

The elasticities approach showed that it is possible for a country to improve its balance of trade through devaluation. Once the exchange rate effects pass through to import and export prices, imports should fall while exports increase, stimulating production of goods and services and income at home. However, this does not always seem to occur. If a country is at the full-employment level of output prior to the devaluation, then it is already producing all it can so that no further output can be forthcoming. What happens in this case following a devaluation? We now turn to the absorption approach to the balance of trade to answer this question.

The *absorption approach to the balance of trade* is a theory that emphasizes how domestic spending on domestic goods changes relative to domestic output. In other words, the balance of trade is viewed as the difference between what the economy produces and what it takes, or absorbs, for domestic use. As commonly treated in introductory economics classes, we can write total output, Y, as being equal to total expenditures, or

$$Y = C + I + G + (X - M) \qquad (12.2)$$

where C is consumption; I, investment; G, government spending; X, exports; and M, imports. We can define absorption, A, as being equal to $C + I + G$, and net exports as $(X - M)$. Thus we can write:

$$Y = A + X - M$$

or

$$Y - A = X - M \qquad (12.3)$$

Absorption, A, is supposed to represent total domestic spending. Thus, if total domestic production, Y, exceeds absorption (the amount of the output consumed at home), then the nation will export the rest of its output and run a balance of trade surplus. In contrast, if absorption exceeds domestic production, then $Y - A$ will be negative; thus by Eq. (12.3), we note that $X - M$ will also be negative, which has the common-sense interpretation that the excess of domestic demand over domestic production will be met through imports.

The analysis of the absorption approach is really broken down into two categories, depending upon whether the economy is at its full-employment level or has unemployed resources. At the full employment, all resources are being used so that the only way for net exports to increase is to have absorption fall. On the other hand, with unemployment, Y is not at its maximum possible value, and thus Y could increase due to increases in exports, X, without changing the domestic absorption, A.

The absorption approach is generally concerned with the effects of a devaluation on the trade balance. If we begin from the case of unemployed resources, we know that domestic output, Y, could increase, so that a devaluation would tend to increase net exports (if the elasticity conditions discussed in the previous section are satisfied) and bring about an increase in output (given a constant absorption). If we start from Y, at the full-employment level, it will not be possible to produce more goods and services. If we devalue, then net exports will tend to increase and the result is strictly inflation. When foreigners try to spend more on our domestic production, and yet there is no increase in output forthcoming, the only result will be a bidding-up of the prices of the goods and services currently being produced.

In the past chapter, we discussed how the IMF has been criticized for imposing conditions that restrict economic growth and lower living standards in borrowing countries. The typical conditionality involves reducing government spending, raising taxes, and restricting money growth. Note that these types of policies are exactly what the absorption approach prescribes. To increase the likelihood of paying back loans, countries need to decrease A. Such policies may be interpreted as austerity imposed by the IMF, but they are intended to reduce A, to make the country more likely to pay back international loans.

Of course, we must realize that the absorption approach is providing a theory of the balance of trade, as did the elasticities approach. The absorption approach can be viewed as a theory of the balance of payments only in a world without capital flows.

SUMMARY

1. This chapter discussed why the domestic currency devaluation does not necessarily improve the balance of trade, especially in the short run.

2. The elasticity of demand (supply) describes how responsive the quantities demanded (supplied) are to a change in price.

3. The elasticities approach to the balance of trade explains how various degrees of elasticities of demand and supply of imported goods could affect the balance of trade.

4. A devaluation of the domestic currency raises the price of foreign goods relative to the domestic goods. As prices of imports are increasing, the total payments to importers could rise or fall depending on the elasticities of demand for imports.

5. The J-curve describes the pattern of the balance of trade after the currency devaluation such that the trade balance falls in the beginning and then rises later.

6. The J-curve effect could be a result of currency contract period and pass-through price adjustment.

7. Since some international exchange contracts are signed before and the payments are collected after the currency devaluation, the devaluation could worsen the balance of trade when the export contracts are written in domestic currency and the import contracts are written in foreign currency.

8. The balance of trade will worsen from a currency devaluation, if there is a full pass-through, resulting in higher import prices and lower export prices.

9. The Marshall–Lerner condition indicates that if the sum of absolute values of the elasticities of demand for imports and demand for exports is greater than one, a currency devaluation could improve the balance of trade.

10. Empirically, there is no consensus whether devaluation of a currency can improve the trade account in the short run.

11. The domestic absorption is the total domestic spending on domestically produced goods by consumers, business firms, and government.

12. According to the absorption approach, the effects of the currency devaluation on trade balance depend not only on whether an economy is operating at its full employment, but also whether the domestic absorption changes during the devaluation. At the full-employment level, if the domestic absorption remains constant, the currency devaluation will not change the balance of trade.

EXERCISES

1. Suppose that the United States is considering devaluing its dollar against a foreign currency to improve the trade balance. What type of currency contracting would have a negative effect on the trade balance?
2. Suppose that the United States is considering devaluing its dollar against a foreign currency to improve the trade balance. What type of pass-through effects would lead to a positive effect on the trade balance?
3. Suppose that the United States is considering devaluing its dollar against a foreign currency to improve the trade balance. Use the absorption approach to explain how the United States can improve its trade balance from the currency devaluation, if the country is currently operating in the full-employment level of output.
4. Give examples of policies that a country could implement to reduce its absorption.
5. What is the J-curve? Explain.
6. How can we use the Marshall–Lerner condition to explain the J-curve effect?

FURTHER READING

Allen, M., 2006. Exchange Rates and Trade Balance Adjustment in Emerging Market Economies. International Monetary Fund. October.

Baek, J., Koo, W.W., Mulik, K., 2009. Exchange rate dynamics and the bilateral trade balance: the case of U.S. agriculture. Agr. Resour. Econ. Rev. 38 (2), 213–228.

Devereaux, M.B., 2000. How does a devaluation affect the current account? J. Int. Money Financ. 19 (6), 833–851.

Devereux, M.B., Engel, C., Storgaard, P.E., 2004. Endogenous exchange rate pass-through when nominal prices are set in advance. J. Int. Econ. 63 (2), 263–291.

Forbes, K., 2002. Cheap labor meets costly capital: the impact of devaluations on commodity firms. J. Dev. Econ. 69, 335–365.

Gagnon, J.E., Knetter, M.M., 1995. Markup adjustment and exchange rate fluctuations: evidence from panel data on automobile exports. J. Int. Money Financ. April.

Gopinath, G., Itskhoki, O., Rigobon, R., 2010. Currency choice and exchange rate pass-through. Am. Econ. Rev. 100 (1), 304–336.

Klitgaard, T., 1996. Coping with the rising yen: Japan's recent export experience. Cur. Issues Econ. Financ. January.

Klitgaard, T., 1999. Exchange rates and profit margins: the case of Japanese exporters. FRBNY Econ. Policy Rev. April.

Koray, F., McMillin, W.D., 1999. Monetary shocks, the exchange rate, and the trade balance. J. Int. Money Financ. December.

Rose, A., 1991. The role of exchange rates in a popular model of international trade: does the 'Marshall–Lerner condition' hold? J. Int. Econ. 3–4, 301–316.

Rose, A., 1996. Are all devaluations alike? FRBSF Econ. Lett. February.

CHAPTER 13

The IS-LM-BP Approach

Contents

An economy open to international trade and payments will face different problems than an economy closed to the rest of the world. The typical introductory economics presentation of macroeconomic equilibrium and policy is a closed-economy view. Discussions of economic adjustments required to combat unemployment or inflation do not consider the rest of the world. Clearly, this is no longer an acceptable approach in an increasingly integrated world.

In the open economy, we can summarize the desirable economic goals as being the attainment of internal and external balance. *Internal balance* means a steady growth of the domestic economy consistent with a low unemployment rate. *External balance* is the achievement of a desired trade balance or desired international capital flows. In principles of economics classes, the emphasis is on internal balance. By concentrating solely on internal goals like inflation, unemployment, and economic growth, simpler-model economies may be used for analysis. A consideration of the joint pursuit of internal and external balance calls for a more detailed view of the economy. The slight increase in complexity yields a big payoff in terms of a more realistic view of the problems facing the modern policy maker. It is no longer a question of changing policy to change unemployment or inflation at home. Now the authorities must also consider the impact on the balance of trade, capital flows, and exchange rates.

THE INTERNAL AND EXTERNAL MACROECONOMIC EQUILIBRIUM

The major tools of macroeconomic policy are fiscal policy (government spending and taxation) and monetary policy (central bank control of the money supply). These tools are used to achieve macroeconomic equilibrium. We assume that macroeconomic equilibrium requires equilibrium in three major sectors of the economy:

1. *Goods market equilibrium.* The quantity of goods and services supplied is equal to the quantity demanded. This is represented by the *IS* curve.
2. *Money market equilibrium.* The quantity of money supplied is equal to the quantity demanded. This is represented by the *LM* curve.
3. *Balance of payments equilibrium.* The current account deficit is equal to the capital account surplus, so that the official settlements definition of the balance of payments equals zero. This is represented by the *BP* curve.

We will analyze the macroeconomic equilibrium with a graph that summarizes equilibrium in each market. Fig. 13.1 displays the *IS-LM-BP* diagram. This graph illustrates various combinations of the domestic interest rate (i) and domestic national income (Y) that yield an equilibrium in the three markets considered here.

THE IS CURVE

First, let us examine the *IS curve*, which represents combinations of i and Y that provide equilibrium in the goods market when everything else (like the price level) is held constant. Y refers to the total output as well as the total income in the economy. Equilibrium occurs when the output of goods and services is equal to the quantity of goods and services demanded. In principles of economics classes, macroeconomic equilibrium is said to exist when the "leakages equal the injections" of spending in the economy. More precisely, domestic saving (S), taxes (T), and imports (IM) represent income received that is not spent on domestic goods and

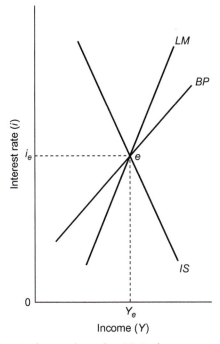

Figure 13.1 Equilibrium in the goods market (*IS*), in the money market (*LM*), and in the balance of payments (*BP*).

services—the leakages from spending. The offsetting injections of spending are represented by investment spending (*I*), government spending (*G*), and exports (*X*). Investment spending is the spending of business firms for new plants and equipment.

Equilibrium occurs when

$$S + T + IM = I + G + X \qquad (13.1)$$

When the leakages from spending equal the injections, then the value of income received from producing goods and services will be equal to total spending, or the quantity of output demanded. The *IS* curve in Fig. 13.1 depicts the various combinations of *i* and *Y* that yield the equality in Eq. (13.1). We now consider why the *IS* curve is downward sloping.

We assume that *S* and *IM* are both functions of income and that taxes are set by governments independent of income. The higher that domestic income, the more domestic residents want to save. Furthermore, the higher income will also enable domestic residents to spend more on

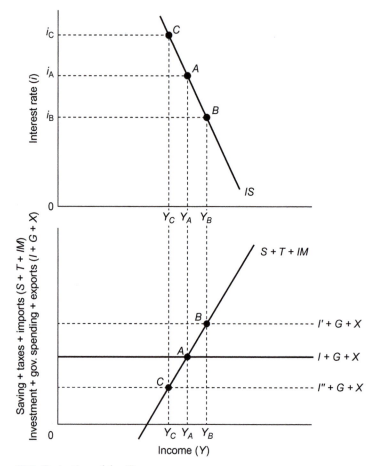

Figure 13.2 Derivation of the *IS* curve.

imports. In the bottom panel of Fig. 13.2, the $S + T + IM$ line is upward sloping. This illustrates that the higher domestic income rises, the greater are savings plus taxes plus imports. Investment is assumed to be a function of the domestic interest rate and so does not change as current domestic income changes. Similarly, exports are assumed to be determined by foreign income (they are foreign imports) and so do not change as domestic income changes. Finally, government spending is set independent of income. Since I, G, and X are all independent of current domestic income, the $I + G + X$ line in the bottom panel of Fig. 13.2 is drawn as a horizontal line.

Eq. (13.1) indicated that equilibrium occurs at that income level where $S + T + IM = I + G + X$. In the bottom panel of Fig. 13.2, point A represents an equilibrium point with an equilibrium level of income Y_A. In the upper panel of the figure, Y_A is shown to be consistent with point A on the IS curve. This point is also associated with a particular interest rate i_A.

To understand why the IS curve slopes downward, consider what happens as the interest rate varies. Suppose the interest rate falls. At the lower interest rate, more potential investment projects become profitable (firms will not require as high a return on investment when the cost of borrowed funds falls), so investment increases as illustrated in the move from $I + G + X$ to $I' + G + X$ in Fig. 13.2. At this higher level of investment spending, equilibrium income increases to Y_B. Point B on the IS curve depicts this new goods market equilibrium, with a lower equilibrium interest rate i_B and higher equilibrium income Y_B.

Finally, consider what happens when the interest rate rises. Investment spending will fall, because fewer potential projects are profitable as the cost of borrowed funds rises. At the lower level of investment spending, the $I + G + X$ curve shifts down to $I'' + G + X$ in Fig. 13.2. The new equilibrium point C is consistent with the level of income Y_C. In the IS diagram in the upper panel we see that point C is consistent with equilibrium income level Y_C and equilibrium interest rate i_C. The other points on the IS curve are consistent with alternative combinations of income and interest rate that yield equilibrium in the goods market.

We must remember that the IS curve is drawn holding the domestic price level constant. A change in the domestic price level will change the price of domestic goods relative to foreign goods. If the domestic price level falls with a given interest rate, then investment, government spending, taxes, and saving will not change. However, domestic goods are now cheaper relative to foreign goods, leading to exports increasing and imports falling. The rise in the $I + G + X$ curve and the fall in the $S + T + IM$ curve would both increase income. Because income increases with a constant interest rate, the IS curve shifts to the right. A rise in the domestic price level would cause the IS curve to shift left.

THE LM CURVE

The LM *curve* in Fig. 13.1 displays the alternative combinations of i and Y at which the demand for money equals the supply. Fig. 13.3 provides a derivation of the LM curve. The left panel shows a money demand curve

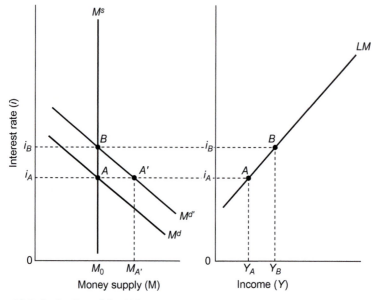

Figure 13.3 Derivation of the *LM* curve.

labeled M^d and a money supply curve labeled M^s. The horizontal axis measures the quantity of money and the vertical axis measures the interest rate. Note that the M^s curve is vertical. This is so because the central bank can choose any money supply it wants, independent of the interest rate. The actual value of the money supply chosen is M_0. The money demand shows, for a fixed amount of wealth, how much people are willing to hold in money form, as opposed to interest-bearing assets. The money demand curve slopes downward, indicating that the higher the interest rate, the lower the quantity of money demanded.

The inverse relationship between the interest rate and quantity of money demanded is a result of the role of interest as the opportunity cost of holding money. Since money earns no interest, the higher the interest rate, the more you must give up to hold money, so less money is held.

The initial money market equilibrium occurs at point A with interest rate i_A. The initial money demand curve, M^d, is drawn for a given level of income. If income increased, then the demand for money would increase, as seen in the shift from M^d to $M^{d'}$. Money demand increases because, at the higher level of income, people want to hold more money to support the increased spending on transactions.

Now let us consider why the *LM* curve has a positive slope. Suppose initially there is equilibrium at point *A* with the interest rate at i_A and income at Y_A in Fig. 13.3. If income increases from Y_A to Y_B, money demand increases from M^d to $M^{d'}$. If the interest rate remains at i_A, there will be an excess demand for money. This is shown in the left panel of Fig. 13.3, as the quantity of money demanded is now $M_{A'}$. With the higher income, money demand is given by $M^{d'}$. At i_A, point A' on the money demand curve is consistent with the higher quantity of money demanded, $M_{A'}$. Since the money supply remains constant at M_0, there will be an excess demand for money given by $M_{A'} - M_0$. The attempt to increase money balances above the quantity of money outstanding will cause the interest rate to rise until a new equilibrium is established at point *B*. This new equilibrium is consistent with a higher interest rate i_B and a higher income Y_B. Points *A* and *B* are both indicated on the *LM* curve in the right panel of Fig. 13.3. The rest of the *LM* curve reflects similar combinations of equilibrium interest rates and income.

The *LM* curve is drawn for a specific money supply. If the supply of money increases, then money demand will have to increase to restore equilibrium. This requires a higher *Y* or lower *i*, or both, so the *LM* curve will shift right. Similarly, a decrease in the money supply will tend to raise *i* and lower *Y*, and the *LM* curve will shift to the left.

THE BP CURVE

The final curve portrayed in Fig. 13.1 is the *BP* curve. The *BP curve* gives the combinations of *i* and *Y* that yield balance of payments equilibrium. The *BP* curve is drawn for a given domestic price level, a given exchange rate, and a given net foreign debt. Equilibrium occurs when the current account surplus is equal to the capital account deficit. Recall from Chapter 3, The Balance of Payments that if there is a current account deficit, then it has to be financed by a capital account surplus.

Fig. 13.4 illustrates the derivation of the *BP* curve. The lower panel of the figure shows a *CS* line, representing the current account surplus, and a *CD* line, representing the capital account deficit. Realistically, the current account surplus may be negative, which would indicate a deficit. Similarly, the capital account deficit may be negative, indicating a surplus. The *CS* line is downward sloping because as income increases, domestic imports increase and the current account surplus falls. The capital account is assumed to be a function of the interest rate and is, therefore, independent of income and a horizontal line.

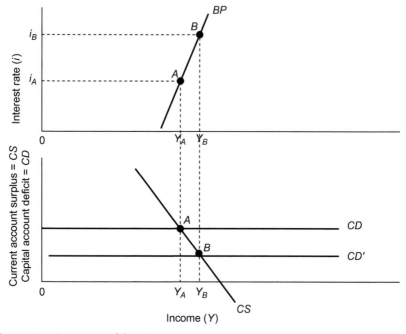

Figure 13.4 Derivation of the *BP* curve.

Equilibrium occurs when the current account surplus equals the capital account deficit, so that the official settlements balance of payments is zero. Initially, equilibrium occurs at point *A* with income level Y_A and interest rate i_A. If the interest rate increases, then domestic financial assets are more attractive to foreign buyers and the capital account deficit falls to *CD'*. At the old income level Y_A, the current account surplus will exceed the capital account deficit, and income must increase to Y_B to provide a new equilibrium at point *B*. Points *A* and *B* on the *BP* curve in Fig. 13.4 illustrate that, as *i* increases, *Y* must also increase to maintain equilibrium. Only an upward sloping *BP* curve will provide combinations of *i* and *Y* consistent with equilibrium.

In deriving the *BP* curve, we assumed that higher interest rates in the domestic economy would attract foreign investors and decrease the capital account deficit. If capital is perfectly mobile for any income level, then any deviation of the domestic interest rate from the foreign rate would cause investors to attempt to hold only the high return assets. Therefore, the *BP* curve becomes perfectly horizontal in the case of perfectly mobile

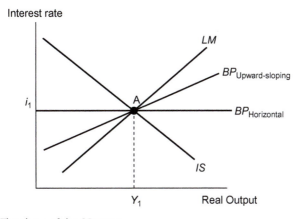

Figure 13.5 The slope of the *BP* curve.

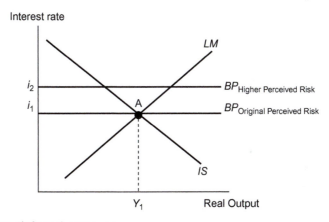

Figure 13.6 Shifts in the *BP* curve.

capital. If foreign capital is not perfectly available then the *BP* curve will be upward sloping. If there are many restrictions to capital mobility then the *BP* curve will become close to vertical. Fig. 13.5 illustrates a perfectly horizontal *BP* curve and an upward sloping *BP* curve.

It is also important to realize that the *BP* curve can shift whether it is upward sloping or horizontal. For example, a changing foreign perception of the substitutability shifts the *BP* curve. This is an intercept change, and thus the entire schedule shifts. For example, in Fig. 13.6 one can see how an increase in the perception of riskiness of a country's assets causes the *BP* curve to shift upward. Thus, interest rates are not equal across countries even with perfect capital mobility. For example, Indonesia may have a positive risk premium, so that investors demand a certain added premium for financing Indonesia's trade deficits. However, as long as that particular risk premium is paid, investors are willing to finance the trade deficit.

EQUILIBRIUM

Equilibrium for the economy requires that all three markets—the goods market, the money market, and the balance of payments—be in equilibrium. This occurs when the *IS, LM,* and *BP* curves intersect at a common equilibrium level of the interest rate and income. In Fig. 13.1, point *e* is the equilibrium point that occurs at the equilibrium interest rate i_e and the equilibrium income level Y_e. Until some change occurs that shifts one of the curves, the *IS-LM-BP* equilibrium will be consistent with all goods produced being sold, money demand equal to money supply, and a current account surplus equal to a capital account deficit that yields a zero balance on the official settlements account.

MONETARY POLICY UNDER FIXED EXCHANGE RATES

With fixed exchange rates, the domestic central bank is not free to conduct monetary policy independently from the rest of the world. If domestic and foreign assets are perfect substitutes, then they must yield the same return to investors. Clearly, in this case there is no room for central banks to conduct an independent monetary policy under fixed exchange rates.

Fig. 13.7 illustrates this situation. With perfect asset substitutability, the *BP* curve is a horizontal line at the domestic interest rate *i*, which equals

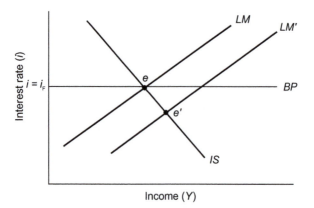

Figure 13.7 Monetary expansion with fixed exchange rates.

the foreign interest rate i_F. Any rate higher than i_F results in large (infinite) capital inflows, while any lower rate yields large capital outflows. Only at i_F is the balance of payments equilibrium obtained.

Suppose the central bank increases the money supply so that the LM curve shifts from LM to LM'. The IS-LM equilibrium is now shifted from e to e'. While e' results in equilibrium in the money and goods market, there will be a large capital outflow and large official settlements balance deficit. This will pressure the domestic currency to depreciate on the foreign exchange market. To maintain the fixed exchange rate, the central bank must intervene and sell foreign exchange to buy domestic currency. The foreign exchange market intervention will decrease the domestic money supply and shift the LM curve back to LM to restore the initial equilibrium at e. With perfect capital mobility, this would all happen instantaneously, so that no movement away from point e is ever observed. Any attempt to lower the money supply and shift the LM curve to the left would have just the reverse effect on the interest rate and intervention activity.

If capital mobility is less than perfect, then the central bank has some opportunity to vary the money supply. Still, the maintenance of the fixed exchange rate will require an ultimate reversal of policy in the face of a constant foreign interest rate. The process is essentially just drawn out over time rather than occurring instantly.

FISCAL POLICY UNDER FIXED EXCHANGE RATES

A change in government spending or taxes will shift the IS curve. Suppose an expansionary fiscal policy is desired. Fig. 13.8 illustrates the effects. With fixed exchange rates, perfect asset substitutability, and perfect capital mobility, the BP curve is a horizontal line at $i = i_F$. An increase in government spending shifts the IS curve right to IS'. The domestic equilibrium shifts from point e to e', which would mean a higher interest rate and higher income. Since point e' is above the BP curve, the official settlements balance of payments moves to a surplus because of a reduced capital account deficit associated with the higher domestic interest rate. To stop the domestic currency from appreciating, the central bank must increase the money supply and buy foreign exchange with domestic money. The increase in the money supply shifts the LM curve to the right. When the money supply has increased enough to move the LM curve to LM' in Fig. 13.8, equilibrium is restored at point e''. Point e'' has the interest rate back at $i = i_F$, and yet income has increased.

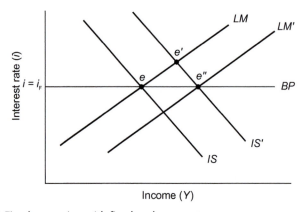

Figure 13.8 Fiscal expansion with fixed exchange rates.

This result is a significant difference from the monetary policy expansion considered in the preceding section. With fixed exchange rates and perfect capital mobility, monetary policy was seen to be ineffective in changing the level of income. This was so because there was no room for independent monetary policy with a fixed exchange rate. In contrast, fiscal policy will have an effect on income and can be used to stimulate the domestic economy.

MONETARY POLICY UNDER FLOATING EXCHANGE RATES

We now consider a world of flexible exchange rates and perfect capital mobility. The notable difference between the analysis in this section and the fixed exchange rate stories of the previous two sections is that with floating rates the central bank is not obliged to intervene in the foreign exchange market to support a particular exchange rate. With no intervention, the current account surplus will equal the capital account deficit so that the official settlements balance equals zero. In addition, since the central bank does not intervene to fix the exchange rate, the money supply can change to any level desired by the monetary authorities. This independence of monetary policy is one of the advantages of flexible exchange rates.

The assumptions of perfect substitutability of assets and perfect capital mobility will result in $i = i_F$ as before. Once again, the BP curve will be a horizontal line at $i = i_F$. Only now, equilibrium in the balance of payments will mean a zero official settlements balance. Changes in the exchange rate will cause shifts in the IS curve. With fixed domestic and foreign goods

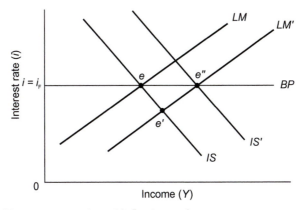

Figure 13.9 Monetary expansion with floating exchange rates.

prices, depreciation of the domestic currency will make domestic goods relatively cheaper and will stimulate domestic exports. Since net exports are part of total spending, the *IS* curve will shift rightward. A domestic currency appreciation will decrease domestic net exports and cause the *IS* curve to shift to the left.

Fig. 13.9 illustrates the effects of an expansionary monetary policy. The increase in the money supply shifts the *LM* curve to the right to *LM'*. The interest rate and income existing at point *e'* would yield equilibrium in the money and goods markets but would cause a larger capital account deficit (and official settlements deficit) since the domestic interest rate would be less than i_F. Since this is a flexible exchange rate system, the official settlements deficit is avoided by adjusting the exchange rate to a level that restores equilibrium. Specifically, the pressure of the official settlements deficit will cause the domestic currency to depreciate. This depreciation is associated with a rightward shift of the *IS* curve as domestic exports increase. When the *IS* curve shifts to *IS'*, the new equilibrium is obtained at *e''*. At e'', income has increased and the domestic interest rate equals the foreign rate.

Had there been a monetary contraction instead of an expansion, the story would have been reversed. A temporarily higher interest rate would decrease the capital account deficit, causing pressure for the domestic currency to appreciate. As domestic net exports are decreased, the *IS* curve shifts to the left until a new equilibrium is established at a lower level of income and the original $i = i_F$ is restored.

In contrast to the fixed exchange rate world, monetary policy can change the level of income with floating exchange rates. Since the exchange rate adjusts to yield balance of payments equilibrium, the central bank can choose its monetary policy independent of other countries' policies. This world of flexible exchange rates and perfect capital mobility is often called the *Mundell–Fleming model* of the open economy. (Robert Mundell, Nobel Laureate in Economics in 1999, and Marcus Fleming were two early researchers who developed models along the lines of those presented here.)

FISCAL POLICY UNDER FLOATING EXCHANGE RATES

An expansionary fiscal policy caused by a tax cut or increased government spending will shift the *IS* curve to the right. Earlier it was shown that with fixed exchange rates, such a policy would result in a higher domestic income level. With flexible exchange rates, we will see that the story is much different.

In Fig. 13.10, the expansionary fiscal policy shifts the *IS* curve right, from *IS* to *IS'*. This shift would result in an intermediate equilibrium at point e'. At e', the goods market and money market will be in equilibrium, but there will be an official settlements surplus because of the lower capital account deficit induced by the higher interest rate at e'. Since the exchange rate is free to adjust to eliminate the balance of payments surplus, the intersection of the *IS* and *LM* curves cannot remain above the *BP* curve.

The official settlements surplus causes the domestic currency to appreciate. This appreciation will reduce domestic exports and increase imports. As net exports fall, the *IS* curve shifts left. When the *IS* curve has returned to the initial equilibrium position that passes through point e, equilibrium is restored

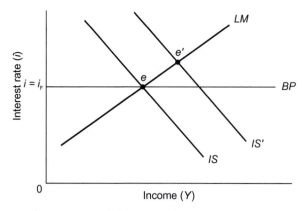

Figure 13.10 Fiscal expansion with floating exchange rates.

in all markets. Note that the final equilibrium occurs at the initial level of i and Y. With floating exchange rates, fiscal policy is ineffective in shifting the level of income. When an expansionary fiscal policy has no effect on income, complete *crowding out* has occurred. Crowding out means that the positive effect on income is offset by a reduction of income from another factor. For example, when the economy moves from e to e' the investment spending will be reduced. This will partially crowd out the positive effect of the expansionary fiscal policy. However, when the domestic currency appreciates and the economy returns to e, then the crowding out effect occurs because the currency appreciation induced by the expansionary fiscal policy reduces net exports to a level that just offsets the fiscal policy effects on income.

USING THE IS-LM-BP APPROACH: THE ASIAN FINANCIAL CRISIS

The Asian financial crisis, illustrated in Fig. 13.11, provides an interesting example of how the IS-LM-BP framework can be used to explain real-world events. In early 1997, foreign investors became worried that assets in Thailand were riskier than in other countries. Thus, the Thai assets and assets in other countries were no longer perfect substitutes. Instead, foreign investors required a positive risk premium to hold Thai assets. This shifted the BP curve up from BP_1 to BP_2. The original starting point A was no longer a viable equilibrium, because capital flows were no longer available at the same interest rates. To protect the fixed exchange rate, the Bank of Thailand had to buy Thai baht and sell dollar foreign reserves, resulting in

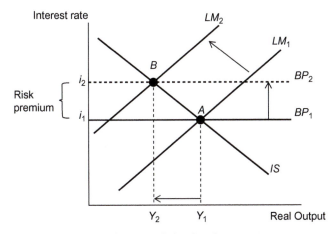

Figure 13.11 The Asian financial crisis with fixed exchange rates.

a reduction in money supply in Thailand. This shifted the *LM* curve from LM_1 to LM_2. This monetary tightening also caused the domestic interest rates to sharply increase, crowding out domestic private investment. Thailand went into a deep recession.

Speculators sensed that the Bank of Thailand could not keep on protecting the Thai baht. Therefore they sold their assets denominated in Thai baht and bought dollar assets. This led to further pressure on the Thai baht to depreciate. After a considerable effort in trying to protect the fixed exchange rate, the Thai government and Bank of Thailand decided to allow the exchange rate to float on July 2, 1997. The Thai baht immediately depreciated from 25 baht per dollar to over 50 baht per dollar. With a floating rate the response to the risk premium demanded by the speculators looks very different. In Fig. 13.12, monetary policy, i.e., the *LM* curve, is unaffected. However, the sharp depreciation that happened once the Thai baht was allowed to float resulted in an increase in the domestic competitiveness, shown in Fig. 13.12 as a shift in the *IS* curve from IS_1 to IS_2. The depreciation led to the beginning of a recovery for Thailand.

Speculators who sold their assets denominated in Thai baht and bought dollar assets were rewarded when the Thai baht sharply depreciated. Therefore they continued their speculation activity in neighboring countries, causing the crisis to spread in Southeast Asia. Within 6 months speculators successfully attacked the fixed exchange rates in four neighboring countries, Indonesia, South Korea, Philippines, and Malaysia. In each case the countries allowed their currencies to float after a considerable effort to try to protect the currency.

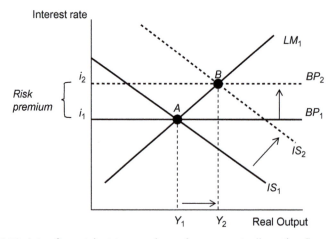

Figure 13.12 Asian financial crisis once the exchange rate is allowed to float.

FAQ: How Did the Asian Financial Crisis Start?

In early 1997, hedge funds believed that the Thai baht was pegged at a too high value and took positions against the baht. The central bank of Thailand did not allow the Thai baht to float, but instead heavily supported it, spending about US$30 billion in a 6-month period. The response by the central bank caused losses to the speculators, but made them even more determined to bet against the Thai baht. The hedge funds knew that the central bank could not maintain its defense over a longer period, and renewed their bets. On one single day alone, on May 14, 1997, speculators had bet US$10 billion against the baht. To compound the problems for Thailand, Japanese banks decided to move assets out of Thailand. The Japanese banks were some of the biggest investors in Thailand, but were already hurt by domestic debt defaults. Therefore, they were quick to withdraw their assets from Thailand.

Pressure from speculators, combined with internal political pressure, finally became too much, and the baht was allowed to float on July 2, 1997. The figure illustrates the collapse of the Thai baht in 1997. The Thai baht fluctuated slightly around about 25 baht per dollar until the central bank announced the float of baht in 1997. After the announcement, the baht depreciated sharply to slightly above 50 baht per dollar, recovering slightly to about 40 baht per dollar.

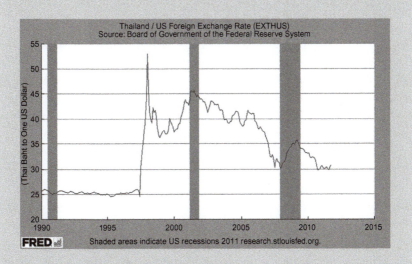

The Thai baht per US dollar from 1990 to 2011.

The speculators who were persistent enough to keep speculating against the Thai baht were handsomely paid when the Thai baht depreciated by almost 20% in a single day.

So why not allow the Thai baht to float earlier? A fixed exchange rate encourages banks and firms not to cover the exchange rate exposure. Thus, banks had short-term loans in dollars and long-term investments in Thai baht. A devaluation of the Thai baht would create difficulty for banks in Thailand, as the cost of paying their debt would exceed the return on their long-term investments. This is typical for many developing countries in that the government encourages local investment and borrows from capital rich developed countries. Thus, banks in Thailand had a large number of loans in dollars and payments in baht. After the depreciation of the dollar, most of the banks and financial firms went bankrupt, with over 50 banks and financial firms taken over by the Thai government in the end of 1997.

INTERNATIONAL POLICY COORDINATION

From the early 1970s onward, the major developed nations have generally operated with floating exchange rates. The IS–LM–BP framework, analyzed in this chapter, has shown that fiscal and monetary policy can generate large swings in floating exchange rates. Economists have been debating how to coordinate policies across countries, because of the potential disruptive effect of exchange rate volatility on world trade.

The high degree of capital mobility existing among the developed countries suggests that fiscal actions that lead to a divergence of the domestic interest rate from the given foreign interest rate will quickly be undone by the influence of exchange rate changes on net exports, as was illustrated in Fig. 13.10. For example, many economists argue that the sharp increase in the dollar value in the early 1980s was due to the expansionary fiscal policy followed by the US government. How could such exchange rate volatility be minimized? If all nations coordinated their domestic policies and simultaneously stimulated their economies, the world interest rate would rise. Thus, the pressure for an exchange rate change for a particular country (in the above case, the United States) would disappear. The problem illustrated in Fig. 13.10 was that of a single country attempting to follow an expansionary policy while the rest of the world retained unchanged policies, so that i_F remains constant. If i_F increased at the same time that i increased, the BP curve would shift upward and the balance of payments equilibrium would be consistent with a higher interest rate.

Similarly, changes in exchange rates and net exports induced by monetary policy can be lessened if central banks coordinate policy so that i_F

shifts with i. There have been instances of coordinated foreign exchange market intervention when a group of central banks jointly followed policies aimed at a depreciation or appreciation of the dollar. These coordinated interventions, intended to achieve a target value of the dollar, also work to bring domestic monetary policies more in line with each other. If the United States has been following an expansionary monetary policy relative to Japan, US interest rates may fall relative to the other country's rates, so that a larger capital account deficit is induced and pressure for a dollar depreciation results. If the central banks decide to work together to stop the dollar depreciation, the Japanese will buy dollars on the foreign exchange market with their domestic currencies, while the Federal Reserve must sell foreign exchange to buy dollars. This will result in a higher money supply in Japan and a lower money supply in the United States. The coordinated intervention works toward a convergence of monetary policy in each country.

The basic argument in favor of international policy coordination is that such coordination would stabilize exchange rates. Whether exchange rate stability offers any substantial benefits over freely floating rates with independent policies is a matter of much debate. Some experts argue that coordinated monetary policy to achieve fixed exchange rates or to reduce exchange rate fluctuations to within narrow target zones would reduce the destabilizing aspects of international trade in goods and financial assets when currencies become overvalued or undervalued. This view emphasizes that in an increasingly integrated world economy, it seems desirable to conduct national economic policy in an international context rather than by simply focusing on domestic policy goals without a view of the international implications.

An alternative view is that most changes in exchange rates result from real economic shocks and should be considered permanent changes. In this view, there is no such thing as an overvalued or undervalued currency because exchange rates always are in equilibrium given current economic conditions. Furthermore, governments cannot change the real relative prices of goods internationally by driving the nominal exchange rate to some particular level through foreign exchange market intervention, because price levels will adjust to the new nominal exchange rate. This view, then, argues that government policy is best aimed at lowering inflation and achieving governmental goals that contribute to a stable domestic economy.

The debate over the appropriate level and form of international policy coordination has been one of the livelier areas of international finance in recent years. Many leading economists have participated, but a problem at the practical level is that different governments emphasize different goals and may view the current economic situation differently. Ours is a more complex world in which to formulate international policy agreements than is typically viewed in scholarly debate, where it is presumed that governments agree on the current problems and on the impact of alternative policies on those problems. Nevertheless, the research of international financial scholars offers much promise in contributing toward a greater understanding of the real-world complexities government officials must address.

SUMMARY

1. The desired economic outcome in an open economy is to achieve both internal balance and external balance at the same time.
2. Internal balance refers to a domestic equilibrium condition such that goods market and money market are in equilibrium and unemployment is at its natural level.
3. External balance requires the balance of payments to be in equilibrium. The condition implies zero balance on the official settlement— the current account surplus must be equal to the capital account deficit.
4. The *IS* curve represents the combinations of income and interest rate levels that bring the good market to equilibrium (i.e., leakages equals to injections).
5. The *LM* curve represents the combinations of income and interest rate levels that bring the money market to equilibrium (i.e., money demand equals to money supply).
6. The *BP* curve represents the combinations of income and interest rate levels that bring the balance of payments to equilibrium (i.e., current account surplus equals to capital account deficit).
7. The internal and external equilibriums occur when three curves intersect at one point.
8. The factors that shift the *IS* curve are a change in domestic price level, a change in exchange rate, and a change in fiscal policy variable.
9. The factor that shifts the *LM* curve is a change in money supply.
10. The slope of the *BP* curve depends on the degree of capital mobility. In the case of perfect capital mobility between countries, the *BP* curve is horizontal.

11. The factor that shifts the *BP* curve is a change in perception of asset substitutability.
12. With perfect substitutability and perfect capital mobility, the domestic interest rate is equal to the foreign interest rate.
13. With fixed exchange rates, a country cannot conduct an independent monetary policy to change domestic income. Only fiscal policy is effective in changing equilibrium income.
14. With floating exchange rates, monetary policy is effective in changing domestic income. However, fiscal policy has no effect on income because of a complete crowding out effect from the balance of payments adjustment.
15. International policy coordination is an idea that aims to stabilize the exchange rates by coordinating each country's fiscal and monetary policies to achieve the best international outcome.

EXERCISES

1. Explain the difference between a closed-economy and an open economy. Explain also how the pursuit of internal equilibrium will be different between the two types of economies.
2. Consider the IS-LM-BP model of an open economy with a constant price level, perfect asset substitutability, and perfect capital mobility. The economy is initially in both internal and external equilibrium.
   a. Explain why the *BP* curve is a horizontal line at $i = i_F$, where i is the domestic nominal interest rate and i_F is the foreign nominal interest rate.
   b. Define the internal equilibrium and external equilibrium of the economy, respectively.
3. From question 2, suppose now that the domestic economy decides to reduce its money supply.
   a. What are the initial effects of this monetary policy on the goods market, the money market, the foreign exchange market, and the balance of payments of the domestic economy? Which curve(s) will shift?
   b. What is the adjustment mechanism under a fixed exchange rate regime? Illustrate and explain which curve(s) will shift during the adjustment, and then compare the new equilibrium with the initial equilibrium.
   c. What is the adjustment mechanism under a flexible exchange rate regime? Illustrate and explain which curve(s) will shift during the adjustment, and then compare the new equilibrium with the initial equilibrium.

4. From question 2, suppose now that the domestic government decides to increase the government spending.

    a. What are the initial effects of this fiscal policy on the goods market, the money market, the foreign exchange market, and the balance of payments of the domestic economy? Which curve(s) will shift?

    b. What is the adjustment mechanism under a fixed exchange rate regime? Illustrate and explain which curve(s) will shift during the adjustment, and then compare the new equilibrium with the initial equilibrium.

    c. What is the adjustment mechanism under a flexible exchange rate regime? Illustrate and explain which curve(s) will shift during the adjustment, and then compare the new equilibrium with the initial equilibrium.

5. If a country has a surplus balance of payments, what will be the appropriate government policy to restore the balance of payments back to equilibrium? What effects might this have on the country's income?

6. What is an international policy coordination? Explain why it is difficult to adopt an international policy coordination in practice.

FURTHER READING

Canzoneri, M., Cumby, R.E., Diba, B.T., 2005. The need for international policy coordination: what's old, what's new, what's yet to come? J. Int. Econ. 66 (2), 363–384.

Fan, L.S., Fan, C.M., 2002. The Mundell–Fleming model revisited. Am. Econ. 46 (1), 42–49.

Fleming, M., 1962. Domestic financial policies under fixed and under floating exchange rates. IMF. Staff. Pap. November.

Ghosh, A., 1986. International policy coordination in an uncertain world. Econ. Lett. (3).

King, M., 2001. Who triggered the Asian financial crisis? Rev. Int. Polit. Econ. 8 (3), 438–466.

Melvin, M., Taylor, M., 2009. The crisis in the foreign exchange market. J. Int. Money Financ. 28 (8), 1317–1330.

Mundell, R.A., 1963. Capital mobility and stabilization policy under fixed and flexible exchange rates. Can. J. Econ. November.

Obstfeld, M., Rogoff, K., 1995. Exchange rate dynamics redux. J. Polit. Econ. June.

Soros, G., 2000. Open Society: Reforming Global Capitalism. PublicAffairs, New York.

APPENDIX A   THE OPEN ECONOMY MULTIPLIER

We can use the macroeconomic model developed in this chapter to analyze the effects of changes in spending on the equilibrium level of national income, assuming the interest rate is unchanged. We begin with the basic macroeconomic equilibrium conditions seen in the bottom half of Fig. 13.2:

$$S + T + IM = I + G + X \qquad (13.A1)$$

In equilibrium, the planned level of saving plus taxes plus imports must equal the planned level of investment plus government spending plus exports. To find the equilibrium levels of national income (Y) and net exports ($X - IM$), we must make some assumptions regarding the variables in Eq. (13.A1). Specifically, we assume that saving and imports both depend on the level of national income. The greater the domestic income, the more people want to save, and the more they want to spend on imports. The fraction of any extra income that people want to save is called the *marginal propensity to save*, which we will denote as s. The fraction of any extra income that people want to spend on imports is called the *marginal propensity to import*, which we will denote as m. So, $S = sY$ and $IM = mY$. The rest of the variables in Eq. (13.A1)—T, I, G, and X—are assumed to be exogenously determined by factors other than domestic income.

With these assumptions, we can substitute the new specifications of S and IM and rewrite Eq. (13.A1) as

$$sY + T + mY = I + G + X \qquad (13.A2)$$

Gathering our Y terms and subtracting T from each side of the equation, we have $(s + m) Y = I + G + X - T$. Solving for the equilibrium level of Y yields

$$Y = (I + G + X - T)/(s + m) \qquad (13.A3)$$

If I, G, or X increased by \$1, the equilibrium level of Y would increase by $1/(s + m)$ times \$1. An increase in T would cause Y to fall. The value of $1/(s + m)$ is known as the *open economy multiplier*. This multiplier is equal to the reciprocal of the marginal propensity to save (s) plus the marginal propensity to import (m). Since s and m will both be some fraction less than 1, we expect this multiplier to exceed 1, so that an increase in I, G, or X spending would cause the equilibrium level of national income to rise by more than the change in spending.

Let us consider an example of this multiplier effect. Suppose that we return to the model of Fig. 13.2 as redrawn in Fig. 13.A1. In this model economy, the marginal propensity to save is 0.3, the marginal propensity to import is 0.2, taxes equal 20, and investment, government spending, and exports each equal 10 (assume the units are billions of dollars). In this case, the macroeconomic model is given by

$$S + T + IM = .3Y + 20 + .2Y = .5Y + 20 \qquad (13.A4)$$

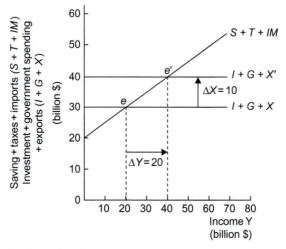

Figure 13.A1 The effect of an increase in exports.

and

$$I + G + X = 10 + 10 + 10 = 30 \qquad (13.\text{A}5)$$

These two equations are drawn in Fig. 13.A1 as the $S + T + IM$ line and the $I + G + X$ line. The point of intersection occurs at e, where the equilibrium level of national income equals $20 billion.

The equilibrium level of income could have been found by using Eq. (13.A3) and substituting the values given for each variable:

$$Y = (I + G + X - T)/(s + m) = 10/.5 = 20 \qquad (13.\text{A}6)$$

Whether we solve for the equilibrium level of Y algebraically or graphically, we find the value of $20 billion.

What would happen if exports increased? For instance, suppose exports increase from $10 to $20 billion. In Fig. 13.A1, the $I + G + X$ line shifts up by the amount of the increase in exports to $I + G + X'$. The two lines are parallel because they differ by a constant $10 billion, the increase in exports, at each level of income. The new equilibrium level of income is found by the new point of intersection e' at an income level of $40 billion. Note that exports increase by 10, yet income increases by 20, from the original equilibrium level of 20 to the new level of 40. Since the increase in equilibrium national income is twice the increase in exports, the open economy multiplier must equal 2. Algebraically, the multiplier is $1/(s + m)$, which, in the example, is $1/(0.3 + 0.2) = 1/0.5 = 2$. An increase in I, G, or X would increase Y by twice the increase in spending in our example.

The intuition behind the multiplier effect is taught in principles of economics courses. If spending, such as export spending, rises in some industry, then there is an increase in the income of factors employed in that industry. These employed resource owners, such as laborers, will increase their spending on goods and services and further stimulate production, which further raises income and spending. This "multiplier effect" has a finite value because not all of the increased income is spent in the domestic economy. Some is saved and some is spent on imports. Saving and imports act as leakages from domestic spending that serve to limit the size of the multiplier. The larger the marginal propensity to save, and the larger the marginal propensity to import, the smaller the multiplier.

In the real-world, such multiplier effects will be more complex due to the presence of taxes and feedback effects from the rest of the world. However, the essential point—that changes in spending may create much larger changes in the national income—remains. Stable growth of the economy requires stable growth of spending.

CHAPTER 14

The Monetary Approach

Contents

The basic premise of the *monetary approach* is that any balance of payments disequilibrium or exchange rate movement is based on a monetary disequilibrium—that is, differences existing between the amount of money people wish to hold and the amount supplied by the monetary authorities. In simple terms, if people demand more money than is being supplied by the central bank, then the excess demand for money would be satisfied by inflows of money from abroad or an appreciation of the currency. On the other hand, if the central bank (the Federal Reserve in the United States) is supplying more money than is demanded, the excess supply of money is eliminated by outflows of money to other countries or a depreciation of the currency. Thus the *monetary approach* emphasizes the determinants of money demand and money supply. The monetary approach can be analyzed separately for fixed and floating exchange rates. If the exchange rate is fixed, then the monetary approach pertains to the balance of payments. In such a case we call the approach the *monetary approach to balance of payments* (MABP). In contrast, if exchange rates are floating then the approach explains exchange rate movements and is called the *monetary approach to exchange rates* (MAER). Both approaches will be discussed in this chapter.

Prior to the monetary approach, it was common to emphasize international trade flows as primary determinants of exchange rates. The traditional approach emphasized the role of exchange rate changes in eliminating international trade imbalances. In this context we should expect countries with current trade surpluses to have appreciating currencies, while countries with trade deficits should have depreciating currencies. It is clear that the world does not work in the simple way just considered. We have seen some instances when countries with trade surpluses have depreciating currencies, while countries with trade deficits have appreciating currencies. This chapter considers an alternative view of the cause of balance of payments disequilibria and exchange rate movements.

SPECIE-FLOW MECHANISM

The monetary approach has a long and distinguished history, so the recent popularity of the approach can be viewed as a rediscovery rather than a modern innovation. In fact, the recent literature often makes use of a quote from *Of the Balance of Trade*, written by David Hume in 1752, to indicate the early understanding of the problem. Hume wrote:

> *Suppose four-fifths of all the money in Great Britain to be annihilated in one night, and the nation reduced to the same condition, with regard to specie, as in the reigns of the Harrys and Edwards, what would be the consequence? Must not the price of all labor and commodities sink in proportion, and everything be sold as cheap as they were in these ages? What nation could then dispute with us in any foreign market, or pretend to navigate or to sell manufactures at the same price, which to us would afford sufficient profit? In how little time, therefore, must this bring back the money which we had lost, and raise us to the level of all the neighboring nations? Where after we have arrived, we immediately lose the advantage of the cheapness of labor and commodities; and the farther flowing in of money is stopped by our fullness and repletion.*

Hume's analysis is a strict monetary approach to prices and the balance of payments. If England's money stock suddenly was reduced by four-fifths, we know from principles of economics that the price level would fall dramatically. The falling price level would give England a price advantage over its foreign competitors, so that its exports would rise and its imports fall. As the foreign money (gold in Hume's day) poured in, England's money supply would rise and its price level would follow. This process continues until England's prices reach the levels of its competitors, after which the system is back in equilibrium.

THE MONETARY APPROACH

Before turning to the model, we should consider some basic concepts and assumptions. In principles of macroeconomics we learn that the Federal Reserve controls the money supply by altering *base money* (currency plus commercial bank reserves held against deposits). As base money changes, the lending ability of commercial banks changes. Increases in base money tend to result in an expansion of the money supply, whereas decreases in base money tend to contract the money supply. For our purposes, it is useful to divide base money into domestic and international components. The domestic component of base money is called *domestic credit*, whereas the remainder is made up of *international reserves* (money items that can be used to settle international debts, primarily foreign exchange).

The international money flows that respond to excess demands or excess supplies of goods or financial assets at home affect base money and then the money supply. For instance, if a US exporter receives payment in foreign currency, this payment will be presented to a US commercial bank to be converted into dollars and deposited in the exporter's account. If the commercial bank has no use for the foreign currency, the bank will exchange the foreign currency for dollars with the Federal Reserve (the Fed). The Fed creates new base money to buy the foreign currency by increasing the commercial bank's reserve deposit with the Fed. Thus, the Fed is accumulating international reserves, and this reserve accumulation brings about an expansion of base money. In the case of an excess supply of money at home, either domestic credit falls to reduce base money, or international reserves will fall in order to lower base money to the desired level.

Now we are ready to construct a simple model of the monetary approach. The usual assumption is that we are analyzing the situation of a small, open economy. A country is defined as "small" when its activities cannot affect the international price of goods or the international interest rate. Openness implies that this country is an active participant in international economic transactions. We could classify nations according to their degree of openness, or the degree to which they depend on international transactions. The United States would be relatively closed, considering the size of the US GDP relative to the value of international trade, whereas Belgium would be relatively open.

A strong assumption of the monetary approach is that there is a stable demand for money. This means that the relationship among money demand, income, and prices does not change significantly over time.

Without a stable demand for money, the monetary approach will not provide a useful framework for analysis. We can begin our model by writing the demand for money as

$$M^d = kPY \qquad (14.1)$$

where M^d is the demand for money, P is the domestic price level, Y is real income or wealth, and k is a constant fraction indicating how money demand will change given a change in P or Y. Eq. (14.1) is often stated as "money demand is a function of prices and income," or "money demand depends on prices and income." The usual story is that the higher the income, the more money people will hold to buy more goods. The higher the price level, the more money is desired to buy any given quantity of goods. So, the demand for money should rise with an increase in either P or Y.

Letting M^s stand for money supply, R for net international reserves (our official holdings of foreign assets less the foreign official holdings of our assets), and D for domestic credit, we can write the money supply relationship as[1]

$$M^s = R + D \qquad (14.2)$$

Letting P stand for the domestic price level, E for the domestic currency price of foreign currency, and P^F for the foreign price level, we can write the *law of one price*, defined in Chapter 7, Prices, Exchange Rates and Purchasing Power Parity as

$$P = EP^F \qquad (14.3)$$

Finally, we need the assumption that equilibrium in the money market holds so that money demand equals money supply, or

$$M^d = M^s \qquad (14.4)$$

The adjustment mechanism that ensures the equilibrium of Eq. (14.4) will vary with the exchange rate regime. With fixed exchange rates, money supply adjusts to money demand through international flows of money via balance of payments imbalances. With flexible exchange rates, money demand will be adjusted to a money supply set by the central bank via exchange rate changes. In the case of a managed float, where theoretically we have floating exchange rates but the central banks intervene

---

[1] We are assuming that base money and the money supply are equal. Realistically, the money supply is some multiple of base money. We assume that this multiple is 1 in order to simplify the analysis.

to keep exchange rates at desired levels, we have both international money flows and exchange rate changes. All three cases will be analyzed subsequently.

Now, we develop the model in a manner that will allow us to analyze the balance of payments and exchange rates in a monetary framework. We begin by substituting Eq. (14.3) into Eq. (14.1).

$$M^d = kEP^F Y \tag{14.5}$$

Substituting Eqs. (14.5) and (14.2) into (14.4) we obtain

$$kEP^F Y = R + D \tag{14.6}$$

Finally, we want to discuss Eq. (14.6), money demand and money supply, in terms of percentage changes. Since k is a constant, the change is zero, and thus k drops out of the analysis and we are left with

$$\hat{E} + \hat{P}^F + \hat{Y} = \hat{R} + \hat{D} \tag{14.7}$$

where the hat (^) over a variable indicates percentage change.[2]

Since the goal of this analysis is to be able to explain changes in the exchange rate or balance of payments, we should have $\hat{R}$ and $\hat{E}$ on the left-hand side of the equation. Rearranging Eq. (14.7) in this manner gives

$$\hat{R} - \hat{E} = \hat{P}^F + \hat{Y} - \hat{D} \tag{14.8}$$

This indicates that the percentage change in net reserves (the balance of payments) minus the percentage change in exchange rates is equal to the foreign inflation rate plus the percentage growth in real income minus the percentage change in domestic credit.

With fixed exchange rates, $\hat{E} = 0$, and we have the MABP. With the exchange rate change equal to zero, the monetary approach Eq. (14.8) simplifies to:

$$\hat{R} = \hat{P}^F + \hat{Y} - \hat{D} \tag{14.9}$$

At the other extreme, a completely flexible exchange rate with no central bank intervention results in a reserve flow $\hat{R}$ equal zero, because

---

[2] In Eq. (14.7), R and D are actually the percentage change as a fraction of total money supply $(R + D)$.

there will not be any changes to reserves. In this case the general Eq. (14.8) is now written for the MAER as

$$-\hat{E} = \hat{P}^F + \hat{Y} - \hat{D} \tag{14.10}$$

THE MONETARY APPROACH TO THE BALANCE OF PAYMENTS

We may draw the line in the balance of payments accounts (see chapter: The Balance of Payments for a review of balance of payments concepts) so that the current and private capital accounts are above the line and only those items that directly affect the money supply are below the line. This balance is often referred to as the *official settlements balance* and refers to net official holdings of gold and foreign exchange, special drawing rights, and changes in reserves at the International Monetary Fund. This allows us to concentrate on the monetary aspects of the balance of payments.

With fixed exchange rates, $\hat{E} = 0$, and we have the MABP. Recall that with the exchange rate change equal to zero, the MABP equation is given in Eq. (14.9). This equation indicates that the change in reserves is equal to the foreign inflation rate, plus the percentage growth of real income, minus the change in domestic credit. Therefore, with fixed exchange rates, an increase in domestic credit with constant prices and income (and thus constant money demand) will lead to a decrease in net international reserves. This means that if the central bank expands domestic credit, creating an excess supply of money, reserves will flow out, or there will be a balance of payments deficit. Conversely, a decrease in domestic credit will lead to an excess demand for money, since money demand is unchanged for a given $\hat{P}^F$ and $\hat{Y}$; yet because D is falling, R will increase by the central bank buying up foreign currency injecting domestic currency, to bring money supply equal to money demand.

Given the framework just developed, we can now consider some of the implications and extensions of the monetary approach. First, the assumption of purchasing power parity (PPP) implies that the central bank must make a policy choice between an exchange rate or a domestic price level. Since $P = EP^F$, under fixed exchange rates, E is constant. Therefore, maintaining the pegged value of E implies that the domestic price level will correspond to that of the rest of the world. This is the case in which people discuss imported inflation. If the foreign price level is increasing rapidly, then our price must follow to maintain the fixed E. On the other hand, with flexible rates E is free to vary to whatever level is necessary to clear the foreign exchange market, and so we can choose our domestic rate of inflation independent of the rest of the world. If we select a lower rate of inflation than foreigners do, then PPP suggests that our currency will tend to appreciate. This issue of choosing between the domestic inflation rate or a preferred exchange rate has important economic as well as political implications and is not made without much thought and consultation among central bankers.

We might mention at this point that there are two views of how PPP operates in the short run, and these two views imply a different mechanism of adjustment to a change in the world economy like a change in the foreign price level. One view is that PPP holds strictly, even in the short run. In this case, a change in the foreign price induces an immediate change in the domestic price and a corresponding change in money demand or money supply. The other view is along the lines of the Hume quote cited previously. The idea here is that prices adjust slowly through the balance of payments effects on the money supply. Thus, if foreign prices rise relative to domestic prices, we tend to sell more to foreigners and run a larger balance of trade surplus. Since we gain international reserves from these goods sales, over time our money supply rises and our prices increase until PPP is restored.

The two approaches differ primarily with regard to timing. The first case assumes that PPP holds in the short run because international reserves flow quickly in response to new events and prices adjust quickly to new equilibrium levels. This fast adjustment is supposedly due to an emphasis on the role of financial assets being bought and sold, resulting in international capital flows. Since financial assets are easily bought and sold, it is easy to understand why many believe that PPP should hold in the short run (ignoring any relative price effects, which we are not discussing in this section). The second case also assumes that PPP holds, but only in the long run. This approach emphasizes the role of goods markets in international adjustment. Since goods prices are supposedly slow to adjust, short-run deviations from PPP will occur that give rise to the balance of trade effects previously discussed. The truth most likely lies between these two extremes. It is reasonable to expect goods prices to adjust slowly over time to changing economic conditions, so it may be reasonable to doubt that PPP holds well in the short run. On the other hand, PPP is not strictly dependent on goods markets. To ignore international capital flows is to miss the potential for a faster adjustment than is possible strictly through goods markets.

We can summarize the policy implications of the MABP as follows:

1. Balance of payments disequilibria are essentially monetary phenomena. Thus, countries would not run long-term (or structural, as they are called) deficits if they did not rely so heavily on inflationary money supply growth to finance government spending.
2. Balance of payments disequilibria must be transitory. If the exchange rate remains fixed, eventually the country must run out of reserves by trying to support a continuing deficit.
3. Balance of payments disequilibria can be handled with domestic monetary policy rather than with adjustments in the exchange rate. Devaluation of the currency exchange rate is a substitute for reducing the growth of domestic credit in that devaluation lowers the value of a country's money relative to the rest of the world (conversely, an appreciation of the currency is a substitute for increasing domestic credit growth). Following any devaluation, if the underlying monetary cause of the devaluation is not corrected, then future devaluations will be required to offset the continued excess supply of the country's money.
4. Domestic balance of payments will be improved by an increase in domestic income via an increase in money demand, if not offset by an increase in domestic credit.

THE MONETARY APPROACH TO THE EXCHANGE RATE

Thus far we have only discussed the MABP, which is fine for a world with fixed exchange rates or a gold standard. For a world with flexible exchange rates, we have the MAER. The dichotomy between fixed and floating exchange rates is an important one. When exchange rates are fixed between countries, we will observe money flowing between countries to adjust to disequilibrium. With floating exchange rates, the exchange rates are allowed to fluctuate with the free-market forces of supply and demand for each currency. The free-market equilibrium exchange rate occurs at a point where the flow of exports just equals the flow of imports so that no net international money flows are required. International economists refer to this choice of money flows or exchange rate changes as the choice of an international *adjustment mechanism*. With fixed exchange rates, the adjustment to changes in international monetary conditions comes through international money flows; whereas with floating rates, the adjustment comes through exchange rate changes.

The MAER equation comes directly from Eq. (14.8). A free-market exchange rate means that no central bank intervention takes place, we have $\hat{R}$ equal zero, so the MAER approach becomes:

$$-\hat{E} = \hat{P}^F + \hat{Y} - \hat{D} \qquad (14.11)$$

With the MAER, an increase in domestic credit, given a constant $\hat{P}^F$ and $\hat{Y}$ (so that money demand is constant), will result in $\hat{E}$ increasing. Since $\hat{E}$ is domestic currency units per foreign currency unit, an increase in $\hat{E}$ means that domestic currency is depreciating. Under the MAER, domestic monetary policy will not cause flows of money internationally but will lead to exchange rate changes. The fact that $\hat{P}^F$ and $\hat{Y}$ have signs opposite that of $\hat{E}$ in Eq. (14.11) indicates that changes in inflation and income growth will cause changes in exchange rates in the opposite direction. For instance, if $\hat{P}^F$ and/or $\hat{Y}$ increase, we know that money demand increases. With constant domestic credit, we have an excess demand for money. As individuals try to increase their money balances, we observe a decrease in $\hat{E}$ or an appreciation of the domestic currency.

THE MONETARY APPROACH FOR A MANAGED FLOATING EXCHANGE RATE

So far, we have discussed the case of fixed or flexible exchange rates, but what is the framework for analysis of a managed float? Remember, a managed float means that although exchange rates are theoretically flexible and determined by the market forces of supply and demand, central banks intervene at times to peg the rates at some desired level. Thus, the managed float has the attributes of both a fixed and a floating exchange rate regime, because changing supply and demand will affect exchange rates, but the actions of the central bank will also allow international reserves to change. To allow for reserve changes, as well as for exchange rate changes, we can simply return to the initial Eq. (14.8). Thus, we can see that given money demand or money supply changes, the central bank can choose to let $\hat{E}$ adjust to the free-market level; or, by holding E at some disequilibrium level, it will allow $\hat{R}$ to adjust.

STERILIZATION

Sterilization is the offsetting of international reserve flows by central banks that wish to follow an independent monetary policy. Under the MABP (with fixed exchange rates), if a country has an excess supply of money, this country would tend to lose international reserves or run a deficit until money supply equals money demand. Central banks often have reasons for desiring either a high money supply growth or a low money supply growth. For example, if the central bank wants to stimulate the economy it might want a high money supply growth. If for some reason the central bank desires a higher money supply and reacts to the deficit by further increasing the money supply, then the deficit will increase and persist as long as the central bank tries to maintain a money supply in excess of money demand. With an excess demand for money, the concept is reversed. The excess demand results in reserve inflows to equate money supply to money demand. If the central bank tries to decrease the money supply so that the excess demand still exists, its efforts will be thwarted by further reserve inflows, which will persist as long as the central bank tries to maintain the policy of a money supply less than money demand.

Sterilization would allow the monetary authorities to stabilize the money supply in the short run without having reserve flows offset their goals. This would be possible if the forces that lead to international arbitrage are slow to operate. For instance, barriers to international capital mobility might exist in a country. In such a case, we might expect international asset return differentials to persist following a change in economic conditions. If the central bank wants to increase the growth of the money supply in the short run, it can do so regardless of money demand and reserve flows. In the long run, when complete adjustment of asset prices is possible, the money supply must grow at a rate consistent with money demand. In the short run, however, the central bank can exercise some discretion.

The actual use of the word *sterilization* derives from the fact that the central bank must be able to neutralize, or sterilize, any reserve flows induced by monetary policy if the policy is to achieve the central bank's money supply goals. For instance, if the central bank is following some money supply growth path, and then money demand increases, leading to reserve inflows, the central bank must be able to sterilize these reserve inflows to keep the money supply from rising to what it considers undesirable levels. This is done by decreasing domestic credit by an amount equal to the growth of international reserves, thus keeping base money and the money supply constant.

Recall again the fixed exchange rate MABP in Eq. (14.9). Given money demand, an increase in domestic credit would be reflected in a fall in $\hat{R}$. Thus, the causality works from $\hat{D}$ to $\hat{R}$. If sterilization occurs, then the causality implied in Eq. (14.9) is no longer true. Instead of the monetary approach equation previously written, where changes in domestic credit ($\hat{D}$, on the right-hand side of the equation) lead to changes in reserves ($\hat{R}$, on the left-hand side), with sterilization we also have changes in reserves inducing changes in domestic credit in order to offset the reserve flows. Sterilization means that there is also a causality flowing from reserve changes to domestic credit, as in

$$\hat{D} = \alpha - \beta\hat{R} \tag{14.12}$$

where β is the sterilization coefficient, ranging in value from 0 (when there is no sterilization) to 1 (complete sterilization). Eq. (14.12) states that the percentage change in domestic credit will be equal to some constant amount (α) determined by the central bank's domestic policy goals, minus the coefficient β, times the percentage change in reserves. The coefficient β will reflect the central bank's ability to use domestic credit to offset reserve flows. Of course, it is possible that the central bank cannot fully offset international reserve flows, and yet some sterilization is possible, in which case β will lie between 0 and 1. Evidence has in fact suggested both extremes as well as an intermediate value for β. It is reasonable to interpret the evidence regarding sterilization as indicating that central banks are able to sterilize a significant fraction of reserve flows in the short run. This means that the monetary authorities can likely choose the growth rate of the money supply in the short run, although long-run money growth must be consistent with money demand requirements.

STERILIZED INTERVENTION

We have, so far, discussed sterilization in the context of fixed exchange rates. Now let us consider how a sterilization operation might occur in a floating exchange rate system. Suppose the Japanese yen is appreciating against the dollar, and the Bank of Japan decides to intervene in the foreign exchange market to increase the value of the dollar and stop the yen appreciation. The Bank of Japan increases domestic credit in order to purchase US dollar-denominated bonds. The increased demand for dollar bonds will lead to an increase in the demand for dollars in the foreign exchange market. This results in the higher foreign exchange value of the dollar. Now suppose that the Bank of Japan has a target level of the Japanese money supply that requires the increase in domestic credit to be offset. The central bank will sell yen-denominated bonds in Japan to reduce the domestic money supply. The domestic Japanese money supply was originally increased by the growth in domestic credit used to buy dollar bonds. The money supply ultimately returns to its initial level because the Bank of Japan uses a domestic open-market operation (the formal term for central bank purchases and sales of domestic bonds) to reduce domestic credit. In this case of managed floating exchange rates, the Bank of Japan uses sterilized intervention to achieve its goal of slowing the appreciation of the yen while keeping the Japanese money supply unchanged. *Sterilized intervention* is ultimately an exchange of domestic bonds for foreign bonds.

It is possible for sterilized intervention with unchanged money supplies to have an effect on the spot exchange rate if money demand changes. The intervention activity could alter the private market view of what to expect in the future. If the intervention changes expectations in a manner that changes money demand (for instance, money demand in Japan falls because the intervention leads people to expect higher Japanese inflation), then the spot rate could change.

SUMMARY

1. The basic premise of the monetary approach is that any balance of payments disequilibrium is based on a monetary disequilibrium.
2. Specie-flow mechanism explains the adjustments to a change in money supply in one country under the fixed exchange rate environment through price movements and international trade flows.
3. According to the specie-flow mechanism, an increase in money supply in Country A will cause a balance of trade deficit in Country A, and a balance of trade surplus in Country B in the short run. In the long run, with the flow of gold from the trade deficit country to the trade surplus country, prices in two countries will adjust to bring both countries back in equilibrium again.
4. Two applications of the monetary approach are: (i) the MABP and (ii) the MAER.
5. The MABP emphasizes money demand and money supply as determinants of the balance of payments under the fixed exchange rate.
6. The MAER emphasizes money demand and money supply as determinants of exchange rate movements.
7. The money supply is composed of domestic credit and international reserves.

8. The money demand is derived from people's willingness to hold money, which is a constant proportion of their nominal income.

9. The MABP implies that the change in international reserves equals to the foreign inflation rate plus the growth rate of domestic output minus the change in domestic money creation.

10. Under the fixed exchange rate, inflation from one country can be transmitted to the other country.

11. The MAER implies that, under the free-floating exchange rate system, a change in monetary policy in one country will not affect the other country's money supply, only causing an adjustment of the exchange rate.

12. The monetary approach in the case of a managed floating exchange rate has attributes of both the MAER and MABP approach.

13. Sterilized intervention is the action by a central bank to offset the effect of a foreign exchange intervention, on the domestic money supply, by using the open-market operations.

EXERCISES

1. "Monetary disequilibrium leads to balance of payments problems under fixed exchange rates, and a currency problem under floating exchange rates." Discuss this statement with reference to the monetary approach.

2. What are the assumptions underlying the MABP? Explain.

3. According to the MABP, what type of economic policies would help a country to resolve a balance of trade deficit?

4. Using the MABP, explain how the Bretton Woods system could break down after the United States increases its money supply too fast.

5. In a perfectly floating exchange rate regime, use the MAER to explain the effect on the dollar price of a Swiss franc ($/SFr) of the following scenarios:
   a. The output in the United States decreases by 3%.
   b. The price level in Switzerland decreases by 2%.

6. Assume that Mexico and the United States are in a fixed exchange rate agreement. Suppose that the Fed increases the money supply by 40%. What would happen to the international reserve position for the United States? Assume that the United States has to intervene to peg the exchange rate; how could they accomplish the intervention?

FURTHER READING

Bahmani-Oskoee, M., Hosny, A., Kishor, N.K., 2015. The exchange rate puzzle revisited. Int. J. Financ. Econ. 20, 126–137.

Baillie, R.T., Osterberg, W.P., 1997. Why do central banks intervene? J. Int. Money Financ. December.

Connolly, M., Putnam, B., Wilford, D.S., 1978. The monetary approach to an open economy: the fundamental theory. In: Putnam, B., Wilford, D.S. (Eds.) The Monetary Approach to International Adjustment, Praeger, New York.

Dominguez, K., 1998. Central bank intervention and exchange rate volatility. J. Int. Money Financ. February.

Hume, D., 1752. Essays, moral, political and literary. In: Cooper, R.N. (Ed.), International Finance, Penguin, Middlesex, 1969.

Neely, C.J., Sarno, L., 2002. How well do monetary fundamentals forecast exchange rates? Fed. Reserve St. Louis Econ. Rev., 51–74. September/October.

Sarno, L., Taylor, M.P., 2001. Official intervention in the foreign exchange: is it effective and, if so, how does it work? J. Econ. Lit. 39 (3), 839–868.

Taylor, M.P., 1995. The economics of exchange rates. J. Econ. Lit. March.

Taylor, M.P., 2003. Why is it so difficult to beat the random walk forecast of exchange rates. J. Int. Econ. 60, 85–107.

CHAPTER 15

Extensions and Challenges to the Monetary Approach

Contents

This chapter considers some of the extensions and challenges to the monetary approach of exchange rate (MAER) determination. The MAER model emphasizes financial asset markets. Rather than the traditional view of exchange rates adjusting to equilibrate international trade in goods, the exchange rate is viewed as adjusting to equilibrate international trade in financial assets. In the MAER model changes to money demand and money supply cause adjustments to goods prices and the exchange rate. Since goods prices adjust slowly relative to financial asset prices, and financial assets are traded continuously each business day, the shift in emphasis from goods markets to asset markets has important implications.

Table 15.1 lists the standard deviation of the percentage changes in prices and exchange rates calculated for four countries. Over the period covered in the table, we observe that spot exchange rates for the four countries studied were four to seven times the volatility of prices. The implication of Table 15.1 is that the basic MAER model is unlikely to capture much of the short run volatility of the exchange rate. This fact has resulted in a number of extensions to the basic MAER approach as well as challenges to the approach.

Table 15.1 The standard deviation of monthly percentage changes in Consumer Price Indexes and spot exchange rates, 1994–2015

Country	Price	Exchange rates
Canada	0.0035	0.0178
Japan	0.0035	0.0262
Mexico	0.0094	0.0395
United Kingdom	0.0037	0.0198

Source: From FRED database.

In this chapter, we will examine five different extensions to the MAER approach. The first is the "news" approach, which allows the MAER to be forward-looking. The portfolio-balance (PB) approach and the trade balance approach add missing variables to the MAER relationships, whereas the overshooting approach and the currency substitution approach extend the MAER approach by adjusting the underlying equation. Finally, we discuss some of the recent challenges to the MAER approach.

THE ROLE OF NEWS

The failure of the MAER to predict a high volatility of the exchange rate has led to extensions and challenges of the MAER approach. However, the high volatility is not difficult to explain. The real world is characterized by unpredictable shocks or surprises. When some unexpected event takes place, we refer to this as *news*. Since interest rates, prices, and incomes are often affected by news, it follows that exchange rates will also be affected by news. By definition, the exchange rate changes linked to news will be unexpected. Thus, we find great difficulty in predicting future spot rates, because we know the exchange rate will be determined in part by events that cannot be foreseen.

The fact that the predicted change in the spot rate, as measured by the MAER approach, varies less over time than does the actual change indicates how much of the change in spot rates is unexpected. Periods dominated by unexpected announcements or realizations of economic policy changes will have great fluctuations in spot and forward exchange rates as expectations are revised subject to the news. Volatile exchange rates simply reflect turbulent times. Even with a good knowledge of the determinants of exchange rates (as discussed in this chapter), without perfect foresight exchange rates will always prove to be difficult to forecast in a dynamic world full of surprises.

The fact that the expected volatility of the exchange rate using the monetary model is less than the actual volatility has led to many extensions of the monetary approach. We discuss these extensions in the rest of the chapter.

THE PB APPROACH

If domestic and foreign bonds are perfect substitutes, then the basic monetary approach, presented in the last chapter, is a useful description of exchange rate determination. However, if domestic and foreign bonds are not perfect substitutes then the MAER has to be modified. The PB approach assumes that assets are imperfect substitutes internationally because investors perceive foreign exchange risk to be attached to foreign-currency-denominated bonds. As the supply of domestic bonds rises relative to foreign bonds, there will be an increased risk premium on the domestic bonds that will cause the domestic currency to depreciate in the spot market. If the spot exchange rate depreciates today, and if the expected future spot rate is unchanged, the expected rate of appreciation over the future will increase.

If the spot exchange rate is a function of relative asset supplies, then the monetary approach Eq. (14.10) should be modified to include the percentage change in the supply of domestic bonds $(\hat{B})$ and the percentage change in the supply of foreign bonds $(\hat{B}^F)$:

$$-\hat{E} = -\hat{D} - \hat{B} + \hat{B}^F + \hat{P}^F + \hat{Y} \qquad (15.1)$$

For instance, if the dollar/pound spot rate is initially $E_{\$/£} = 2.00$, and the expected spot rate from the MAER approach in 1 year is $E_{\$/£} = 1.90$, then the expected rate of dollar appreciation is 5% $[(1.90 - 2.00)/2.00]$. Now suppose that an increase in the outstanding stock of dollar-denominated bonds results in a depreciation of the spot rate today to $E_{\$/£} = 2.05$. The expected rate of dollar appreciation is now approximately 7.3% $[(1.90 - 2.05)/2.05]$. Thus, the addition of the imperfect substitution between the domestic and foreign bond portfolio can explain higher variability in the foreign exchange rate.

Recall in the last chapter that we discussed the sterilized intervention. It is difficult to explain in terms of the basic monetary approach model why a country would pursue sterilized intervention. However, in terms of the PB approach in Eq. (15.1), sterilization makes more sense. Suppose the Japanese yen is appreciating against the dollar, and the Bank of Japan decides to intervene in the foreign exchange market to increase the value of the dollar and stop the yen appreciation. The Bank of Japan increases domestic credit in order to purchase US dollar-denominated bonds. This should cause the yen to depreciate. This effect is reinforced by the open market sale of yen securities by the Bank of Japan. Thus, the yen can depreciate even with a sterilized intervention.

This broader PB view might be expected to explain exchange rate changes better than the simple MAER equation. However, the empirical evidence is not at all clear on this matter.

THE TRADE BALANCE APPROACH

The introduction to this chapter discussed the modern shift in emphasis away from exchange rate models that rely on international trade in goods to exchange rate models based on financial assets. However, there is still a useful role for trade flows in asset approach models, since trade flows have implications for financial asset flows.

If balance of trade deficits are financed by depleting domestic stocks of foreign currency, and trade surpluses are associated with increases in domestic holdings of foreign money, we can see the role for the trade account. If the exchange rate adjusts so that the stocks of domestic and foreign money are willingly held, then the country with a trade surplus will be accumulating foreign currency. As holdings of foreign money increase relative to domestic, the relative value of foreign money will fall or the foreign currency will depreciate.

Although realized trade flows and the consequent changes in currency holdings will affect the current spot exchange rate, the expected future change in the spot rate will be affected by expectations regarding the future balance of trade and its implied currency holdings. An important aspect of this analysis is that changes in the future expected value of a currency can have an immediate impact on current spot rates. For instance, suppose there is a sudden change in the world economy that leads to expectations of a larger trade deficit in the future, say, an international oil cartel develops and there is an expectation that the domestic economy will have to pay much more for oil imports. In this case forward-looking individuals will anticipate a decrease in domestic holdings of foreign money over time. This, in turn, will cause expectations of a higher rate of appreciation in the value of foreign currency, or a faster expected depreciation of the domestic currency. This higher expected rate of depreciation of the domestic currency leads to an immediate attempt by individuals and firms to shift from domestic into foreign money. Because, at this moment, the total stocks of foreign and domestic money are constant, the attempt to exchange domestic for foreign money will cause an immediate appreciation of the foreign currency to maintain equilibrium, and so the existing supplies of domestic and foreign money are willingly held.

We note that current spot exchange rates are affected by changes in expectations concerning future trade flows, as well as by current international trade flows. As is often the case in economic phenomena, the short run effect of some new event determining the balance of trade can differ from the long-run result. Suppose the long-run equilibrium under floating exchange rates is balanced trade, where exports equal imports. If we are initially in equilibrium and then experience a disturbance like an oil cartel formation, in the short run we expect large balance of trade deficits, but in the long run, as all prices and quantities adjust to the situation, we return to the long-run equilibrium of balanced trade. The new long-run equilibrium exchange rate will be higher than the old rate, since, as a result of the period of the trade deficit, foreigners will have larger stocks of domestic currency while domestic residents hold less foreign currency. The exchange rate need not move to the new equilibrium immediately. In the short run during which trade deficits are experienced, the exchange rate will tend to be below the new equilibrium rate. Thus, as the outflow of money from the domestic economy proceeds with the deficits, there is a steady depreciation of the domestic currency to maintain the short-run equilibrium where quantities of monies demanded and supplied are equal.

Fig. 15.1 illustrates the effects just discussed. Some unexpected event occurs at time t_0 that causes a balance of trade deficit. The initial exchange rate is E_0. With the deficit, and the consequent outflow of money from home to abroad, the domestic currency will depreciate. Eventually, as prices and quantities adjust to the changes in the structure of trade, a new long-run equilibrium is reached at E_1, where the trade balance is restored. This move to the new long-run exchange rate, E_1, does not have to come instantaneously, because the deficit will persist for some time. However, the forward rate could jump to E_1 at time t_0 as the market now expects

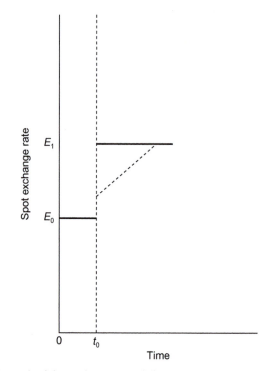

Figure 15.1 The path of the exchange rate following a new event that causes balance of trade deficits.

E_1 to be the long-run equilibrium exchange rate. The dashed line in Fig. 15.1 represents the path taken by the spot exchange rate in the short run. At t_0, there is an instantaneous jump in the exchange rate even before any trade deficits are realized, because individuals try to exchange domestic money for foreign in anticipation of the domestic currency depreciation. Over time, as the trade deficits occur, there is a steady depreciation of the domestic currency, with the exchange rate approaching its new long-run steady-state value, E_1, as the trade deficit approaches zero.

The inclusion of the balance of trade as a determinant of exchange rates is particularly useful since the popular press often emphasizes the trade account in explanations of exchange rate behavior. As previously shown, it is possible to make sense of balance of trade flows in a model where the exchange rate is determined by desired and actual financial asset flows, so that the role of trade flows in exchange rate determination may be consistent with the modern asset approach to the exchange rate.

THE OVERSHOOTING APPROACH

Fig. 15.1 indicates that with news regarding a higher trade deficit for the domestic country, the spot exchange rate will jump immediately above E_0 and will then rise steadily until the new long-run equilibrium, E_1, is reached. It is possible that the exchange rate may not always move in such an orderly fashion to the new long-run equilibrium following a disturbance.

We know that purchasing power parity does not hold well under flexible exchange rates. Exchange rates exhibit much more volatile behavior than do prices. We might expect that in the short run, following some disturbance to equilibrium, prices will adjust slowly to the new equilibrium level, whereas exchange rates and interest rates adjust quickly. Dornbusch (1976) shows that the different speed of adjustment to equilibrium allows for some interesting behavior regarding exchange rates and prices.

At times it appears that spot exchange rates move too much, given some economic disturbance. Moreover, we have observed instances when country A has a higher inflation rate than country B, yet A's currency appreciates relative to B's. Such anomalies can be explained in the context of an "overshooting" exchange rate model. We assume that financial markets adjust instantaneously to an exogenous shock, whereas goods markets adjust slowly over time. With this setting, we analyze what happens when country A increases its money supply.

For equilibrium in the money market, money demand must equal money supply. Thus, if the money supply increases, something must happen to increase money demand. We assume money demand depends on income and the interest rate, so we can write a money demand function like

$$M^d = aY + bi \qquad (15.2)$$

where M^d is the real stock of money demanded (the nominal stock of money divided by the price level), Y is income, and i is the interest rate. Money demand is positively related to income, so a exceeds zero. As Y increases, people tend to demand more of everything, including money. Since the interest rate is the opportunity cost of holding money, there is an inverse relationship between money demand and i, or b is negative. It is commonly believed that in the short run following an increase in the money supply, both income and the price level are relatively constant. As a result, interest rates must drop to equate money demand to money supply.

The interest rate parity relation for countries A and B may be written as

$$i_A = i_B + (F - E)/E \qquad (15.3)$$

Thus, if i_A falls, for a given foreign interest rate i_B, the expected change in the currency value, $(F - E)/E$, must be negative. However, when the money supply in country A increases, we expect that eventually prices there will rise, since we have more A currency chasing the limited quantity of goods available for purchase. This higher future price in A will imply a higher future exchange rate to achieve purchasing power parity:

$$E = P_A/P_B$$

Since P_A is expected to rise over time, given P_B, E will also rise. This higher expected future spot rate will be reflected in a higher forward rate now. But if F rises, while at the same time $(F-E)/E$ falls to maintain interest rate parity, E will have to increase more than F. Then, once prices start rising, real money balances fall and the domestic interest rate rises. Over time, as the interest rate increases, E will fall to maintain interest rate parity. Therefore, the initial rise in E will be in excess of the long-run E, or E will overshoot its long-run value.

If the discussion seems overwhelming at this point, the reader will be relieved to know that a concise summary can be given graphically. Fig. 15.2 summarizes the discussion thus far. The initial equilibrium is given by E_0, F_0, P_0, and i_0. When the money supply increases at time t_0, the domestic interest rate falls, and the spot and forward exchange rates increase while the price level remains fixed. The eventual equilibrium price and exchange rate will rise in proportion to the increase in the money supply. Although the forward rate will move immediately to its new equilibrium, F_1, the spot rate will increase above the eventual equilibrium, E_1, because of the need to maintain interest parity (remember i has fallen in the short run). Over time, as prices start rising, the interest rate increases and the exchange rate converges to the new equilibrium, E_1.

As a result of the overshooting E, we observe a period where country A has rising prices relative to the fixed price of country B, yet A's currency appreciates along the solid line converging to E_1. We might explain this period as one in which prices increase, lowering real money balances and raising interest rates. Country A experiences capital inflows in response to the higher interest rates, so that A's currency appreciates steadily at the same rate as the interest rate increase in order to maintain interest rate parity.

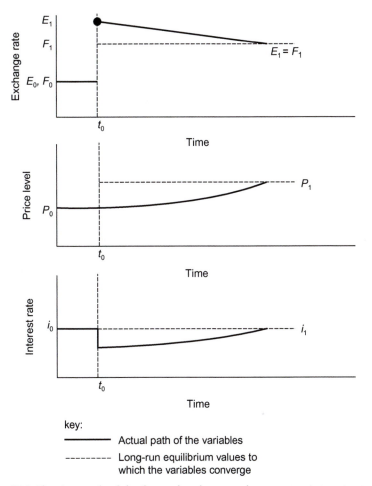

Figure 15.2 The time path of the forward and spot exchange rates, interest rate, and price level following an increase in the domestic money supply at time t_0.

THE CURRENCY SUBSTITUTION APPROACH

Economists have long argued that one of the advantages of flexible exchange rates is that countries become independent in terms of their ability to formulate domestic monetary policy. This is obviously not true when exchange rates are fixed. If country A must maintain a fixed exchange rate with country B, then A must follow a monetary policy similar to B's. Should A follow an inflationary policy in which prices are rising 20% per year while B follows a policy aimed at price stability, then a fixed rate of exchange between the money of A and B will prove very difficult to maintain. Yet with flexible exchange rates, A and B can each choose any monetary policy they like, and the exchange rate will simply change over time to adjust for the inflation differentials.

This independence of domestic policy under flexible exchange rates may be reduced if there is an international demand for monies. Suppose country B residents desire to hold currency A to use for future transactions or simply to hold as part of their investment portfolio. As demand for money shifts between currencies A and B, the exchange rate will shift as well. In a region with substitutable currencies, shifts in money demand between currencies will add an additional element of exchange rate variability.

With fixed exchange rates, central banks make currencies perfect substitutes on the supply side. They alter the supplies of currency to maintain the exchange rate peg. The issue of currency substitution deals with the substitutability among currencies on the demand side of the market. If currencies were perfect substitutes to money demanders, then all currencies would have to have the same inflation rates, or demand for the high-inflation currency would fall to zero (since the inflation rate determines the loss of purchasing power of a money). Perfectly substitutable monies indicate that demanders are indifferent between the use of one currency and another. If the cost of holding currency A rises relative to the cost of holding B, say because of a higher inflation rate for currency A, then demand will shift away from A to B, when A and B are substitutes. This would cause the A currency to depreciate even more than was initially called for by the inflation differential between A and B.

For instance, suppose Canada has a 10% annual inflation rate while the United States has a 5% rate. With no currency substitution, we would expect the US dollar to appreciate against the Canadian dollar on purchasing power parity grounds. Now suppose that Canadian citizens hold stocks of US dollar currency, and these US dollars are good substitutes for Canadian dollars. The higher inflation rate on the Canadian dollar means that stocks of Canadian dollars held will lose value more rapidly than US dollars, so there is an increased demand for US dollar currency. This attempt to exchange Canadian dollar currency for US dollars results in a further depreciation of the Canadian dollar. Such shifts in demand between currencies can result in volatile exchange rates and can be very unsettling to central banks desiring exchange rate stability.

Although central banks may attempt to follow independent monetary policies, they will not be able to do so with high currency substitution.

Money demanders will adjust their portfolio holdings away from high-inflation currencies to low-inflation currencies. This currency substitution leads to more volatile exchange rates, since not only does the exchange rate adjust to compensate for the original inflation differential, but it also adjusts as currency portfolios are altered. Therefore, one implication of a high degree of currency substitution is a need for international coordination of monetary policy. If money demanders substitute between currencies to force each currency to follow a similar inflation rate, then the supposed independence of monetary policy under flexible exchange rates is largely illusory.

We should expect currency substitution to be most important in a regional setting where there is a relatively high degree of mobility of resources between countries. For instance, the use of the euro by countries in Western Europe may be evidence of a high degree of currency substitution that once existed among the former European currencies. Alternatively, there is evidence of a high degree of currency substitution existing between the US dollar and Latin American currencies. In many Latin American countries, dollars serve as an important substitute currency, both as a store of value (the dollar being more stable than the typical Latin American currency) and as a medium of exchange used for transactions. This latter effect is particularly pronounced in border areas. Aside from regional settings, it is not clear that currency substitution should be a potentially important source of exchange rate variability. At this point it is probably safe to treat currency substitution as a potentially important source of exchange rate variability, but one that may not be relevant to all country pairs.

RECENT INNOVATIONS TO OPEN-ECONOMY MACROECONOMICS

The recent advances in open-economy macroeconomics come in two general types. The first assumes that the economy responds quickly so that an equilibrium is reached quickly, whereas the other type of models have some short-run restriction to prevent an equilibrium in the short run.

The so-called *equilibrium approach* to exchange rates assumes that prices, interest rates, and exchange rates are always at their market clearing equilibrium levels. In this approach, changes in exchange rates occur because of changes in tastes or technology and are part of the adjustment to a shock to the world economy. For instance, suppose an improvement in technology in Switzerland increases Swiss output, and at the higher level of productivity the price of Swiss goods relative to other countries' goods falls through a depreciation of the franc. The lower relative price of Swiss output is associated with rising Swiss exports. In this scenario, the franc did not depreciate in order to make Swiss goods more competitive on world markets; instead it depreciated because the higher level of Swiss productivity made the relative price of Swiss goods fall.

According to the equilibrium approach, changes in exchange rates are caused by changes in tastes or technology, so the franc depreciation did not cause the increase in Swiss exports and output but instead was a result of these changes. Similarly, if tastes had changed so that Swiss goods were now more favored by consumers, this would increase the relative price of Swiss goods and would be associated with a franc appreciation. In this view of the world, exchange rate changes can never be viewed as good or bad—they simply occur in response to some other event and are part of the adjustment to a new equilibrium.

Another recent approach to explaining exchange rates assumes that in the long run the equilibrium approach is reached, but in the short run restrictions to price movements result in temporary disequilibria that result in large exchange rate variability. Essentially these models combine elements of the *IS-LM-BP* framework from Chapter 13, The IS-LM-BP Approach with the monetary approach. While these new models are too complex to be covered in detail here, we should realize where economic thought is moving and the implications of this new thinking. *The New International Macroeconomics* carefully considers the details of the economy to the level of individual firms and households and how their actions aggregate to macroeconomic phenomena.

The *IS-LM-BP* model focused on one country and abstracted from the rest of the world, which is in the background. The New International Macroeconomics typically examines two countries (you might think of one as the rest of the world) and the determination of key macroeconomic variables like incomes, prices, and the exchange rate. The predictions of this type of model would include the following effects of a surprising increase in the domestic money supply: consumer spending increases at home and abroad; domestic income increases by more than foreign income; the domestic currency depreciates and purchasing power parity is maintained continuously.

The *IS-LM-BP* model was developed holding the price level constant. In many New International Macroeconomic models the price level is held fixed for a short run and then allowed to change in the long run as in the monetary approach. So the short-run fixed price is like the old model, but the long run allows for a dynamic adjustment of prices over time that is missing from the static models of the *IS-LM-BP* type. In many New International Macroeconomic models, if prices were perfectly flexible, then money supply shocks would have no effects on real variables like income or consumption due to the assumption of purchasing power parity. In this case, prices would change in proportion to changes in the money supply and the exchange rate would change to leave relative prices at home and abroad unchanged (the "law of one price") so that there is no inducement for changes in consumption or production. So the assumption of "sticky prices" is important to generate changes in spending and output.

Since there is much evidence against the law of one price, some research has focused on a modified version of a New International Macroeconomic model that allows for *pricing to market*. This occurs when local currency pricing reflects local market conditions in each country and allows for price discrimination across countries. In this case, purchasing power parity does not hold and so changes in the money supply of one country may result in bigger exchange rate changes due to the relative lack of responsiveness of price levels across countries. This is an important change since we observe real-world exchange rates having much greater volatility than relative prices across countries.

SUMMARY

1. The monetary approach to the exchange rate does not predict the high volatility of exchange rates.
2. Five approaches trying to explain excessive exchange rate variation are: (i) the news approach, (ii) the PB approach, (iii) the trade balance approach, (iv) the overshooting approach, and (v) the currency substitution approach.
3. The volatility of exchange rate is affected by news—unforeseeable events or shocks. News about future policies immediately affects the exchange rate.
4. The PB approach extends the MAER by including the relative supply of domestic bonds to foreign bonds into the analysis of the exchange rate determination. The domestic and foreign assets are *imperfect* substitutes (there is a risk premium to holding foreign assets).

The changes in the demand and supply of domestic and foreign bond markets will lead to exchange rate movements.

5. Sterilized intervention that leaves money supply unchanged can affect exchange rates through PB channel of shifting relative bond supplies.

6. In the trade balance approach, the future expected value of a currency can have an immediate impact on current spot rates. Any news that changes the expectations about the future directions of the balance of trade will affect the expected value of the future spot exchange rates and hence will affect the current spot rates.

7. The overshooting approach assumes the perfect capital mobility such that financial markets adjust immediately, but the good market adjusts slowly to shocks. As a result, when the money supply increases, the domestic currency depreciates more than the necessary long-run level because of the overreaction from financial markets in the short run. As time passes, the goods prices will rise in proportion to the increase in money supply. The exchange rate will return to its long-run level.

8. The independence of domestic monetary policy under flexible exchange rates may be reduced if there is currency substitution.

9. If people are willing to substitute between the domestic currency and other currencies, then demand for the domestic currency might be affected by money supply changes. As a result, substitutability between currencies constrains monetary policy action and increases exchange rate volatility.

10. Currency substitution is important in a regional setting and it may require international coordination of monetary policy.

11. The recent trends in the open economy macroeconomics focus on two modeling types: (i) the general equilibrium approach—prices, interest rates, and exchange rates adjust instantaneously to restore an equilibrium; and (ii) the *IS-LM-BP* framework—which describes the sluggishness of adjustments toward the equilibrium in the short run causing temporary disequilibrium and exchange rate variability.

EXERCISES

1. In each of the five approaches, list the underlying assumptions (e.g., what is assumed in terms of speed of adjustment in goods markets and financial markets, expectations, asset substitutability, and currency substitutability).

2. Suppose that a central bank buys bonds on the open market and uses money to pay for them, thereby increasing the supply of money and decreasing the supply of bonds. Use the PB approach to explain what would happen to (i) domestic interest rate, (ii) demand for foreign bonds, (iii) foreign interest rate, and (iv) the spot exchange rate.

3. Explain why a high currency substitution would cause the US dollar exchange rate to depreciate more than the expected level when the Fed increases money supply in the United States.

4. Suppose that the Fed unexpectedly decreases the money supply in the United States. Use the overshooting approach to explain how the spot exchange rate, forward rate, domestic interest rate, and the domestic price level would change in response to the policy change. Draw graphs to illustrate the time paths of the adjustments.

5. Assume that a country increases its domestic money supply. If the "overshooting" theory is correct, how could a central bank prevent the exchange rate from depreciating too much in the short run?

6. Suppose the United States discovers a new technology that will improve its exports. Therefore, there are rumors that this technology will bring the US trade balance from trade deficits to expected long-term surpluses. What would happen to the exchange rate value of the US dollar from this news? Do you anticipate any difference in the dollar values between short run and long run?

FURTHER READING

Aivazian, V.A., Callen, J.L., Krinsky, I., Kwan, C.C.Y., 1986. International exchange risk and asset substitutability. J. Int. Money Financ. December.

Baillie, R.T., Osterberg, W.P., 1997. Why do central banks intervene? J. Int. Money Financ. December.

Chari, V., Kehoe, P.J., McGrattan, E.R., 2002. Can sticky price models generate volatile and persistent exchange rates? Rev. Econ. Stud. 69 (3), 533–563.

Dominguez, K., 1998. Central bank intervention and exchange rate volatility. J. Int. Money Financ. February.

Dornbusch, R., 1976. Expectations and exchange rate dynamics. J. Pol. Econ. 84 (6), 1161–1176.

Ize, A., Yeyati, E.L., 2003. Financial dollarization. J. Int. Econ. 59, 323–347.

Lane, P.R., 2001. The new open economy macroeconomics: a survey J. Int. Econ. August.

Levin, J.H., 1986. Trade flow lags, monetary and fiscal policy, and exchange rate overshooting. J. Int. Money Financ. December.

Moura, G., 2011. Testing the equilibrium exchange rate model. Appl. Math. Sci. 5 (20), 981–993.

Sarno, L., Taylor, M.P., 2002. New Developments in Exchange Rate Economics. Elgar, Cheltenham.

Solow, R.M., Touffut, J. (Eds.), 2012. What's Right with Macroeconomics? Elgar, Cheltenham.

Steinsson, J., 2008. The dynamic behavior of the real exchange rate in sticky price models. Am. Econ. Rev. 98 (1), 519–533.

Stockman, A.C., 1987. The equilibrium approach to exchange rates. Fed. Reserve. Bank of Richmond Econ. Rev. April.

Taylor, M., 1995. The economics of exchange rates J. Econ. Lit. March.

GLOSSARY

Absorption approach to the balance of trade A theory based on domestic spending for domestic goods (absorption) relative to domestic output.

Adjustable peg A system of fixed exchange rates, with periodic devaluations allowed when conditions warrant.

Adjusted present value The value today of future cash flows from operations plus related financial effects.

Adjustment mechanism The method by which the international economy reacts to remove a disequilibrium.

Airbill A bill of lading for goods shipped by air.

American depositary receipts (ADRs) Negotiable instruments certifying shares of a foreign stock held by a foreign custodian.

Arbitrage Buying in a market where the price is low and then selling in a market with a higher price.

Arm's-length pricing Prices that an unrelated buyer and seller would willingly pay.

Asymmetric information Causes exchange rates to change due to traders' fear that they are quoting prices to someone who knows more about current market conditions than they do.

Autocorrelation The errors from a regression equation are related over time.

Balance of payments A balance sheet recording a nation's international transactions.

Balance of payments equilibrium When credits equal debits on some sub-account of the balance of payments.

Balance of trade Merchandise exports minus merchandise imports.

Bankers' acceptance A time draft drawn on and accepted by a particular bank, to be paid at maturity.

Bank notes Actual paper currency.

Base money Currency plus commercial bank reserves held against deposits.

Basel rules Rules set by the Bank for International Settlements (BIS) to ensure banks have sufficient backing of their liabilities.

Basic balance The sum of the balances on the merchandise, services, unilateral transfers, and long-term capital accounts.

Basis point One-hundredth of a percent, or 0.0001.

Basket pegger A country that maintains a fixed exchange rate with a composite or weighted average of foreign currencies rather than against a single foreign currency.

Beta A measure of the portfolio risk associated with an individual asset.

Big Mac index An index produced by *The Economist* measuring the exchange rate adjusted cost of a good across countries.

Bill of lading Agreement issued by a shipping company to carry goods to a destination port.

Bimetallism Two metals, like gold and silver, serving as backing for the money supply.

Black market An illegal market in foreign exchange.

Bretton Woods agreement An adjustable peg agreement with the U.S. dollar as the anchor currency.

Broker An intermediary in the foreign exchange market.

Call option The right to buy currency at a stated price on or before a future date.

Capital account That part of the balance of payments that records trade in financial assets.

Capital budgeting Evaluating prospective investment alternatives in order to fund preferred Projects.

Capital controls Restrictions on international capital flows, like taxes or quotas.

Capital flight Large investment outflows associated with increased risk in a country.

Capital flow Funds that cross a geographic border.

Central bank The official bank of a government. For example, the Federal Reserve in the United States.

Chartists Forecasters who use the past history of exchange rates to predict future movements.

Closed economy An economy with little or no economic activity involving the rest of the world.

Commodity money standard Money has a fixed value relative to some commodity.

Comparative advantage A determinant of the pattern of world trade in terms of which country exports which goods.

Compensating balances Bank deposits that must be held as a form of compensation to the bank.

Country risk analysis An evaluation of the potential for default or rescheduling on loans made to a particular country.

Covariance A measure of the degree to which two variables move together.

Covered interest arbitrage Buying or selling assets internationally and using the forward market to eliminate exchange risk in order to take advantage of return differentials.

Crawling peg A system in which the exchange rate is held fixed in the short run but is adjusted at regular intervals to reflect supply and demand pressures.

Credit default swap A contract that ensures that a payment will be made on loan.

Cross rate The implied third exchange rate, given two exchange rates involving three currencies.

Currency board A government institution that exchanges domestic currency for foreign currency at a fixed rate of exchange.

Currency contract period The period immediately following a devaluation when contracts negotiated prior to the devaluation come due.

Currency swap Where two counterparties exchange streams of interest payments in different currencies for an agreed period of time and exchange principal amounts in the respective currencies at an agreed exchange rate at maturity.

Currency union A region within which exchange rates are fixed.

Current account In the balance of payments the sum of the merchandise, services, and unilateral transfers accounts.

Debt-equity swaps An exchange of debt for the debtor's domestic currency, which is then used to buy equity positions in the debtor country.

Deep market A market with a large number of buyers and sellers, and assets traded, so that trading occurs at all times.

Depreciation A decrease in a currency's value.

Destabilizing speculation Speculation causing exchange rates to fluctuate more than they would in the absence of such speculation.

Direct foreign investment Expenditures related to the establishment of foreign operating units, where the investment exceeds 10% ownership of the company.

Discount The forward pricing of a currency at less than the spot price.

Discount rate Rate of interest used to determine present value of future cash flow.

Diversified portfolio A mix of investments that lowers an investor's risk.

Dock receipt A document issued by a shipping company listing the quantity and quality of the goods delivered to the dock.

Dollarization Occurs when a country unilaterally adopts another country's currency in place of its own currency.

Domestic credit The domestic component of base money.

Durable goods Goods with useful lives of more than one year.

Economic exposure The exposure of the value of the firm to changes in exchange rates.

Effective return The foreign interest rate of a foreign investment plus the forward premium or discount.

Efficient market A market in which prices reflect all available information.

Elasticities approach to the balance of trade An analysis that addresses the conditions necessary for a devaluation to improve the trade balance.

Elasticity The responsiveness of quantity to changes in price.

Endogenous Determined by factors within a model.

Equation of exchange An equation stating that the money supply times the velocity of money is equal to the price level times the quantity of transactions.

Equilibrium approach An approach that says that changes in exchange rates are largely due to changing tastes or technology.

Eurobank A bank that accepts deposits and makes loans in foreign currencies.

Eurobond market The market engaging in direct offshore borrowing and lending through the sale of bonds denominated in one currency yet sold in many countries.

Eurocurrency market The offshore banking market where commercial banks accept deposits and make loans in foreign currencies.

European Central Bank The central bank that oversees the monetary policy of all countries included in the euro system.

European currency unit (ECU) A unit that preceded the euro, but was never issued in tangible form. An average of the values of EMS currencies.

European Monetary System (EMS) A monetary system within which exchange rates were fixed, since the countries involved floated jointly against the rest of the world.

Exchange rate The price of one nation's currency in terms of another nation's currency.

Exchange rate index A measure of the weighted average value of a currency.

Exchange risk The risk arising from uncertainty regarding future exchange rates.

Exogenous Determined by factors given to a model, outside of or independent of other variables in the model.

External balance A desired trade balance or desired international capital flows.

Factors Firms that buy accounts receivable and assume responsibility for collection.

Fisher effect The expected effect of inflation on the nominal interest rate.

Fisher equation An equation stating that the nominal interest rate is equal to the real rate plus expected inflation.

Fixed exchange rates When central banks set exchange rates at particular levels.

Flexible exchange rates Free market supply and demand determine the exchange rate.

Foreign exchange Bank deposits and currency denominated in foreign monetary units.

Foreign exchange market A market mostly comprising large commercial banks buying and selling foreign exchange from and to each other.

Foreign exchange swap The simultaneous exchange of two currencies on a specific date at a rate agreed at the time of the contract and a reverse exchange of the same two currencies at a date further in the future at a rate agreed at the time of contracting.

Forward discount A forward rate at less than the spot rate.

Forward exchange market A market for trading currencies among banks where delivery occurs at a future date.

Forward exchange rate The price of a currency to be delivered sometime in the future.

Forward premium A forward rate in excess of the spot rate.

Fundamental model Forecasts exchange rates based on variables that are believed to be important determinants of exchange rates.

Futures Contracts to buy and sell currency for future delivery that are traded on organized exchanges.

Gold exchange standard A standard whereby a currency is valued in terms of a gold equivalent and every other currency is to maintain fixed exchange rates against that currency.

Gold standard Currencies maintain a fixed price relative to gold.

Great recession The sharp slowdown in the end of 2007, following the financial crisis in the U.S.

Gresham's law A law stating that cheap money drives out good money.

Hedging Taking a position to reduce risk.

IBFs International banking facilities—units of banks located in the United States that conduct Eurocurrency business.

IMF conditionality Economic adjustments imposed on a country by the IMF (International Monetary Fund) before loans will be made.

Inflation–adjusted exchange rate The exchange rate minus the inflation differential between two countries.

Interest rate parity The equivalence of the interest differential between two currencies to the forward premium or discount.

Internal balance Domestic economic growth consistent with a low unemployment rate.

International Monetary Fund (IMF) An international organization that provides loans to countries experiencing balance of payments problems.

International reserves The international component of base money, primarily foreign exchange.

Intervention The buying and selling of currencies by central banks to affect the exchange rate.

Inventory control Effect on exchange rates when traders alter quotes to maintain a balance between amount of currency bought and sold.

J-curve effect Following a devaluation, an initial decrease in the trade balance followed by an increase.

Law of one price A law stating that all goods sell for the same price worldwide when converted to a common currency.

Letter of credit A letter issued by a bank that obligates the bank to pay a specific amount of money to an exporter.

LIBOR London interbank offer rate—the interest rate that banks charge each other for short-term loans.

Liquid assets Assets that can easily be spent, like cash or checking account money.

Long position Buying a currency to be delivered in the future.

Managed float The floating of exchange rates with central bank intervention.

Margin Money deposited with a broker to finance futures trading.

Marginal propensity to import The change in imports given a change in income.

Marshall–Lerner condition The necessary international demand elasticities that will ensure an improvement in the trade balance following a devaluation.

Monetary approach to the balance of payments (MABP); monetary approach to the exchange rate (MAER) An analysis emphasizing money demand and money supply as determinants of the balance of payments under fixed exchange rates and of the exchange rate under floating rates.

Money multiplier The ratio of the money supply to base money.

Moral hazard An inducement to greater risk taking that occurs when the decision maker does not expect to bear the full cost of bad decisions.

Mortgage-backed security (MBS) A securitized instrument grouping a number of mortgages into a financial instrument that can be resold.

Multinational firm A business firm operating in more than one country.

Mundell–Fleming model A model of an economy with flexible exchange rates and perfect capital mobility.

Netting Consolidating payables and receivables in a currency so that only the difference must be bought or sold.

Nominal interest rate The interest rate actually observed in the market.

Nonsystematic risk Risk unique to an individual asset, which can be diversified away.

Official settlements balance The balance of payments account measuring the change in short-term capital held by foreign monetary authorities and official reserve asset transactions.

Offshore banking Accepting deposits and making loans in foreign currency—the Eurocurrency market.

Open economy An economy actively involved in international trade.

Opportunity cost The next-best alternative when undertaking some activity.

Optimum currency area The area that maximizes the economic gains of having exchange rates that are fixed among currencies in the area and flexible rates with other areas.

Options Contracts that give the right to buy or sell a certain amount of currency at a stated price on or before a future date.

Overshooting model A foreign exchange rate model that allows the exchange rate to overadjust by having prices staying fixed in the short run whereas capital markets are flexible.

Parallel market A free foreign exchange market that exists as an alternative to a regulated official market.

Paris Club An arrangement whereby creditor governments meet with debtor nations in Paris to restructure debts.

Pass-through The effects of a devaluation on prices—the devaluing country sees its import prices rise while export prices to foreign buyers fall.

Percent per annum The percentage return on a 12-month basis.

Perfect capital mobility The free flow of capital between nations because there are no significant transactions costs or capital controls.

Petrodollars Dollars earned by the export of oil, generally the earnings of the Organization of Petroleum Exporting Countries (OPEC).

Portfolio-balance approach A theory of exchange rate determination that considers relative supply and demand for bonds.

Premium The forward pricing of a currency at more than the spot price.

Present value The value today of some amount to be received in the future.

Pricing to market Adjusting domestic currency prices in response to exchange rate changes in order to maintain market share.

Purchasing power parity *Absolute*: the equivalence of the exchange rate to the ratio of the foreign and domestic price levels. *Relative*: the equivalence of the percentage change in the exchange rate to the inflation differential between two nations.

Put option The right to sell currency at a stated price on or before a future date.

Real exchange rate The nominal exchange rate for two currencies divided by the ratio of their price levels.

Real interest rate The nominal interest rate minus the rate of inflation.

Regression analysis A statistical technique for estimating the relationship between a dependent variable and one or more independent variables.

Relative price The price of one good relative to the price of another good.

Risk aversion The degree to which people wish to avoid risk.

Risk lover or risk preferrer An economics agent who enjoys risk.

Risk premium The difference between the forward exchange rate and the expected future spot rate.

Rogue trader A trader who does not follow the rules and regulations set up by the company.

Seigniorage The difference between the cost of issuing money and the real resources acquired by the money issuer.

Short position Selling a currency forward for future delivery.

Smithsonian agreement A December 1971 proclamation that the dollar was officially devalued and that currencies would now be allowed to fluctuate within ±2.25 percent of the new parity values.

Special drawing right (SDR) An international reserve asset created by the IMF.

Specie-flow mechanism A model showing that specie, e.g. gold, flows to create an equilibrium in the balance of payments.

Spot exchange rate The price of a currency for current delivery.

Spot market Buying and selling currency for immediate delivery.

Spread The difference between the buying and selling price of a currency or the differential between the interest rate on loans and deposits.

Stable-valued money A currency with a stable and low inflation rate.

Statistical significance A concept that allows one to relate estimated values to a hypothesized true value.

Sterilization The offsetting of international reserve flows with domestic credit.

Sterilized intervention Using open-market operations to offset the effect of intervention on the domestic money supply.

Strike price The price at which currency may be bought or sold in an option contract.

Swap The trade of one currency for another currency, combining a spot and forward transaction (or two forwards) in one deal.

Systematic risk The risk common to all assets.

Technical trading model Uses the past history of exchange rates to predict future movements.

Term structure of interest rates The return on an asset over different maturity dates.

Thin market A market with a small number of buyers and sellers, and assets traded.

Tiered exchange rates Different exchange rates applied to different classes of transactions.

Trade flow model An exchange rate model based on trade flows.

Transaction costs The costs associated with buying and selling activity.

Transaction exposure The foreign exchange risk associated with a particular transaction to be completed sometime in the future.

Transfer price The price charged to a subsidiary for internal goods transfers.

Translation The conversion of monetary values from one currency to another.

Translation exposure The difference between a firm's foreign-currency-denominated assets and its foreign-currency-denominated liabilities.

Triangular arbitrage Infer cross rate from two currencies to compare with another, then buying where price is low and selling where price is high.

Unbiased The property of being correct on average.

Unilateral transfers A current account entry that represents one-sided transactions such as gifts, pensions, foreign aid.

Variance A measure of how a variable changes in value about its mean.

INDEX

Note: Page numbers followed by "*f*," "*t*," and "*b*" refer to figures, tables, and boxes, respectively.